the **UNAUTHORIZED GUIDE** to

Pocket PC

Michael Morrison

201 West 103rd Street, Indianapolis, Indiana 46290

The Unauthorized Guide to Pocket PC

Copyright © 2001 by Que

International Standard Book Number: 0-7897-2472-3

Library of Congress Catalog Card Number: 00-106256

Printed in the United States of America

First Printing: November, 2000

02 01 00   4 3 2

Trademarks

Warning and Disclaimer

Associate Publisher
Greg Wiegand

Acquisitions Editor
Angelina Ward

Development Editor
Todd Brakke

Managing Editor
Thomas F. Hayes

Project Editor
Heather McNeill

Copy Editor
Julie A. McNamee

Indexer
Kelly Castell

Proofreader
Maribeth Echard

Technical Editor
Tom Gibson

Team Coordinator
Sharry Lee Gregory

Interior Designer
Kevin Spear

Cover Designer
Karen Ruggles

Editorial Assistant
Angela Boley

Production
Darin Crone

Contents

Appendixes

Michael Morrison is a writer, developer, toy inventor, and author of a variety of books including *Java in Plain English 3rd Edition* (IDG Books, 2000), *XML Unleashed* (Sams Publishing, 1999), and *The Complete Idiot's Guide to Java 2* (Que Publishing, 1999). Michael is the instructor of several Web-based courses including DigitalThink's Introduction to Java 2 series, JavaBeans for Programmers series, and Win32 Fundamentals series. Michael also serves as a technical director for ReviewNet, a company that provides Web-based staffing tools for information technology personnel. Finally, Michael is the creative lead at Gas Hound Games, a toy company he cofounded that is located on the Web at http://www.gashound.com.

When not risking life and limb on his skateboard or mountain bike, trying to avoid the penalty box in hockey, or watching movies with his wife, Masheed, Michael enjoys daydreaming next to his koi pond. You can visit Michael on the Web at http://www.thetribe.com. He also encourages you to check out his board game, Inc. The Game of Business, at http://www.incthegame.com.

About the Author

Dedication

To my wife Masheed, the best friend I've ever had, the most loving person I've ever known, and the person who made my writing career possible.

Acknowledgments

I want to thank Angelina Ward and Sharry Lee Gregory for doing their best to keep me on track as I watched the deadlines fly by. Thanks also to Todd Brakke, whose numerous editorial and content suggestions have made this a much stronger book. I know there are lots of other folks I haven't met at Pearson Technology Group to whom I am indebted for this book, and I thank you all.

Thanks to Cheryl at Casio for being so helpful in providing me with information and a very capable Cassiopeia device to use while writing the book. Equal thanks go to Amanda at Pretec Electronics for being so forthcoming with product information and allowing me to use one of Pretec's excellent modems.

A huge thanks goes to Chris Van Buren for making this project happen, orchestrating my writing career, and keeping me busy, all while jet-setting in Brazil.

I would like to thank my teammates on the Café Coco hockey team: Chuck, Brian K., Brian B., David, Mike, Chris C., Chris M., Ray, Jake, Ken, Fergy, Larry, Andy, Kevin, Steve, Greg, and Jamie. You guys helped provide me with a wonderful outlet for physical aggression, and I thank you for it.

My parents deserve a big thanks for always being so supportive of everything I do. This especially applies to my dad, who spent a great deal of time showing me how not to hit a golf ball during my infrequent writing breaks.

I couldn't have possibly maintained any sanity during the development of this book without the help of music—yes, I like to listen while I write. Thanks to The Trash Can Sinatras, Mr. Bungle, and The Smiths for keeping me entertained and energized while writing into the wee hours of the night.

Finally, the biggest thank you of all goes to my wife Masheed, who literally camped out in my office during some of the late-night writing sessions so that we could be near each other. I am truly blessed to have you in my life.

Tell Us What You Think!

As the reader of this book, *you* are our most important critic and commentator. We value your opinion and want to know what we're doing right, what we could do better, what areas you'd like to see us publish in, and any other words of wisdom you're willing to pass our way.

As an Associate Publisher for Que, I welcome your comments. You can fax, email, or write me directly to let me know what you did or didn't like about this book—as well as what we can do to make our books stronger.

Please note that I cannot help you with technical problems related to the topic of this book, and that due to the high volume of mail I receive, I might not be able to reply to every message.

When you write, please be sure to include this book's title and author as well as your name and phone or fax number. I will carefully review your comments and share them with the author and editors who worked on the book.

Fax: 317-581-4666

Email: greg.wiegand@macmillanusa.com

Mail: Greg Wiegand
            Que
            201 West 103rd Street
            Indianapolis, IN 46290 USA

WHEN I FIRST HEARD ABOUT POCKET PC, the latest incarnation of Microsoft's Windows CE operating system, my initial reaction was that it was just Windows CE 3.0 with a new name. Although there is some truth to the fact that Pocket PC is technically Windows CE 3.0 under the hood, the differences between Pocket PC and prior versions of Windows CE are dramatic. Windows CE was put through the wringer by many users and deservedly received a great deal of criticism. Microsoft has taken several media beatings over its failures in the handheld marketplace. For these reasons and more, Microsoft set out to develop a completely new handheld operating system when it went back to the drawing board for Pocket PC.

It's important to understand that Pocket PC is not just Windows scaled down to fit in your hand. Lest you think Microsoft was swayed by the success of the Palm operating system, let me clarify that Pocket PC is not a thin operating system designed to house a personal information management application, either. Pocket PC literally is a new breed of operating system that is based on the notion that it is possible to perform a much wider range of computing tasks on a palm-size computer than anyone had previously believed possible. Prior to the Pocket PC, palm-size computers were thought of us fancy electronic address books, and in many cases that's all they were. Microsoft aimed to take advantage of the fact that hardware exists to create a device that is powerful enough to do all kinds of interesting things, such as run productivity applications, browse the Web, check email, play digital music, and allow you to read digital books, among other things.

Even with its powerful arsenal of hardware and software capabilities, Pocket PC still has a significant challenge ahead. As of this writing, Palm-compatible devices still enjoy a growing lion's share of the handheld computer market. Many Palm users are also die-hard Macintosh users; a group that is unlikely to be swayed to use a Microsoft product no matter what it is has to offer. However, there are also significant numbers of Palm users who will find it increasingly difficult to resist the allure of a device that can do so many things so well. Microsoft has quite likely finally gotten it right with Pocket PC. This is important to know, because no one wants to buy into a technology product that isn't successful. The potential success or failure of Pocket PC is an inevitable concern looming over this new technology (and any new technology, for that matter) that is up against firmly entrenched competition.

You might be glad to learn that very little of this book concerns itself with the market issues associated with Pocket PC. Instead, the book delves into the Pocket PC technology and explores the details of each component of these devices. The current crop of Pocket PC devices is examined, along with the differences between each. The majority of the book focuses on the different applications that are either included in the Pocket PC ROM, or are shipped standard on the CD-ROM accompanying every Pocket PC device. I made a considerable effort to reveal tips and tricks that aren't necessarily documented or obvious to the casual user. The hope is that this book will reveal new and interesting things about your Pocket PC that you didn't previously know or understand, and ultimately help you get more out of your device and use it more productively.

Structure of the Book

This book is designed to be read sequentially, but that doesn't mean you can't jump around if you want to learn something specific. Although I've attempted to present the material in a logical order that addresses the needs of most Pocket PC users, you might have a particular topic about which you are interested in learning first. By all means, start wherever you're comfortable and tackle the topics most important to you first.

The book uses cross-references to tie together related topics, so you should be able to refer to an earlier chapter if you miss something and need to refresh your memory.

The book is broken down into the following parts:

- Part I, "Getting Started with Your Pocket PC," introduces you to the Pocket PC operating system and clarifies its relationship to earlier versions of Windows CE, as well as the Palm operating system. You also take a look at the hardware that goes into specific Pocket PC devices, and learn how to set up and personalize a Pocket PC device.

- Part II, "Pocket PC: The Next Generation PDA," examines the Pocket PC in its role as a next-generation personal digital assistant (PDA). Although Pocket PC devices are much more than PDAs, this part of the book makes the argument that the applications that comprise Pocket Outlook make for an extremely high-powered PDA.

- Part III, "Pocket PC: The Network Appliance," digs into the specifics of networking and how it impacts Pocket PC computing. You first learn how to get connected with a Pocket PC and a modem or Ethernet CompactFlash (CF) card. You then move on to learning the ins and outs of managing email, browsing the Web, and making use of wireless networking options.

- Part IV, "Pocket PC: The Portable Office," takes a look at the role of Pocket PC as a mobile productivity tool. This part begins by introducing you to a powerful natural handwriting-recognition tool that is included on the CD-ROM accompanying your Pocket PC. It then delves into the details of using Pocket Word and Pocket Excel to create and manage documents and spreadsheets. You also learn how to manage finances on your Pocket PC with Pocket Money, and find your way around strange towns with Pocket Streets.

- Part V, "Pocket PC: The Multimedia Entertainer," explores the fun side of Pocket PC by showing you how to play digital music with the Windows Media Player. You then learn how to read digital eBooks and listen to audible eBooks with Microsoft Reader. This part of the book concludes by touring several popular Pocket PC games, as well as demonstrating how to use a Pocket PC device as a digital camera.

Special Features

There are several features that you'll see consistently used throughout the book. These features call out particularly important pieces of information, and are presented to give you an idea as to the immediate relevance of the information. Following are the features used throughout the book, along with their meanings:

- **Inside Scoop**—Presents information that isn't readily apparent or that is likely not covered in other Pocket PC publications; this information was gathered after extensive research into Pocket PC, and often reveals background knowledge not available elsewhere.

- **Undocumented**—Presents practical information that isn't covered in the documentation for Pocket PCs; this information was gathered during extensive use of Pocket PC devices, and often reveals hidden tricks and tips for getting the most out of your Pocket PC.

- **Watch Out**—Illuminates potential pitfalls you might encounter while using your Pocket PC.

- **Remember**—Clarifies important information that is relevant to the current discussion; although not critical to understanding a given topic, this information can serve as a valuable supplement.

- **See Also**—Directs you to another section of the book that covers a topic related to the current discussion.

Getting Started with Your Pocket PC

PART I

GET THE SCOOP ON...
Pocket PC and the Uncertain Future
of PDAs ▪ Pocket PC and Windows CE ▪ Where
Pocket PC Might Turn Up ▪ Pocket PC and
Internet Connectivity

Pocket PC Fundamentals

P OCKET PC REPRESENTS IN MANY ways the first of a new breed of handheld computers that offer desktop features in the palm of your hand. Although there certainly have been many previous incarnations of handheld computing devices, none have been as ambitious both in terms of hardware and software as Pocket PC. Whether the average handheld computer user desires this much sizzle in a handheld device has yet to be seen, but computer users have rarely subscribed to the "less is more" theory when it comes to power and flexibility.

This chapter takes a look at the big picture of Pocket PC and how it fits into the handheld-computing landscape. Pocket PC is competing in a market with a very dominant leader, which in many ways explains the aggressive set of features packed into the device. This chapter also puts into perspective the relationship between Pocket PC and Windows CE, Microsoft's handheld operating system that has struggled for years to find its place in the hand of every mobile computer user.

Pocket PC: The PDA Killer

It is currently impossible to speak of handheld computers without addressing the incredibly popular Palm line of handheld devices. As of this writing, the Palm line of devices and compatible clones running the Palm OS represent the lion's share of the handheld computer market. This is due to a number of

7

Remember
Just in case you aren't a PDA guru, the idea behind a PDA is to serve as an electronic organizer by providing a convenient place to manage contacts, schedule meetings, keep up with tasks, and so on. PDAs are designed to provide roughly the functionality of a desktop application such as Microsoft Outlook, but in a more simplified and compact manner. Desktop applications such as Microsoft Outlook are sometimes referred to as PIMs (Personal Information Managers).

reasons, not limited to a sleek design, great marketing, and a very affordable price tag. Palm devices basically set the standard for modern Personal Digital Assistants, or PDAs. As PDAs, Palm devices provide a rich set of features that are intuitive and easy to use. Unfortunately, the Palm operating system was designed purely around the PDA concept, and doesn't necessarily scale well to the demands of a full-blown handheld computer.

In today's hectic workplace, PDAs are a necessity for some, which explains the popularity of the Palm devices. However, I want to make the argument that the PDA approach to handheld computing is no different from the original spreadsheet approach to personal computing. In case you weren't wired for the early days of PC history, most of the original PCs were sold purely because of spreadsheet software that allowed people to crunch numbers much more effectively than using calculators. The spreadsheet was the killer application that initially put computers on so many desks. However, spreadsheet software eventually settled in as one of many important computer applications. Do you still perceive the spreadsheet as the killer PC application? I doubt it.

The same usage shift is currently taking place in the handheld world as Palm devices cling to their killer application (PDA software), while Pocket PC introduces a complete computing experience. In addition to functioning as a traditional PDA, a Pocket PC device also serves as a word processor, spreadsheet, navigational map, financial manager, email client, Web client, digital Walkman™, digital voice recorder, digital book reader, and portable video game. These features are due to both the hardware and software of the Pocket PC platform, which are much more in line with a full-featured computer than with a PDA such as a Palm device. It's worth noting that some of the functionality built into Pocket PC devices can be added to Palm devices via third-party hardware and software, but these add-ons still run contrary to the original PDA design of Palm devices.

Although the feature list of the Pocket PC operating system is certainly a clear indicator of its technical superiority over the Palm operating system, let's dig a little deeper and really see why Pocket PCs are more powerful devices. Following is a list of the major aspects of Pocket PC devices that make them clear-cut winners over Palm devices:

- **Faster processor**—Pocket PCs all have 32-bit processors with speeds in the range of 70Mhz to 206MHz, whereas the fastest Palm devices have 20MHz processors.

- **More memory**—Pocket PCs all have between 16MB and 32MB of RAM and 16MB of ROM, whereas the most powerful Palm devices have 8MB of RAM and 2MB of ROM.

- **Better screens**—Pocket PCs all have screens that are 240×320 in resolution, whereas Palms have 160×160 resolution. Also, most Pocket PCs have color screens; however, only a couple of the newer Palm devices have color screens. The end result is that a lot of the Palm software was developed without color in mind.

- **Standard expansion slot**—Most Pocket PCs include a standard CompactFlash expansion slot, whereas most of the Palm devices do not; the TRGPro Palm-compatible device includes a CompactFlash slot, and the Handspring Visor device includes a proprietary Springboard expansion slot. The Compaq iPAQ Pocket PC doesn't include a CompactFlash expansion slot, but it supports an expansion sleeve that allows you to use CompactFlash cards.

- **Natural handwriting recognition**—Pocket PCs include natural handwriting recognition software, which allows you to write very closely to how you're accustomed to writing and have it automatically translated into text. For some reason, the Pocket PC natural handwriting recognition software (Transcriber) is not built into the operating system, although it is shipped on the CD-ROM that accompanies every device. Palm devices use a special Graffiti language for handwriting recognition; although many

Remember
"Pocket PC" is a trademarked name that refers to a software platform created by Microsoft for handheld devices. This software dictates certain minimal hardware requirements. A Pocket PC is a handheld device that runs the Pocket PC operating system and adheres to Pocket PC hardware standards.

Palm users are fond of the Graffiti language, it has a fairly steep learning curve.

■ **Full Web browsing**—Pocket PCs include Pocket Internet Explorer, which allows you to view any Web page provided you don't mind scrolling around a little; there is a "fit to screen" option that does a fairly decent job of scaling pages down to fit on the Pocket PC screen. Palm devices don't support any direct Web browsing; you must view Web content as text snippets.

Remember
Everyone has his or her own opinion about the potential success or failure of the Pocket PC technology, and you've just heard mine. Obviously, no one knows what is going to happen in regard to Pocket PC and its attempt to replace Palm as the handheld operating system of choice. I can tell you that my motivation for writing this book has to do with the fact that I finally feel that Microsoft got it right with Pocket PC. Even so, I'm not religious about Pocket PC and I encourage you to choose the OS that makes the most sense for you.

This list isn't intended to be all-inclusive; there are obviously other areas in which Pocket PC devices shine over Palm devices. However, it does reveal the most significant areas in which Pocket PC excels over Palm. Keep in mind that this information is current as of this writing. I fully expect both Pocket PCs and Palm devices to continue to evolve rapidly and acquire more features.

Although there is little doubt that Pocket PC is a superior technology to Palm's offerings, one unfortunate reality of the computer business is that the best technology doesn't always win. Market share reigns supreme in the computer business, which puts Microsoft in an unfamiliar position with regard to Pocket PC. Microsoft has relied on market share to dominate the computer world with DOS and then Windows. Many have criticized Microsoft in the past for having an inferior product (DOS and early versions of Windows) but forcing it on users by the sheer power of its dominant market share. Now Microsoft finds itself on the other side of the fence with a superior technology and very little market share; Microsoft has much work ahead as it tries to dethrone Palm and steal away market share with Pocket PC.

As it stands right now, I think the Pocket PC technology is sufficiently superior to eventually win out in the long run. A new generation of handheld computer user is emerging that will demand the capabilities that are built into Pocket PCs. There are considerable doubts as to whether the Palm operating system can sufficiently evolve to meet the needs of these users. Also, you have to consider the strength of Microsoft and its commitment to Windows. Short of buying Palm, there is no reason for Microsoft to ever back away from making some incarnation of Windows the de facto standard for handheld computing. Speaking of Windows, let's turn our attention to Windows CE, a technology that has consistently proven troublesome for Microsoft.

Pocket PC and Windows CE

Windows CE got its start back in 1994 when Microsoft began developing a PDA known as the WinPad. The WinPad was initially conceived to compete against the Apple Newton, a PDA that eventually crashed and burned due to numerous problems. Many of the Newton's problems had to do with memory, or the lack of it, which led Microsoft to realize that affordable technology wasn't quite there to make the WinPad a success. So, Microsoft cancelled the WinPad project and abandoned the thought of a mobile operating system, at least for the time being.

A few years after the WinPad fizzled, Microsoft turned its attention to set-top Internet devices, which were interesting because they had some of the same hardware and software requirements as the WinPad. The idea behind set-top Internet devices was that they would sit on top of a television set like a cable box. As part of its set-top Internet device development efforts, Microsoft developed an initiative called SIPC, which stood for Simply Interactive PCs. Microsoft took a stab at developing an SIPC but eventually aborted the project. Although the SIPC initiative ultimately failed, it rekindled Microsoft's desire to build a compact operating system that would run on handheld devices.

Microsoft's new attempt at a compact operating system was codenamed Project Pegasus, and in many ways picked up where the WinPad software left off. However, by now Windows 95 was a big success and Microsoft wanted the Pegasus GUI (Graphical User Interface) to have a similar look and feel as Windows 95. Pegasus did in fact take on the look and feel of Windows 95, and was publicly unveiled as Windows CE 1.0 at Fall Comdex 1996.

Undocumented Although Microsoft has never officially divulged the meaning of the "CE" in Windows CE, it is reported to have originally stood for "Consumer Electronics." I've also heard that it stands for "Compact Edition." Because either meaning makes sense, I'll leave it up to you to decide what you want it to mean. Microsoft's official stance is that it means nothing.

Inside Scoop
Although Windows CE originally had a similar look and feel as Windows 95/NT, it has more in common with Windows NT in terms of the nuts and bolts of its architecture.

It's important to note at this point that Windows CE 1.0 was never perceived as a PDA operating system. Microsoft always had a bigger picture in mind, and therefore always looked at Windows CE as a compact version of Windows, not a fancy contact manager. This perspective is evident in the fact that Windows CE 1.0 had no handwriting recognition support. Most PDAs on the market used some form of handwriting recognition, but Microsoft was concerned about the quality of handwriting recognition software, and decided to wait on incorporating it into Windows CE. In addition to not including support for handwriting recognition, Microsoft also set Windows CE apart from PDAs by including desktop productivity applications such as Word and Excel.

Although Windows CE was ultimately just an operating system, Microsoft laid out strict guidelines regarding the hardware configuration of devices that could support Windows CE. A Windows CE 1.0 device was required to have a grayscale screen with 480×480 resolution, 2MB of RAM, 4MB of ROM for Windows CE and standard applications, a serial port, an infrared port, a PCMCIA slot, and a keyboard. Clearly this was no PDA, but just as clear was the fact that there was no market for such a device at the time; Windows CE 1.0 never caught on.

Windows CE 2.0 was released in September of 1997, and although it had been revamped in several ways, it still didn't make much of an impact on the handheld market. Many critics complained that it felt too much like the desktop Windows, which felt clunky on a small screen with no mouse. It was in fact designed to be a lot like the desktop Windows, Windows 95, and Microsoft still had not learned that this wasn't really a good thing. Windows CE 2.0 also was noted for being sluggish in terms of performance. Microsoft would later release a much-improved Windows CE 2.1 and still suffer from the same complaints from users who didn't want to use Windows 95/98 on anything but their desktop or notebook computers.

"
To be honest, we haven't done things so well before.
—Phil Holden, Windows CE Group Product Manager
"

Then the light bulb went on in Redmond. It was realized that not only did Windows CE need a major GUI facelift, but it also had taken enough of a media beating that it needed a whole new image. This brings us to the Pocket PC, which is really

Windows CE 3.0. By changing the name from Windows CE to Pocket PC, Microsoft is hoping to start over again and try to establish a recognizable brand with no negative history to drag it down. As of this writing, it's too early to tell whether the renaming strategy will really work, but early returns are positive. "Pocket PC" is a catchier name anyway, so I don't mind the fact that I'm really using Windows CE 3.0, the fourth release of a product with a troubled past. Microsoft has a history of getting it wrong a few times and then hitting a home run on the third or fourth revision. If history repeats itself, the Pocket PC will be a winner.

Outside of the Pocket

I've heard the question asked that with Pocket PCs having so much power, will they threaten traditional PCs? In a word, no. Although Pocket PCs pack a lot of punch in a small footprint, they still serve as complementary devices to a traditional PC. Granted, you can buy a keyboard for your Pocket PC, plug in one of IBM's CompactFlash 1GB micro hard drives, and use the suite of Pocket applications to the max, but at some point you will undoubtedly want to have a desktop PC on which to do serious work. Pocket PCs are designed for mobility, and for those times when you're mobile they are incredibly useful. Few of us are so nomadic to be on the run all the time, which is why we typically also have a desktop or laptop computer. With its advanced synchronization features, Pocket PC makes it easy to share information between a Pocket PC device and a desktop or laptop PC.

While we're on the subject of Pocket PC and its impact on traditional PCs, it's worth revisiting the original focus of Windows CE because Microsoft might come full-circle with its plans. I mentioned earlier that one of the iterations of Windows CE was designed for use in set-top Internet devices. Although Microsoft bailed on the effort at the time, Internet technology has now evolved to the point that set-top Internet devices are much more feasible. Not only that, but the general public is much more accustomed to using the Internet, so the learning curve of using such a device is much lower.

Inside Scoop
Pocket PC, or Windows CE 3.0, was code-named Rapier prior to its release. Interestingly enough, Microsoft originally tried to use the name "Palm PC" for an earlier version of Windows CE, but Palm Computing, and its parent 3Com, promptly took them to court to defend the Palm name. The lawsuit was eventually settled, and Microsoft was able to take home the name "Palm-size PC." The name "Pocket PC" didn't come about until later, when Microsoft was able to obtain the name from a company called Pocket PC, Inc.

Inside Scoop
IBM recently announced the imminent availability of a 1GB Microdrive that resides in a Type II CompactFlash card. 170MB and 340MB versions of the Microdrive were already available, but the 1GB drive is large enough to really impact the way Pocket PCs are used. You learn more about Pocket PC hardware in Chapter 2, "Inside a Pocket PC."

Remember
Networked computers are also sometimes referred to as Internet appliances.

Inside Scoop
For more information on Microsoft's Xbox video game system, check out the Xbox Web site at http://www.xbox.com.

What I'm basically getting at is that it is quite possible that we'll see Windows CE alive again in set-top Internet devices. This will most likely come in the form of networked computers, also known as NCs. Networked Computers are minimal computers that primarily serve as Internet clients. It could be that Pocket PC will eventually make its way onto these computers, although Microsoft might shy away from using the "Pocket PC" name to keep from confusing the handheld brand name.

Another arena in which Windows CE/Pocket PC might eventually reveal itself is in home video games. Microsoft has already announced its Xbox video game system, which will obviously require some sort of compact operating system. When released for Christmas 2001, the Xbox video game system will likely be the most powerful home video game system to date. Microsoft has intentionally one-upped other game systems in practically every aspect of the Xbox's design. Microsoft hasn't revealed the specific operating system driving the Xbox, but I wouldn't be surprised if it resembles a jazzed-up version of Pocket PC. Even though games require stellar graphics and sound support, they also require the utmost in software performance, which usually comes from a very efficient, compact operating system.

The Significance of Pocket PC Connectivity

The feature set of Pocket PC devices is clearly impressive, and is a major reason the devices will finally put Microsoft on the map in the handheld world. However, all the pint-sized productivity applications in the world won't make Pocket PC a success without one ingredient that in the past hasn't been much of an issue with handheld devices: connectivity. Some previous handheld devices have supported modems, and you can obviously connect most devices to a desktop computer and share information, but the allure of the Internet in the handheld world is something entirely new.

The ability to send and receive email with attachments, retrieve stock quotes, shop, and view full Web pages, all from the convenience of your pocket is something few of us would imagine possible at the moment, especially in such a small device.

The Pocket PC not only makes these activities possible, but it is nearly as seamless to connect to the Internet with a Pocket PC as it is with a traditional desktop or laptop computer. Whereas the PDA was the original killer application to create the niche market for handheld devices, connectivity will be the killer application to put handheld devices in the hands of average computer users.

As of this writing, the easiest way to connect a Pocket PC to the Internet is through either a wired modem, which obviously requires a physical phone line, or through a mobile phone. The mobile phone option requires a mobile phone with a suitable data port that can communicate with a Pocket PC. One of the more interesting approaches to communicating via a mobile phone is infrared, which involves a Pocket PC linking up with a mobile phone via infrared ports on both devices. Because no one likes wires, this is a particularly elegant approach that works great provided the devices are placed close to each other with a clear line of sight between the ports.

In addition to the wired modem and mobile phone approaches to connecting a Pocket PC to the Internet, there is a huge push to bring a more standardized, ideally built-in form of wireless connectivity to the Pocket PC platform. For example, the Palm VII device includes a special wireless service that is specially designed for Palm VII users. The wireless hardware is built into the device; all you must do is sign up and pay the monthly fee to have wireless email and Internet support. Of course, the Palm platform still doesn't have true Web browsing, and there are limitations in its email support, but the fact remains that users appreciate the simplicity of buying a device with everything they need to go wireless.

Compaq is the first Pocket PC manufacturer to offer a wireless bundle that approximates the simplicity of the Palm VII. The Wireless iPAQ is a Compaq iPAQ Pocket PC with a Sierra Wireless AirCard 300 wireless Internet card and Infowave communication software. The AirCard 300 is a wireless modem implemented in a PC card that can be used with the Compaq iPAQ thanks to the iPAQ's PC card expansion jacket. This wireless bundle is a major step in the right direction in terms of the positioning Pocket PC as a serious contender in the world of wireless mobile Internet access. Hewlett-Packard also has a wireless bundle in the works for their Jornada line of Pocket PCs.

Even though the bundled approach to wireless connectivity plays an important role for Pocket PCs in the short term, Microsoft has alluded to the fact that Pocket PCs will eventually include wireless support standard in each device. Regardless of how wireless connectivity for Pocket PC unfolds, it will be something anxiously anticipated by all Pocket PC users.

Inside Scoop
For more information on Compaq's Wireless iPAQ bundle, please visit the Compaq Pocket PC Web site at http:// www.compaq.com/ products/ handhelds/ pocketpc.

Essential Information

- With its massive set of features, Pocket PC introduces a new type of handheld device that goes far beyond the limited functionality of traditional PDAs such as Palm devices.

- Although Microsoft's marketing machine would probably prefer you not know the connection, the Pocket PC operating system is really Windows CE 3.0. This isn't really a bad thing, however, because Microsoft is known for getting it right after three or four iterations.

- Pocket PCs certainly pack a punch in terms of productivity applications and connectivity, but they are designed as a lightweight mobile companion to a traditional desktop or laptop computer, not a replacement for it.

- Productivity and multimedia applications clearly are exciting components of the Pocket PC equation, but the real killer application for Pocket PCs is wireless connectivity to the Internet.

GET THE SCOOP ON...
Types of Pocket PC Processors ▪ The Significance of
Memory to Pocket PCs ▪ Other Facets of Pocket PC
Hardware ▪ The Structure of the Pocket PC
Graphical User Interface

Inside a Pocket PC

P OCKET PCS ARE INTERESTING DEVICES that differ from many of the other types of handheld devices you might have seen or used in the past. In terms of hardware, Pocket PCs include an unprecedented array of features packed into a small footprint. On the software side of things, the Pocket PC operating system presents a highly intuitive graphical user interface (GUI) that addresses the complaints voiced over previous versions of Windows CE. This chapter delves into the guts of Pocket PCs to find out exactly what kind of hardware goes into each device, along with examining the main components of the Pocket PC GUI.

Pocket PC Hardware Essentials

To fully understand Pocket PCs and get the most out of them, you must have a solid grasp on what they are made of. More specifically, it's important to understand exactly what hardware goes into a Pocket PC device, which in turn gives it the power to carry out all its dynamic functionality. The hardware portion of a Pocket PC can be broken down into the following major components:

▪ Processor

▪ Memory

▪ Power

▪ Screen

- Stylus

- I/O Ports

- Multimedia hardware

The next few sections explore each of these facets of Pocket PC hardware and examine their roles in making Pocket PCs such powerful handheld devices. Before getting into each hardware component, I'd like to point out that there are currently seven Pocket PC devices on the market as of this writing:

- Casio Cassiopeia E-115

- HP Jornada 540

- HP Jornada 545

- HP Jornada 548

- Compaq Aero 1550

- Compaq iPAQ H3650 (same as H3630)

- Symbol PPT 2700

I'll be referring to these devices throughout the hardware discussion to illuminate similarities and differences between them. My goal is to simultaneously reveal the hardware that drives Pocket PCs in general as well as point out the different hardware approaches taken by each Pocket PC manufacturer.

Processor

The processor is the brain of Pocket PC devices, and therefore is critical in determining how much power is packed into them. I'm sure you are familiar with desktop and laptop processor speeds, which passed the 1GHz (1,000MHz) threshold in 2000. It was only a couple of years ago when a 200MHz PC was considered speedy for most applications. Knowing this, it's pretty impressive that Pocket PCs currently use processors up to 206MHz. (There is no one standard processor for Pocket PCs.)

Unlike desktop PCs, which all use x86-based processors manufactured by either Intel or AMD, Pocket PCs are more diverse

Inside Scoop
Keep in mind that although certain core specifications must be met by all Pocket PCs, device manufacturers certainly vary in the hardware used in their different devices. For example, there are five different processors currently used in Pocket PCs. Manufacturers are also free to include various custom software applications in addition to the standard Pocket PC applications.

in their usage of processors. Currently, there are five main processors used in Pocket PCs, which are shown in Table 2.1 along with their respective speeds and the Pocket PCs in which they are found. To find out where to look for the most up-to-date information on Pocket PC processors and related hardware, please refer to Appendix B, "Pocket PC Resources."

TABLE 2.1: PROCESSORS CURRENTLY USED IN POCKET PC DEVICES

Processor	Speed	Pocket PC
NEC MIPS VR4111	70MHz	Compaq Aero 1550
NEC MIPS VR4181	80MHz	Symbol PPT 2700
NEC MIPS VR4121	131MHz	Casio Cassiopeia E-115
SH3 7709	133MHz	HP Jornada 540/545/548
Intel StrongARM	206MHz	Compaq iPAQ H3650

Although it's nice to know that diversity is alive and well in the Pocket PC processor market, this is bad news in terms of software distribution. One thing that Intel's monopoly over PC processors has done is standardize the instruction set for PCs, which means that all software compiled to the x86 instruction set will work on all Intel processors, including compatible processors manufactured by AMD. Pocket PC processors are each distinctively different, and therefore require an application to be compiled to a specific processor. So, for example, if you developed a Pocket PC game and you wanted all Pocket PC users to be able to purchase and play it, you would have to offer three different versions of the game: one for MIPS, one for SH3, and one for StrongARM.

From the development end of things, building a different executable for each processor is a matter of throwing a software switch, but from the user's perspective it can cause considerable confusion. Ideally, the user shouldn't have to be concerned about the type of processor in her Pocket PC, but for the time being it is something users have to accept.

It might be logical to assume that the processor speed of a Pocket PC completely dictates the device's performance, but that's not entirely true. It is possible for a Pocket PC to perform

Inside Scoop
For the record, it's possible that a dominant processor will emerge from the pack and eventually assert itself as the processor of choice for Pocket PCs. MIPS processors have been somewhat of a standard in earlier Windows CE devices, but I wouldn't rule out Pocket PC newcomer Intel, because it is a household name and its processor has the most horsepower.

Remember
Benchmark results weren't available for the Symbol PPT 2700 Pocket PC as of this writing.

quite well in a particular operation, such as graphics processing, even though it doesn't have the most juiced-up processor. As you probably know, it is possible for a desktop PC to outperform a similar PC with a faster processor due to more efficient hardware subsystems and drivers. This is why PC magazines and review services use benchmark tests to assess performance differences between similar PCs. Fortunately, it is also possible to perform such benchmarks on Pocket PCs. One such Pocket PC benchmarking application is called VOBenchmark, and is freely available from Virtual Office Systems, Inc. at http://www.voscorp.com/PPC. Although you are free to try out VOBenchmark on your own Pocket PC, Timothy Tripp has already done the work for you. The results of his benchmark tests on each of the four major Pocket PC devices are shown in Table 2.2. Because the number indicates the time to complete an operation, a lower number is better.

TABLE 2.2: A BENCHMARK COMPARISON OF THE MAJOR POCKET PC DEVICES

Operation	Compaq 1550	Casio E-115	HP 540/545/548	Compaq iPAQ H3650
Ellipse	3.05	0.59	2.34	5.52
Rectangle	2.30	0.36	2.54	1.20
Rounded Rect.	3.39	0.85	2.95	7.88
Text	3.17	1.35	1.31	1.26
Integer	0.57	0.32	0.81	0.20
Floating Point	9.63	5.62	3.81	2.06
Memory	0.82	0.48	0.51	0.25

It's important to understand that the benchmark results are measured in seconds, which means that each number in the table represents how long it takes a particular device to carry out a particular benchmark operation. The first four benchmark operations are highly graphics intensive, which reveals more about the graphics subsystem of a given device than it does about the main processor. In other words, if a device performs well graphically, yet has a slower processor than another device, then it likely has an efficient graphics driver. A good example of this is the Casio E-115, which literally smoked the competition in the graphics benchmarks. Both the HP and Compaq H3650 have faster processors but the Casio still beats them handily in terms of graphics processing. The last three benchmarks are more in line with what you would expect based purely on processor speed; the speedier Compaq H3650 wins them all hands-down, whereas the slower Compaq 1550 trails in two of the three benchmarks .

Memory

Perhaps the only hardware component of a Pocket PC even more important than processor speed is memory. Because Pocket PCs are inherently compact devices with every design decision carefully weighed against size, cost, weight, and ruggedness, it stands to reason that memory is the only real Pocket PC bottleneck. All Pocket PCs are required to have at least 16MB of ROM and 16MB of RAM. Although the ROM is sufficient for storing the Pocket PC operating system and standard applications, the RAM is where things quickly get tight. When you consider that desktop computers have exploded in terms of their memory and hard disk capacities, it's really no surprise that people haven't argued much as applications and data files have continued to balloon in size. When you literally have gigabytes of hard disk space to spare, who cares if a file is 120KB or 120MB? Obviously, there are reasons to care, but in the big picture, it isn't that big of a deal when you almost always have room to spare.

Mobile devices live by a very different set of rules than desktop computers, and memory is the one area where this is painfully evident. The primary issue is the cost of compact memory, which is higher than the cost of normal desktop computer memory, and incredibly higher than the cost of hard disk space. The comparison to hard disk space is important because Pocket PCs typically don't have hard drives, in which case they must rely on some form of RAM as residual storage. When you look at trying to replace the storage space of a hard drive with RAM, cost suddenly becomes a big problem.

Because compact RAM for handheld devices is relatively expensive, Pocket PC manufacturers decided to design them

Inside Scoop
In the previous discussion about hard drives and Pocket PCs, I mentioned that Pocket PCs typically don't have hard drives. I used the word "typically" because although RAM serves as the default storage in Pocket PCs, IBM is manufacturing miniature hard drives in the form of CompactFlash cards that can plug into the expansion slot of Pocket PCs. These hard drives are called Microdrives, and are currently available in 170MB, 340MB, and 1GB sizes, with the 1GB drive costing under $500. I would be shocked if Microdrives don't become one of the most popular Pocket PC add-ons, possibly only second in line behind modems. For more information on the IBM Microdrives, take a look at the Micro-drive Web site at http://www. storage.ibm.com/ hardsoft/ diskdrdl/micro.

with enough RAM to handle average usage, but not enough to handle extreme applications such as storing a lot of MP3 music content. For those users with large memory requirements, the extensibility of Pocket PCs saves the day. More specifically, all Pocket PCs are required to support some form of RAM expansion, whether it be a CompactFlash slot or a PC card slot. This allows users to buy extra RAM and plug it into their Pocket PCs for plenty of extra storage room. It's basically a matter of economics when it comes to how much memory is enough; if you can afford it, get a bunch and you won't have to worry so much about running out.

You will most likely expand the memory of your Pocket PC via the CompactFlash slot on the device. CompactFlash RAM is packaged in CompactFlash cards (CF cards), and is currently available in sizes ranging from 4MB to 256MB. CF cards are available in two different types: CF Type I and CF Type II. CF Type I cards are roughly the size of a matchbook and weigh about half an ounce, while Type II cards are slightly thicker and weigh a little more. Devices with Type II slots will also accept Type I cards, but devices that support only Type I cards will not accept Type II cards. RAM is typically packaged in CF Type I cards, which makes it usable in the widest range of devices. Table 2.3 lists the current crop of Pocket PCs and their support for CF cards.

TABLE 2.3: COMPACTFLASH CARD SUPPORT IN THE CURRENT POCKET PC DEVICES

Pocket PC	CF Support
Symbol PPT 2700	None
Compaq Aero 1550	CF Type I
HP Jornada 540/545/548	CF Type I
Compaq iPAQ H3650	CF Type II via CF Expansion Pack
Casio Cassiopeia E-115	CF Type II

Inside Scoop
You might be familiar with CF cards in digital cameras because some digital cameras use them to store digital photographs. If you happen to have a digital camera that uses a CF card, you can remove the card, place it in your Pocket PC, and view the pictures.

As Table 2.3 shows, the Casio E-115 is the only Pocket PC that includes support for CF Type II cards straight out of the box. The Compaq H3650 also supports CF Type II cards, but you must buy the Compaq CF Expansion Pack. Compaq's thought is that the expansion pack approach gives you more flexibility and allows the Pocket PC to be thinner and lighter weight if you don't use a CF card. Compaq also offers a PC Expansion Pack that allows you to use standard PC cards with the iPAQ H3650. This is very interesting because there is enormous support for PC cards due to their usage in laptop computers. Getting back to the CF cards, the Compaq 1550 and HP Pocket PCs all support CF Type I cards.

Even though CF memory cards ultimately contain RAM, you really can think of them as removable disk drives because data is stored on them persistently. In other words, if all power to your Pocket PC is lost or if you perform a full reset on the device, the data on a CF card will still be intact. For this reason, CF cards are ideally suited as a means of backing up your Pocket PC, especially when you are going to be away from a desktop computer for a while. If you are in close proximity to a desktop computer, it probably makes more sense to back up to it.

→ **See Also** Appendix C, "Resetting Your Pocket PC," **p. 379**.

Because CF cards function more as disk drives, as opposed to traditional memory, you will likely want to store both applications and data files on CF cards. The most obvious usage for CF memory cards is storing MP3 music files, which are notorious for taking up a lot of space. You might also decide to store maps for Pocket Streets, email attachments, or eBooks on the CF card. Basically, any data can be stored on a CF card, and most applications can be safely installed and executed from a CF card as well. I say "most" applications because there are a few applications that look to a specific area of built-in RAM for their data files. The Avantgo client in Pocket Internet Explorer is a good example of this; it expects Web files to be located in a specific directory within the main RAM of a device. Fortunately, there is a workaround for this problem that you learn about in Chapter 10, "Using Pocket Internet Explorer."

Power

A Pocket PC with no power wouldn't be of much use, so power is certainly an important part of the Pocket PC hardware

Remember
The Symbol Pocket PC is targeted to a much different user than the other devices, which explains the absence of a CF expansion slot. The Symbol Pocket PC is geared toward heavy-duty industrial applications where it might be exposed to extreme physical conditions. This results in a feature set and price point that might not be appealing to the average handheld user. On the other hand, industrial users demand the ruggedness of the Symbol device, and probably wouldn't consider one of the others.

picture. All Pocket PCs include two power sources: a main battery that is used to power the device during normal use and a backup battery that the device uses when the main battery isn't functioning. Your Pocket PC keeps close tabs on battery power and informs you of either batteries going low. It's important to heed these warnings and either recharge/replace the main battery or replace the backup battery in response to the respective warnings.

The most important battery in a Pocket PC is obviously the main battery, which is typically a rechargeable battery. Table 2.4 lists the different types of main batteries used in current Pocket PCs, along with the main battery life of each device.

TABLE 2.4: BATTERY TYPES AND APPROXIMATE BATTERY LIFE

Pocket PC	Battery Type	Battery Life (Hours)
Casio Cassiopeia E-115	Lithium Ion	6
HP Jornada 540/545/548	Lithium Ion	8
Compaq iPAQ H3650	Lithium Polymer	12
Compaq Aero 1550	Lithium Ion	14

The table reveals that Lithium Ion batteries are the more popular battery type in Pocket PCs. However, the Compaq H3650 uses the newer lithium polymer batteries, which offer significantly improved battery life. The only reason the Compaq 1550 has a longer battery life with the older lithium ion batteries is because it has a much slower processor and a grayscale screen, two hardware components that significantly reduce power consumption.

Each Pocket PC differs slightly in how the main and backup batteries are accessed and replaced. Furthermore, there is some variance in how the main batteries are recharged; most devices support charging the main battery through a cradle, and some also allow you to use an AC adapter cord. Be sure not to touch the batteries unless the unit is turned off and you have a backup of any important data.

Screen

Few people can look at a Pocket PC without appreciating the screen. At least in comparison to other handheld devices, the screen on most Pocket PCs is a treat to view. All Pocket PCs are required to support a screen resolution of 240×320 pixels. Although not a strict requirement, most Pocket PCs also include color screens, which adds significantly to the usability of the devices. Perhaps the most common criticism of Pocket PC screens is the image degradation when viewing the screen at a sharp angle, a common weakness associated with LCD screens. Even so, the screen quality on Pocket PCs rivals that of the best laptop and notebook computers.

Screens are perhaps the one area in which Pocket PC devices differ the most. Table 2.5 shows the different display technologies employed in the current Pocket PC devices.

TABLE 2.5: DISPLAY TECHNOLOGIES IN THE CURRENT POCKET PC DEVICES

Pocket PC	Display Technology
Compaq Aero 1550	STN
Symbol PPT 2700	CSTN
HP Jornada 540/545/548	CSTN
Casio Cassiopeia E-115	TFT
Compaq iPAQ H3650	Reflective TFT

The Compaq 1550 uses the Super Twist Nematic (STN) display technology, which is also known as a passive-matrix display. STN displays attempt to improve the image quality on the screen by twisting light rays. The STN display on the Compaq 1550 is a grayscale screen, and is easy to read under a variety of different lighting conditions such as both indoors and outdoors. The Symbol 2700 and HP Jornada Pocket PCs use a Color Super Twist Nematic (CSTN) display, which works especially well with Pocket PC's ClearType technology for reading eBooks. Although not quite as bright as the Casio E-115's TFT display, the CSTN displays are a little more viewable in direct light. The Casio E-115 takes an active-matrix approach with a Thin Film Transistor (TFT) display. TFT displays are brighter

Inside Scoop
A new type of storage card known as a MultiMediaCard (MMC) is currently gaining momentum and offers an interesting alternative to CF cards. MMCs are smaller than CF cards (about the size of a postage stamp), have similar capacities as CF cards, and include encryption support for securing data. A new line of Casio Pocket PCs is planned to use MMCs instead of CF cards in order to reduce the size of the devices. I don't think you have to worry about CF cards going away any time soon, but MMCs are an interesting technology that will likely have a significant impact on future Pocket PC devices.

Remember
Battery life information wasn't available for the Symbol PPT 2700 Pocket PC as of this writing.

Watch Out!
Be careful when cleaning the screen of your Pocket PC. Some commercial glass cleaners such as Formula 409 contain solvents that can damage the top layer of the LCD screen, which is made of plastic; more specifically, avoid using a cleaner that contains acetone, ethanol, isopropyl alcohol, or toluene. Kensington Computer Screen Cleaner is a safe option, as is Concept Kitchen's PDA Screen Clean. Kensington Computer Screen Cleaner is available at most computer stores, and you can order Concept Kitchen's PDA Screen Clean directly from Concept Kitchen at http://www.conceptkitchen.com.

than their passive-matrix counterparts but they tend to wash out more in direct light such as outdoor sunlight. The Compaq H3650 likely has the best display technology in terms of balancing brightness with performance in different lighting. Its reflective TFT display includes an ambient light sensor that adjusts the display according to the intensity of light in its surroundings.

Regardless of the specific display technologies employed by the different Pocket PC screens, the good news is that they all have screens that are quite viewable, especially when compared to other handheld devices. However, the display technologies employed by Pocket PC screens don't tell the entire story in regard to image quality. There is the issue of color, which isn't consistent across Pocket PC devices. The Pocket PC operating system is designed around 16-bit color graphics, which results in more than 65,000 different colors. Initially, it was planned that all Pocket PC devices would support 16-bit color to meet the requirements of the operating system. However, things didn't quite work out as planned.

HP marketed their Jornada line of Pocket PCs as supporting 16-bit color, but when users complained about problems with image quality when viewing images with a lot of colors, a weakness was revealed. HP realized and admitted that although the Jornada screen itself can display 16-bit color, the Jornada's display electronics are designed to support 12-bit color. 12-bit color allows only 4,096 different colors, which can make a big difference when viewing photographic images. The 12-bit limitation in the Jornada display reveals itself only when viewing images with a wide range of colors, so it won't impact all users the same. However, it has caused enough of a public relations problem that HP is offering to make amends with customers who bought the device prior to the issue surfacing.

Although the support for 12-bit color in HP's Jornada devices appears to have been an accident, Compaq actively designed the Compaq H3650 to support 12-bit color. It's not really clear why they chose to go this route given that the Pocket PC platform targets 16-bit color, but there is presumably a manufacturing cost savings. Given that the H3650 is priced roughly

$100 lower than its functional competitors, it might turn out being a smart move.

I/O Ports

The Pocket PC platform dictates that all Pocket PCs have several input/output (I/O) ports to provide the utmost in flexibility when it comes to communicating with the outside world. In the earlier "Memory" section, I already covered the CompactFlash expansion slot, which is commonly available in most Pocket PCs. Whereas the CompactFlash slot is critical in providing expansion capabilities to Pocket PCs, I/O ports such as serial, USB, and infrared are important in allowing Pocket PCs to connect and communicate with desktop PCs and other mobile devices. Serial and USB ports are the most commonly used Pocket PC I/O ports, but not all devices support both. Table 2.6 reveals the types of ports supported in the current crop of Pocket PCs.

TABLE 2.6: COMPACTFLASH CARD SUPPORT

Pocket PC	I/O Support
Compaq Aero 1550	Serial port
Casio Cassiopeia E-115	Serial port
Symbol PPT 2700	Serial port
HP Jornada 540/545/548	USB/Serial port
Compaq iPAQ H3650	USB/Serial port

Although serial and USB ports are equally useful for synchronizing a Pocket PC with a desktop or laptop computer, USB ports are significantly faster. More specifically, a Pocket PC serial port is limited to a data transfer rate of 115Kbps (kilobits per second), whereas a USB port can move data at speeds of 1500Kbps. That's over 10 times as fast, which can make a big difference when transferring large files such as digital MP3 or WMA music files.

Beyond serial and USB ports, all Pocket PCs include an infrared port that can be used to communicate with other devices via an invisible beam of light. The infrared port is convenient because it doesn't require a physical connection for

Undocumented
Because the top layer of a Pocket PC screen is plastic, it is relatively easy to scratch it, which can be very frustrating. Believe it or not, an inexpensive way to fix minor scratches on your Pocket PC's screen is to spray a little STP Son of a Gun tire cleaner on the screen and lightly buff it off. It contains a polymer that bonds with the top layer of the LCD screen and fills minor scratches.

Undocumented
Although the HP Jornada 540 series of Pocket PCs include a USB port, for some reason the port is limited to using serial speeds of 115Kbps. Consequently, the Compaq iPAQ's USB port functions much faster than the Jornada's.

Undocumented
One common complaint from some HP Jornada users is that the screen's surface is a little rough, which can result in the stylus not moving as smoothly as it could. This isn't an issue when tapping to navigate the Pocket PC GUI, but it can potentially be annoying when handwriting with the stylus. A simple solution to this problem is to place a screen protector over the Jornada's screen. There are some commercial screen protectors available, or you can make your own by cutting a piece of Avery Self-Adhesive Laminating Sheets to fit the screen. Laminate It! is a similar product that also works well as a Pocket PC screen protector.

two devices to communicate with each other. The speed of the infrared port clocks in at 115Kbps, which is the same as the serial port. This isn't quite as big of an issue with the infrared port, however, because it is designed more for mobile communication between devices, as opposed to desktop synchronization. For example, you can use the infrared port with some mobile phones, effectively establishing a wireless Internet connection.

Multimedia Hardware

The last hardware facet of Pocket PCs is multimedia hardware, which is somewhat of a catchall for portions of the Pocket PC device that somehow aid in viewing and/or interacting with multimedia content. Following are the major multimedia hardware components of a Pocket PC device:

- Stylus

- Speaker

- Headphone jack

- Microphone

- Buttons

The stylus might not seem to qualify as a multimedia component of a Pocket PC, but you have to consider the fact that the majority of interaction carried out with the device is done through the stylus. Along with serving as an intuitive means of navigating through the Pocket PC GUI, the stylus can serve as an interesting control for games and other interactive multimedia applications.

The speaker is an obvious piece of hardware that is a necessity for hearing sounds emitted by a Pocket PC. Similarly, the headphone jack provides a convenient way to hear a Pocket PC through headphones without disturbing anyone else. The microphone can be used for verbal note taking, dictation, recording meetings, or maybe even recording your child's first word.

Buttons are where you see the most disparity among different Pocket PC devices. Each manufacturer has their own opinion about what types of buttons are useful and the ergonomics of where they are located. I don't have too strong of an opinion regarding button styles or placement other than to say that I really like Pocket PCs that include a multidirectional gamepad button. Many Pocket PC users will enjoy using their devices to play games, and a gamepad is practically a necessity for many games. Currently, the Casio Cassiopeia E-115 and the Compaq iPAQ H3650 are the only Pocket PCs with gamepads.

One button common to all Pocket PCs is the Record button, which is used to record audio via the microphone. Every Pocket PC also has an Action button on the side of the device. This button is used primarily to scroll a screen up and down, or to select an item in a list above or below the currently selected item. Pressing the Action button is akin to hitting the Enter key on the keyboard; it activates a selected item. The combination of being able to use this button to both navigate and select items makes it possible to use a Pocket PC with one hand.

The Pocket PC Graphical User Interface

If you are a user of earlier versions of Windows CE, then you will probably recognize a lot of changes in the Pocket PC GUI (Graphical User Interface). The GUI of earlier versions of Windows CE was the primary area of complaint by most users because they felt like Microsoft had taken Windows 95/98 and crammed it into a smaller screen. After taking a lot of abuse, Microsoft did their homework and completely revamped the Pocket PC GUI. One of the simplest changes was to get rid of the 3D look in all the graphical components such as buttons and toolbars. Although the 3D look is certainly more appealing, Microsoft conceded that it was an unnecessary luxury in Pocket PC that wasted valuable screen real estate. The resulting flat look is still very clean and aesthetically pleasing.

The Pocket PC GUI can be broken down into four major areas:

Inside Scoop

A neat feature of the infrared support in Pocket PCs is that you can continue working on a Pocket PC while communicating via the infrared port.

- Today Screen

- Navigation Bar

- Command Bar

- Text Input

Figure 2.1 shows how the first three parts of the Pocket PC GUI fit into the overall scheme of things; the fourth is accessible only within the context of an application. The next few sections explore each of these pieces of the Pocket PC GUI puzzle.

Figure 2.1
The major components of the Pocket PC GUI are the Today Screen, the Navigation Bar, and the Command Bar. Navigation Bar— Solid horizontal blue bar at the top of the image Command Bar— Solid horizontal gray bar at the bottom of the image Today Screen— Large portion of screen between the two bars

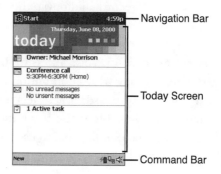

The Navigation Bar is located at the top of the screen, and is visible in most applications. In addition to displaying the current time on the right side of the screen, the Navigation Bar is responsible for housing the Start menu on the left side. The Start menu is very similar to the Start menu in Windows 95/98 in that it provides a convenient place to launch applications. When you run an application, the word "Start" in the Start menu changes to reflect the name of the application; you can still access the Start menu by clicking the Start menu icon to the left of the application name. Figure 2.2 shows the opened Start menu.

The contents of the Start menu are pretty straightforward in that they are applications you can launch. One neat feature of the Start menu that isn't quite so obvious is the line of icons at the top of the menu just above the Today menu item. These icons indicate the last six applications that were run, and provide a quick way to launch any of the applications again. This icon list constantly changes to reflect the last six applications you've used.

→ **See Also** "Customizing the Start Menu," **p. 40**.

Figure 2.2
The Start menu provides a convenient starting point for launching Pocket PC applications.

The Today screen is located just below the Navigation Bar, and serves as the default screen that is displayed when you first turn on your Pocket PC. The Today screen displays the owner of the Pocket PC along with any upcoming appointments, messages, and tasks for the day. In conjunction with the Navigation Bar and Command Bar, the Today screen serves as a great starting point for performing most Pocket PC operations. It is possible to customize the Today screen by altering the graphics near the top of the window, and also by installing third-party applications that present personalized information such as stock quotes.

→ **See Also** "Customizing the Today Screen," **p. 59**.

Below the Today screen you'll find the Command Bar, which is used to display system information, perform application-specific operations, and enter text information via the Soft Input Panel (SIP) button. To the left of the Command Bar is a menu that changes with respect to the currently active application. For example, on the Today Screen the menu consists solely of a New submenu, which displays a list of menu items allowing you to create a new appointment, contact, task, note, email message, Excel workbook, or Word document. On the right side of the Command Bar, there are several icons that display system information. Following are the different pieces

Undocumented
Some Pocket
PCs, such as the
Casio Cassiopeia
E-115, have been
criticized for not
having powerful
enough audio to
listen to digital
music, especially
when there is
background noise
such as riding in
a car or plane. If
you feel you
aren't getting
enough volume
out of your
Pocket PC, you
might want to
check out the
Boostaroo audio
amplifier. It is a
small device that
increases the
gain of a Pocket
PC's headphone
jack, thereby giv-
ing you more vol-
ume. The
Boostaroo also
includes three
headphone jacks,
which allows sev-
eral people to lis-
ten in together.
For more informa-
tion, visit the
Boostaroo Web
site at
http://www.
boostaroo.com.

of system information represented by icons that might appear in this portion of the Command Bar:

- Sounds on/off.

- Main battery is charging.

- Main battery is very low.

- Backup battery is low.

- Backup battery is very low.

- External (AC) power source is connected.

- Dial-up connection is active.

- Direct connection is active.

The Command Bar icons are displayed only when the Today Screen is active; if an application is executing, the SIP button is displayed instead. This button allows you to select the method of input used to enter text. Although the SIP button provides access to only two types of text input by default, there are actually three different approaches supported by Pocket PC:

- Soft keyboard

- Character Recognizer

- Transcriber (must be installed separately)

The soft keyboard is a scaled-down keyboard that is shown on the screen. You can type on the soft keyboard by tapping its keys with the stylus. The Character Recognizer is a handwriting interface that allows you to write individual characters and have them recognized and converted into text. Although the handwriting recognition is quite effective, it can be time-consuming writing individual characters one at a time. Transcriber provides a more powerful means of entering hand-written text; it allows you to write anywhere on the screen. Transcriber is not installed on Pocket PCs by default, but it is available on the ActiveSync CD-ROM that ships with all Pocket PCs. After installing Transcriber, you can access it via the Soft

Input Panel button. You learn much more about Transcriber in Chapter 12, "Transcriber: Handwriting Recognition That Works."

Closing Applications

Although this doesn't technically have anything to do with setting up your Pocket PC, I want to take a moment to explain a facet of the Pocket PC operating system that is somewhat confusing if you are a desktop Windows user. Unlike desktop applications, Pocket PC applications are designed without a means of closing them manually. In other words, you won't find an X in the upper-right corner or an Exit command anywhere in the menus of Pocket PC applications. This can be very frustrating to first-time Pocket PC users who are accustomed to shutting down applications in Windows and are concerned about leaving applications open on their Pocket PC. I struggled for some time trying to figure out how to close applications the first time I used a Pocket PC, so I'm speaking from experience.

The reason for this seemingly strange functionality has to do with the way the Pocket PC operating system manages memory. Pocket PC is constantly assessing available memory and will automatically shut down unused applications as memory is needed. The idea is to simplify the user interface and allow you to focus on tasks instead of applications. In other words, you shouldn't have to concern yourself with what applications are running, but instead focus on what things you need to accomplish. Pocket PC takes on the role of determining when an open application has been idle long enough to warrant being closed.

Another more subtle reason for the lack of a means of explicitly closing applications has to do with the screen size of Pocket PCs. On a desktop computer, it is possible to resize most application windows and have multiple applications in view at any given time. It is common for many users to have several applications running at once, and then switch back and forth between the applications. The screen size of a desktop computer provides enough space to see and work with multiple applications. Pocket PCs, on the other hand, have very limited screen space and don't support the resizing of windows. Consequently, you tend to think of a Pocket PC application as the sole application running at any given time. Of course, you can run multiple applications concurrently on a Pocket PC and share work between them, but the lack of window resizing support still gives the effect of only one application running at any given time.

If you are struggling with the whole notion of allowing the operating system to shut down applications for you, then I encourage you to be patient and try to get used to it. It's actually a pretty convenient feature after you learn to trust it. Even so, there still may be situations where you want to explicitly close an application, usually to free up memory. In these situations, you have two options for closing manually closing applications:

1. Use the Ctrl+C keyboard combination

2. Use the Memory tab in the system settings

The first approach for manually closing applications involves using the keyboard on the Soft Input Panel to enter the Ctrl+C key combination. The Ctrl+C key combination results in the current application being shut down. To enter the combination, select the soft keyboard on the SIP, tap the Ctl key (same as the Ctrl key on a full-size keyboard) in the lower-left corner, and then tap the C key. The current application will then be shut down and removed from memory.

The second approach to shutting down applications manually involves using the system Settings screen. Follow these steps to shut down an application using the system Settings screen:

1. Tap Start, and then tap Settings.

2. Tap the System tab, and then tap the Memory icon.

3. Tap the Running Programs tab.

4. Tap the application you'd like to shut down in the list of running applications.

5. Tap the Stop button to close the application. You can also tap Stop All to close all running applications.

Watch Out!
On the Memory Settings screen, there is an option to remove programs. Although your first impression may be that this removes a program from memory, it actually removes the selected application from your device.

Essential Information

- Although Pocket PCs are unified in their operating system, the processors used in different devices vary widely among manufacturers.

- Because Pocket PCs aren't designed with a hard drive in mind, memory is the most important hardware component of a Pocket PC.

- Even with the confusion and negative press brought on by color problems with the screen in HP's Jornada line of Pocket PCs, the overall screen quality of Pocket PCs is significantly better than other handheld devices.

- The Pocket PC graphical user interface revolves around the Today screen, which provides a window into daily activities and commitments, not to mention a convenient place to launch applications and survey system information at a glance.

GET THE SCOOP ON...
Personalizing Your Pocket PC ▪ Customizing Pocket
PC Menus ▪ Extending the Backlight and Power ▪
Synchronizing and Exploring with ActiveSync ▪
Decorating Your Pocket PC with Custom Graphics

Setting Up Your Pocket PC

IF YOU'RE LIKE ME, IT'S HARD to be patient and learn how to use a new gadget when you first get it. I want to immediately turn it on and begin tinkering. If you're not a tinkerer, that's okay, too. Fortunately, this chapter is for both tinkerers and the tinkering impaired because it addresses the basics of setting up a Pocket PC, along with some interesting customizations that you won't find in the manual that came with the device. You can think of this chapter as an insider's look at how to set up and tweak your Pocket PC so that it's perfectly tailored to you.

If you're already an avid Pocket PC user and are long past the setup phase, you'll find some interesting pieces of information in this chapter. For example, you might not have known that it's possible to customize the graphics on the Today screen to suit your own tastes.

Personalizing Your Pocket PC

The first step in setting up a Pocket PC is to personalize it by telling it who you are and what time zone you live in. Before you can begin personalizing your device, however, you must take care of a small bit of technical housekeeping. When your Pocket PC first powers up out of the box, it guides you through aligning the screen. This is necessary to properly align the screen within the device's display. You perform the screen alignment by tapping the stylus on a series of crosshairs as they appear on the screen.

After aligning the screen, you are prompted to enter your city and time zone. This information is important to keep the system clock running properly. Keep in mind that the system clock is used to schedule appointments and meetings, which is why accuracy is a must. Speaking of the system clock, you'll probably have to set it unless your device magically has the correct date and time already set when you get it. Following are the steps required to set the date and time on your device:

1. Go to the Today screen (tap Start, and then tap Today).

2. Tap the date just below the time in the upper-right corner, which brings up the Clock Settings page.

3. Use the arrows to set the correct date and time.

4. Tap OK in the upper-right corner, and then tap Yes to save changes to the clock settings.

With the date and time set, you are ready to enter owner information, which is very important should you ever misplace the device. The following steps guide you through entering owner information:

1. Go to the Today screen.

2. Tap the Owner band just below the Today graphic.

3. Fill in the text fields with your name, company, street address, telephone number, and email address. The Soft Input Panel (virtual keyboard) automatically appears when you tap one of the text fields.

4. Check the check box below the text fields if you want the device to display owner information on a Power-On screen when it is first turned on. The idea is that someone would immediately know to whom a lost device belongs when it's first turned on. This option is a necessity if you plan on setting a password on the device (covered in the next section).

Watch Out!
Make sure the time zone is set properly on your desktop computer or you will find that your Pocket PC's clock will get reset each time you synchronize.

Remember
The process of aligning the screen and establishing the city/time zone, as well as personalizing your device, must also be repeated when you perform a hard reset of the device.

5. Tap the Notes tab at the bottom of the screen if you want to add any notes about yourself. The check box on the Notes page allows you to designate that the notes are displayed when the device is first turned on.

6. Tap OK in the upper-right corner to accept the owner information.

Now that your Pocket PC knows your name, it's time for you to give your device a name of its own. Naming your device is important because this name is used to identify the device when you synchronize with a desktop computer. It is more difficult to alter the name after you've set up the ActiveSync synchronization software, so I encourage you to do it now. The device name also comes into play if you perform a hard reset after having set up the device for synchronization; you'll need to restore the original device name in order to synchronize and restore the device from a backup.

1. Tap Start, and then tap Settings.

2. Tap the System tab, and then tap the About icon.

3. Tap the Device ID tab.

4. Enter a name for the device (no spaces), along with a device description.

5. Tap OK in the upper-right corner to accept the device name and description.

Your Pocket PC is now personalized in terms of knowing who you are and having a name for itself. Now, you must consider whether you need to protect information on the device from the prying eyes of others.

Password Protecting the Device

The Pocket PC operating system allows you to set a system password that is requested each time the device is turned on. If the password is entered incorrectly, the device won't let you get past the password-entry screen. Setting a password is a personal preference, and has a lot to do with how you plan to use your

Watch Out!
If you plan on setting a password for your Pocket PC, be sure to check the check box on the Owner Information screen that displays owner information when the device is turned on. If you don't, if the device is lost, the person who finds it won't be able to get past the password screen to find out who owns the device.

Remember
The Pocket PC device name must start with a letter and consist of the letters A-Z and numbers 0-9. Underscores are also allowed, and can be used instead of spaces if you want to separate words.

40   Part I · Getting Started with Your Pocket PC

Remember
If you decide to password protect your Pocket PC, be sure to set the device so it displays owner information when turned on.

Watch Out!
Be sure to select a password that you won't forget. If you should forget your password, the only way to get back into your Pocket PC is to perform a hard reset, which blitzes the device memory. If you're like me and still run the risk of forgetting the password, just be sure to back up your device regularly. Then, if you ever have to perform a hard reset, you can still restore everything. For more information on how to perform a hard reset for your particular device, refer to Appendix C, "Resetting Your Pocket PC," or check the manuals that came with your device.

Pocket PC. If you will store sensitive information such as credit card numbers or business information that could be detrimental in the wrong hands, then a password is a necessity. You also might want to set a password if you plan on using Pocket Money, because your personal finance information should be protected.

The Pocket PC password is actually more of a PIN number. It's a four-digit number that you must enter by tapping on numeric keys on the screen, much like you would enter your PIN number for a bank account at an ATM. To set a password and password protect your device, follow these steps:

1. Tap Start, and then tap Settings.

2. Tap the Password icon (this icon is labeled "HP security" on the HP Jornada series of Pocket PCs).

3. Enter a four-digit password by tapping the numeric keys on the screen. Be sure to select a password that you won't forget.

4. Tap OK in the upper-right corner, and then tap Yes to save the password settings.

Now that your Pocket PC is safe and secure, the next step is to do some tweaking to the Start menu to tailor things a little more to your liking.

Customizing the Start Menu

The Start menu is the anchor of the Pocket PC user interface, and is typically used a great deal to launch applications or open folders. In fact, the Start menu allows you to be only two taps away from any application or folder. Therefore, it is important that it contain exactly the applications and folders you plan to use regularly, and nothing more. Fortunately, it's easy to customize the Start menu. The following steps explain how:

1. Tap Start, and then tap Settings.

2. Tap the Menus icon.

3. Check and uncheck appropriate applications and folders to customize the contents of the Start menu (Figure 3.1).

4. Tap OK in the upper-right corner to accept the Start menu changes.

Figure 3.1
Customizing the Start menu is as simple as checking and unchecking the applications that you'd like to appear in the menu.

The first item displayed in the Start menu is a series of icons that indicate the last six applications you've used. This is intended to provide a quick means of accessing recently used applications; tap an icon to launch the given application.

Customizing the New Menu

Another important part of the Pocket PC user interface is the New menu, which is located in the lower-left corner of the screen, that provides a convenient place to create new documents. Following are the types of documents that can be created with the New menu, along with the applications used to modify them:

- Appointments, Calendar

- Tasks, Tasks

- Contacts, Contacts

- Notes, Notes

- Email messages, Inbox

- Excel workbooks, Pocket Excel

- Word documents, Pocket Word

Watch Out!
The Start menu is capable of holding only eight applications/ folders and still fit on the screen. If you check more than eight applications/ folders you'll have to scroll down in the Start menu to access some of the menu items.

The New menu helps add a document-centric feel to Pocket PCs, which means that you think in terms of documents rather than applications. As an example, the New menu allows you to focus on creating a spreadsheet or email message, as opposed to focusing on running Pocket Excel or Inbox. The shift from applications to documents is subtle, but has been taking place in the desktop Windows environment for the past several years.

The New menu can be customized, in which case you specify which types of documents you want to be able to create via the menu. The other customization available with the New menu is enabling the New menu button, which is a small up arrow that appears next to the New menu. On the Today screen, the button doesn't add any functionality, but within an application, the button allows you to create new documents of any of the previous types listed. Without having the button enabled, which is the default setting, you can use the New button only to create new documents of the same type as the application you are using. Of course, you always have full access to creating different document types via the New menu when you are on the Today screen.

To customize the New menu, follow these steps:

1. Tap Start, and then tap Settings.

2. Tap the Menus icon, and then tap the New Menu tab.

3. Check the check box above the document types to turn on the New menu button.

4. Check and uncheck appropriate document types to customize the contents of the New menu.

5. Tap OK in the upper-right corner to accept the New menu changes.

Your New button is now customized and ready to help you create new documents with ease. Let's now turn our attention to the backlight that many find annoying because it seems to be constantly dimming itself.

Extending the Backlight

With battery life a consistent concern for any PDA owner, your Pocket PC, by default, is most likely set up to preserve power to its fullest. One of the features that preserves battery life is the automatic dimming of the backlight on the screen when the device sits inactive for a given period of time. Although Auto Dim is a handy and valuable feature, I think you'll agree that the default timeout period of 15 seconds is way too short. I don't mind a little extra battery drain if it means not having to worry about tapping the screen every 15 seconds. Besides, even the most battery-hungry Pocket PCs still have reasonable battery life. The battery life of Pocket PCs currently ranges from 6 to 14 hours, depending upon a variety of different things such as the type of battery and the type of screen, to name a couple.

→ **See Also** "Power," **p. 23**.

To alter the backlight timeout period for the backlight, follow these steps:

1. Tap Start, and then tap Settings.

2. Tap the System tab, and then tap the Brightness icon; this icon is named Backlight on some devices.

3. Tap the Auto Dim tab.

4. Tap the combo box below the Battery Power check box and select a new timeout period for the Auto Dim feature; I prefer 2 minutes.

5. Tap OK in the upper-right corner to accept the Auto Dim changes.

You might have noticed that you can also set Auto Dim to work with an external power source. This option is unchecked by default because there really isn't much of a power savings issue when running a Pocket PC off an external power source.

Extending the Power

Similar to the Auto Dim feature, in my opinion the default setting for the Power Off feature is too short. The Power Off feature is responsible for automatically turning off the device

Watch Out!
Not all Pocket PCs have an Auto Dim feature but most of them allow you to somehow control the backlight. If your device doesn't have an AutoDim tab in the Brightness/Backli ght settings, then look for a setting that allows you to alter the back- light. For example, Compaq iPAQ devices allow you to select the level of brightness from several settings, although you might want to stick with the Auto setting because it does a good job of adjust- ing the backlight automatically.

Remember
If you have a Casio E-115 device and really want to fine-tune the screen proper-ties of your Pocket PC, you can alter the con-trast and bright-ness from the same Brightness Properties page. To do so, just tap the Contrast or Brightness tabs that appear at the bottom of the screen next to the Auto Dim tab.

when it sits idle for a certain period of time. By default, this timeout period is set to three minutes. Although I can appre-ciate the logic behind wanting to save precious battery life, three minutes is likely too short for the tastes of most users. I would rather lose a little battery life than have to constantly keep turning the device back on. This is ultimately a personal preference, however, so by all means feel free to be as miserly as you want with battery life.

To change the Power Off timeout period, follow these steps:

1. Tap Start, and then tap Settings.

2. Tap the System tab, and then tap the Power icon.

3. Tap the Power Off tab.

4. Tap the first combo box and select a new timeout period for the Power Off feature; I prefer 5 minutes (Figure 3.2).

5. Tap OK in the upper-right corner to accept the Power Off changes.

Figure 3.2
The Power Off tab on the Power Properties screen allows you to adjust the timeout period for the Power Off feature.

Similar to Auto Dim, you can also set Power Off to work with an external power source. Not surprisingly, this option is unchecked by default because power savings isn't a big deal when running a Pocket PC off an external power source.

Tweaking the Soft Input Panel

The last stop on this tour of Pocket PC setup and customiza-tion is to tweak the Soft Input Panel (SIP) to suit your style of input. As you might already know, the SIP supports two standard approaches to text input:

- Character Recognizer

- Keyboard

The SIP automatically appears in context at the lower-right corner of the screen when you are in an application that requires text entry. The first SIP customization has to do with the Keyboard input method. You can change the size of the virtual keyboard keys and establish gestures with the stylus that correspond to commonly used keys such as Shift and Enter. Gestures are special strokes that you make with the stylus that perform a special function such as capitalizing a letter, deleting a character, or imitating a control key such as Shift or Enter. Gestures are performed over the soft keyboard in the SIP, and are interpreted as control entries rather than character entries.

Gestures are available only with large keys, but I encourage you to try them out. I got used to them in a matter of minutes and found them to be quite efficient in avoiding having to peck the Space, Shift, Backspace, and Enter keys; you can perform the gestures anywhere on the keyboard. The main benefit is the Shift gesture, which applies to the key that you perform the gesture over. For example, to enter a capital M, you tap on the M key and drag upward with the stylus.

→ **See Also** "KeySync Keyboard," **p. 370**.

To customize the Keyboard input method, follow these steps:

1. Launch any application that involves text entry, such as Notes.

2. Tap the up arrow on the SIP, and then tap Options.

3. To use large keys, tap the Large keys radio button (Small Keys is the default setting).

4. To enable gestures, tap the Gestures check box.

5. Tap OK in the upper-right corner to accept the Keyboard input method changes.

Another customization that is useful in regard to user input involves the Word Completion feature. Word Completion is the feature that suggests words in a pop-up window while you're entering text. Ideally, Word Completion suggests the word you're entering and you can quickly tap it to avoid the extra text entry. The default setting for Word Completion is to suggest one word after you enter two letters. Although the two-letter settings seems to work well, I prefer having more words from which to choose.

To raise the number of words suggested by the Word Completion feature, follow these steps:

1. Tap the up arrow on the SIP, and then tap Options.

2. Tap the Word Completion tab.

3. Tap the first combo box and select a new number of words for the Word Completion feature; I prefer four words. I've found the default settings for the other preferences on this page to work well, but you are free to change them if you like. As an example, you can change the number of letters that are entered before the Word Completion feature kicks in (two is the default).

4. Tap OK in the upper-right corner to accept the Word Completion changes.

You might have noticed an Options tab at the bottom of the screen when setting the previous input options. This tab allows you to customize input settings such as the audio format used for voice recording, the zoom level used for writing and typing text, and a couple of other neat text-entry features. I find it beneficial to make a slight modification to these settings. First, I think 8,000 Hz, 16 Bit, Mono (16 KB/s) audio provides a better tradeoff of quality and storage space for voice recordings than the default setting. If you aren't so concerned about minimizing storage space and you prefer higher-quality audio, then you may consider changing this setting to a higher quality such as "11,025 Hz, 16 Bit, Stereo (43 KB/s)." Just keep in mind that these settings apply to voice recordings, which rarely have to be of superior sound quality.

To alter the input settings within the Options tab on the Input Settings screen, follow these steps:

1. Tap the up arrow on the SIP, and then tap Options.

2. Tap the Options tab.

3. Tap the first combo box and select 8,000 Hz, 16 Bit, Mono (16 KB/s) for the voice recording format; feel free to adjust this setting for your own purposes if you are familiar with audio formats.

4. Tap the second and third combo boxes and select 150% for each.

5. Tap OK in the upper-right corner to accept the input Options changes.

That wraps up the setup and most of the personalization of your Pocket PC device. I encourage you to tinker with the settings and tailor them to your own needs and preferences. Even so, I've tried to provide you with what I've found to be the most useful customization changes. Later in the chapter in the section titled "Decorating Your Pocket PC," you learn how to personalize the look of your device by changing the graphics on the Power-On and Today screen.

Synchronizing with the ActiveSync Software

The Pocket PC operating system comes standard with a wide range of applications and interesting features. Because these applications and features are implemented in ROM, you don't ever have to worry about reinstalling them. Even with this rich set of functionality built into your Pocket PC, you will undoubtedly want to expand its horizons by installing new software. Perhaps even more important is the capability of sharing and synchronizing data with your desktop PC. To accomplish any of this, you must establish a connection between your Pocket PC and your desktop PC.

The physical connection between a Pocket PC and a desktop PC is pretty straightforward, and involves one of the following types of connections:

- USB

- Serial

- Infrared

- Ethernet

Inside Scoop
Because most
desktop PCs don't
have an infrared
port, an infrared
connection with a
Pocket PC is usu-
ally established
with an infrared
USB adapter. An
infrared USB
adapter plugs into
the USB port of
the desktop com-
puter and provides
an infrared port;
you align the
Pocket PC's
infrared port with
it and you're good
to go.

USB is the preferred connection type for most users because it's the fastest among non-Ethernet connections. However, not all Pocket PCs support USB, in which case you must rely on a serial or infrared connection. If you have the capability of connecting to your desktop computer via an Ethernet connection, then you might want to consider purchasing an Ethernet CF card for your Pocket PC. Ethernet connections are extremely fast (up to 10MB/s) and result in very quick synchronization. Short of Ethernet, a USB connection is your best bet for reasonably speedy synchronization.

Your device most likely came with a cradle, which is used to establish the physical connection between it and the desktop PC. Additionally, the cradle for most Pocket PCs also serves as a recharging unit for the main batteries of the device. The first step in connecting your Pocket PC to a desktop PC is to connect the cradle to the desktop PC. After that's done, you can go ahead and set the Pocket PC in the cradle, in which case its batteries will probably start charging.

Now that the Pocket PC's physical connection is established with the desktop PC, you're ready to tackle the software side of the equation. This is carried out with Microsoft's ActiveSync software, which ships on a CD-ROM standard with all Pocket PCs. ActiveSync is responsible for detecting a Pocket PC connection and allowing you to synchronize and share data between a Pocket PC device and a desktop computer. Synchronization is quite powerful, and is handled at the application level. In other words, you set the applications whose data you would like to have synchronized. You'll quickly learn that ActiveSync is a very straightforward application to use.

Before installing ActiveSync, it's worth making a slight modification to the connection settings for your device. By default, your Pocket PC's synchronization connection speed is set to 57,600Kbps. This speed isn't too bad, but why not go faster if possible? You can go faster by raising the connection speed. Follow these steps to raise the connection speed of your device to 115,200Kbps:

1. Tap Start, and then tap Settings.

2. Tap the Connections tab.

3. Tap the Power Off tab.

4. Tap the combo box and select 115200 Default as the connection speed.

5. Tap OK in the upper-right corner to accept the connection speed changes.

Your Pocket PC is now ready to establish a relationship with the desktop PC.

Setting Up and Synchronizing

To begin installing the ActiveSync software, insert the ActiveSync CD-ROM into the CD-ROM drive of the desktop PC with which you are synchronizing your Pocket PC. After a few moments, you will see the window shown in Figure 3.3, which is the beginning of the ActiveSync Installation Wizard.

Clicking the Next button proceeds to start the installation process. The next window displayed allows you to select the

Undocumented
You may be wondering whether the ActiveSync software is available for Macintosh computers. Unfortunately, as of this writing it is not. However, it is possible to use the Windows version of ActiveSync on a Macintosh with the help of a Windows emulation software package called Virtual PC. Virtual PC emulates a Windows environment within the Macintosh operating system, and allows you to install ActiveSync and use it as if it was actually running on a Windows system.

Figure 3.3
The beginning of the ActiveSync Installation Wizard is the first window you see when installing the ActiveSync software.

Remember
If you have the Autorun feature of Windows disabled, you'll need to manually run the ActiveSync setup program by clicking Run on the Start menu, and then selecting Setup.exe from the CD-ROM.

installation folder for ActiveSync. I recommend keeping the default setting, but clicking the Change button allows you to put ActiveSync anywhere you want.

Clicking Next moves you along to a screen that confirms you have physically connected your Pocket PC to the desktop PC. Upon clicking Next on this window, the Installation Wizard searches for a connected Pocket PC device on the available COM (serial) ports and USB ports. If the device isn't found, double check that the cradle is properly connected to the desktop PC, the Pocket PC is firmly seated in the cradle, and the Pocket PC has a charge on its batteries.

When the device is found, the window in Figure 3.4 is displayed, which asks whether you want to set up a partnership. To synchronize application data, such as the email in your Inbox or tasks in the Tasks application, you must create a partnership between the two machines. Although a partnership is not required to establish a connection and share information between the Pocket PC and the desktop PC, without a partnership you are limited to copying or moving files back and forth between the machines and installing applications. In other words, you won't be able to synchronize data with an application.

Figure 3.4
The next window of the ActiveSync Installation Wizard allows you to set up a partnership, which is necessary for synchronizing application data.

Assuming you selected the Yes radio button to set up a partnership, the Select a Personal Information Manager window appears next. This window prompts you to select the desktop application to be used for synchronizing appointments, contacts, and tasks. You will probably want to keep the default settings of Microsoft Outlook, unless you use some other personal information manager.

The guts of the partnership are established in the Synchronization Settings window, which is displayed next (see Figure 3.5). This window allows you to select the specific applications you want synchronize with. Resist the temptation to select all of them, because you will likely only be interested in synchronizing certain types of information. As an example, I typically synchronize only the Calendar, Contacts, Inbox, and Tasks applications. Following are the applications that can be synchronized:

- AvantGo

- Calendar

- Contacts

- Favorite

- Files

- Inbox

- Notes

- Tasks

Figure 3.5
The Synchronization Settings window allows you to select applications you want to synchronize with.

You can fine-tune the settings of the synchronized applications by selecting an application in the list and then clicking the

Settings button. Figure 3.6 shows the settings available for the Inbox application.

Figure 3.6
The Inbox Synchronization Settings window allows you to customize the manner in which email messages are synchronized via the Inbox application.

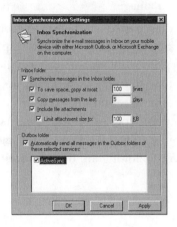

If you compare the options selected in this figure to the default settings of your Pocket PC, you can see that I made a few changes to the default settings. The Include File Attachments option allows you to receive attachments along with email messages. Although this is a very useful feature, you need to be careful about limiting the size of the attachments so that you don't receive enormous files along with email. The ActiveSync check box under the Outbox Folder options allows you to send email from your Pocket PC through your desktop email client, which in this case is Microsoft Outlook. In other words, you can enter email messages while out and about with your Pocket PC, and then when you get home set the Pocket PC in its cradle and have the email automatically sent through your desktop PC's email service.

Click OK to accept the Inbox Synchronization Settings, and then Next to accept the Synchronization Settings. You will then see Figure 3.7, which is the end of the ActiveSync Installation Wizard.

At this point, you can click the Finish button to finish the installation and begin using ActiveSync. ActiveSync automatically begins synchronizing the applications you selected during installation, which might take a few minutes depending on how much information you have stored in each application

Inside Scoop
I've found that it is useful to turn on the Include File Attachments option and limit the attachment size to 100KB. That way, when a relative sends you a whopping 2MB MPEG video of junior's first steps, you won't be wasting precious RAM or synchronization time.

(see Figure 3.8). The really neat thing about ActiveSync is that it's automatic in its approach to synchronization. To test it out, try modifying a piece of synchronized information on the desktop PC and watch for Active Sync to spring into action and synchronize it on the Pocket PC. The same thing applies to modifying synchronized data on the Pocket PC.

Figure 3.7
The final step of the ActiveSync Installation Wizard clarifies the completion of the ActiveSync installation.

Figure 3.8
Synchronization can take a few minutes if you have a lot of information to be synchronized.

You can tell that synchronization is complete because the circular green icon in the upper-right corner of the ActiveSync window stops its animation; the small green ActiveSync icon in the system tray also stops its animation. More importantly, the status of each of the types of synchronized information turns to Synchronized as shown in Figure 3.8 for the Calendar type.

One thorny issue in regard to synchronization is the potential conflict that arises if you modify a piece of synchronized data on both the Pocket PC and the desktop PC before synchronization takes place. Which version of the data does ActiveSync accept and use as the basis for synchronization? When this type of conflict occurs, ActiveSync flags the data item as

Inside Scoop

If your Inbox consists of several subfolders of archived email, you might be concerned about all this mail getting synchronized with the Pocket PC. This is not a problem because ActiveSync synchronizes only with the Inbox of the desktop mail client, meaning that the only email synchronized with the Pocket PC is email present in the Inbox folder of your Pocket PC; any other mail folders are ignored.

"unresolved" during synchronization. Then, you must resolve the conflict by selecting one of the versions of the item as the correct one.

One option for handling synchronization conflict resolution is to always let your desktop computer win. In other words, you're saying that in the event of a synchronization conflict, always replace the version on the Pocket PC with the desktop version. This makes sense for many users because your desktop PC is likely to have the latest versions of all application data. To set this option in ActiveSync, follow these steps:

1. Click the Options button on the main toolbar.

2. Click the Rules tab.

3. Click the middle radio button, which indicates that the item on the device should always be replaced. The other radio buttons correspond to options that allow you to leave a conflict unresolved or replace the version on the computer with the Pocket PC version.

4. Click OK to accept the Conflict Resolution options.

Another synchronization option that you might want to consider is the synchronization mode, which is available under the Sync Mode tab in the ActiveSync Options dialog box. There are three possible settings for the synchronization mode, which determine when synchronization takes place:

- Continuously while the device is connected

- Only upon connection

- Manually

The default setting is the first one, which is guaranteed to provide the most accurate level of synchronization because the device is constantly synchronizing as data changes. If you aren't so concerned about up-to-the-minute synchronization, then the second option is reasonable, too. In this case, the device is synchronized upon being connected to the desktop PC. Keep in mind that you can still manually synchronize whenever you want by clicking the Sync button on the main ActiveSync toolbar.

Exploring from a Desktop PC

Synchronizing via ActiveSync is the automated way to keep your Pocket PC and your desktop PC on the same track in terms of application data. ActiveSync also supports exploring the Pocket PC, which basically lets you use Windows Explorer on your desktop PC to explore the file system of the Pocket PC. In doing so, you can move, copy, or delete files between the Pocket PC and the desktop PC. To explore your Pocket PC, open ActiveSync by clicking Start, Programs, and then Microsoft ActiveSync, followed by the Explore button on the main ActiveSync toolbar. This results in an Explorer window appearing that shows the My Documents folder in the Pocket PC file system (Figure 3.9).

Double-clicking the My Pocket PC icon takes you to the root level of the file system where you can directly access the familiar My Documents and Program Files folders, among others.

Because the standard Windows Explorer application is used to explore the Pocket PC, you are free to copy and move files by dragging and dropping them between Explorer instances. So, to copy or move files between the Pocket PC and the desktop PC, you just open another Explorer window and explore your hard drive. From there you can drag and drop between the two Explorer instances with ease. Behind the scenes, ActiveSync is handling the actual file transfers, but it is seamless from your perspective .

Watch Out!
Unfortunately, it might be necessary for you to switch the synchronization mode to Only Upon Connection to circumvent a bug in Pocket Money. Although I've yet to cover Pocket Money, it's worth pointing out that the current version is very sensitive about continuous synchronization and can corrupt its own database. The safest thing to do is set the synchronization mode to Only Upon Connection. This information is covered in more detail in Chapter 15, "Using Pocket Money."

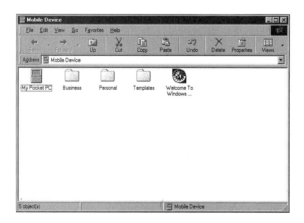

Figure 3.9
Exploring a Pocket PC device begins with the My Documents folder in Explorer.

Backing Up Your Pocket PC

Remember
ActiveSync can also be launched by double-clicking the ActiveSync icon in the desktop system tray.

ActiveSync includes a powerful backup feature that I encourage you to explore and use on a regular basis. By regularly backing up your Pocket PC, you minimize the chances of losing valuable data due to a battery problem or some other more serious accident such as dropping your device in water. The backup feature in ActiveSync is accessed via the Tools menu; the Backup/Restore command on the Tools menu takes you to the Backup/Restore dialog box, which is shown in Figure 3.10.

Figure 3.10
The Backup/Restore dialog box in the ActiveSync application allows you to perform a backup on your device or restore a previous backup to your device.

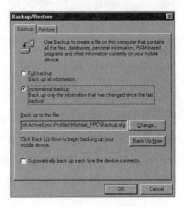

Undocumented
As long as ActiveSync is running, you can also explore your Pocket PC from Windows Explorer by clicking the Mobile Device icon in the My Computer window. You can open the Mobile Device icon to reveal the entire file system of the Pocket PC.

The two radio buttons in the Backup/Restore dialog box allow you to choose between a full or incremental backup. A full backup always backs up everything on your device regardless of whether you've backed it up before, whereas an incremental backup backs up only information that has changed since the previous backup. Incremental backups are faster and take up less space on your desktop computer's hard drive, and are probably the best backup approach to use unless you don't plan to back up your device frequently.

Near the bottom of the Backup/Restore dialog box is a check box that allows you to automatically back up your device each time it connects via ActiveSync. Although this might seem like a lot of overhead in terms of information transfer, if you choose the incremental backup approach, then automatic backups are pretty quick. This is a great way to guarantee that your device's contents are always safely stored away on your desktop computer in the case of a problem. The Change button in the Backup/Restore dialog box allows you to change the name and location of the backup file on the desktop computer.

When you are ready to perform a backup, click the Back Up Now button in the Backup/Restore dialog box. Figure 3.11 shows the backup process taking place.

Figure 3.11
The backup process can take a while if your device is full of data.

After performing a backup, it is very easy to restore information to your device. To restore a previous backup, click the Restore tab in the Backup/Restore dialog box. Figure 3.12 shows this dialog box, which is pretty simple.

Figure 3.12
The Restore tab in the Backup/Restore dialog box allows you to restore backed-up data.

To restore backed-up data to your device, close all applications running on the device and then click the Restore Now button in the Restore tab of the Backup/Restore dialog box in ActiveSync. Unlike the backup process, you can't abort the restore process after it begins. It is important that you don't use your device until the restore process finishes.

→ **See Also** "Closing Applications," **p. 33**.

Inside Scoop
It's generally a good idea to back up your Pocket PC at least once a month.

Decorating Your Pocket PC

You've covered a lot of territory in this chapter, so let's lighten things up with a couple of somewhat esoteric Pocket PC customizations to the graphics on the Power-On and Today screens. These graphics can be easily set by copying appropriately named files onto your Pocket PC.

Watch Out!
The previous steps to customizing the Power-On screen won't work on the HP Jornada series of Pocket PCs due to HP's implementation of the Power-On screen. Jornada Pocket PCs do allow you to customize the Power-On screen but they use a different name and format for the image file. In fact, the image used on the Jornada Power-On screen is actually much larger, measuring 240×295 in size. To customize the Power-On screen of a Jornada Pocket PC, follow the previous steps but create a bitmap (BMP) image that is 240×295 in size and name it hpstart.bmp. It is important that this image be stored in the Windows Bitmap format and not GIF.

Customizing the Power-On Screen

If you recall, the Power-On screen is displayed when a Pocket PC is first turned on, provided that you have checked the option on the Owner Information screen that displays owner information when the device is turned on. Please refer to the "Personalizing Your Pocket PC" section earlier in this chapter for more information on setting this option. It is possible to customize the graphical image displayed on the Power-On screen, which isn't a huge functional issue but does add a touch of personalization to your device.

The image displayed on the Power-On screen is a GIF image of size 240×60. To change the look of the Power-On screen, you create a GIF image that is 240×60 in size using whatever graphical program you have at your disposal and copy it over the default image on the device. The default image is named myinfo.gif, and is located in the \Windows folder on the device. You can change the image as much as you want. Following are the steps required to customize the Power-On screen:

1. Create a GIF image that is 240×60 in size and name it myinfo.gif.

2. Use ActiveSync to explore to the \Windows folder on your Pocket PC.

3. Copy the myinfo.gif file from your desktop PC to the \Windows folder on your Pocket PC, making sure to confirm the replacement of the existing file.

4. Turn the device off and back on to see the results.

Figure 3.13 shows the Power-On screen of my Pocket PC customized with a mountain image.

Figure 3.13

Figure 3.13
You can customize the image on the Power-On screen to give your Pocket PC a more personal feel when it is turned on.

Customizing the Today Screen

Like the Power-On screen, the Today screen is also customizable in terms of the graphics you see in the background near the top of the screen. Unlike the Power-On screen, the Today screen uses two images: one that is displayed behind the date and another larger image that appears just below the date and includes the word "Today." Following are the names and sizes of these two images:

- tdydate.gif: 240×20

- tdybnr.gif: 240×40

Similar to customization of the Power-On screen, customizing the Today screen images involves replacing the images in the \Windows folder of the Pocket PC with images of your own. Following are the steps required to change the Today screen images:

1. Create a GIF image that is 240×20 in size and name it tdydate.gif.

2. Create a GIF image that is 240×40 in size and name it tdybnr.gif.

3. Use ActiveSync to explore to the \Windows folder on your Pocket PC.

4. Copy the GIF files from your desktop PC to the \Windows folder on your Pocket PC, making sure to confirm the replacement of the existing files.

Inside Scoop
If you aren't too artistically inclined or don't have the desire to create your own Today screen images, you'll be glad to know that there are images readily available for you to download off the Web. James Feck has a Web page located at http://www.thefecks.com/pocketpc/today_page.html that includes Today screen images that he created. The Pocket PC software company DeveloperOne also hosts a Web page containing Today screen images, which is located at http://www.developerone.com/pocketpc/tips/today.

5. Perform a soft reset of the device for the Today screen changes to take effect.

Figure 3.14 shows the Today screen of my Pocket PC customized with images of a scenic lake.

Figure 3.14
You can customize the images on the Today screen to personalize your Pocket PC.

In addition to customizing the background images on the Today screen, you might also want to consider making an additional, more practical change to the way the Today screen is accessed. Because the Today screen serves as a starting point in the Pocket PC user interface, it makes sense that it should be readily available. Granted, you can always get to it from the top of the Start menu, but I like the idea of my Pocket PC automatically taking me back to the Today screen if I haven't used the device for a while. Fortunately, this feature is built in to the Pocket PC operating system, and you can alter it to have the Today screen displayed more often.

By default, your Pocket PC is set up so the Today screen is displayed if the device is idle for four hours. I prefer the minimum setting for this feature, which is one hour. To change the idle period for the Today screen, follow these steps:

1. Go to the Today screen.

2. Tab the Today graphic near the top of the screen just below the date.

3. Select the idle period in the combo box near the bottom of the screen.

4. Click OK to accept the Today Settings changes.

You might have noticed in the Today Settings screen that you can customize the information that is displayed on the Today screen. To do so, you check and uncheck the information that you want to have displayed. By default, all the items are checked, which results in the most information being displayed on the Today screen. This is my personal preference because there is plenty of room on the Today screen and you might as well use it.

Essential Information

- Set the owner information for your Pocket PC so you can be contacted if your Pocket PC is lost and found.

- The Start menu provides quick access to any application with two taps of the stylus, and can be customized to suit your own tastes.

- Password protecting your Pocket PC is a good idea if you plan to keep sensitive information on the device, such as credit card numbers or business information.

- The ActiveSync software allows you to synchronize application data between your Pocket PC and a desktop PC, explore the Pocket PC file system, copy and move files, and install applications.

- Altering the visual appearance of the Power-On and Today screens is as simple as replacing a few images in the \Windows folder on your Pocket PC.

Pocket PC: The Next Generation PDA

PART II

GET THE SCOOP ON...
The Relationship Between Pocket Outlook and Outlook
2000 ▪ How to Use the Basic Features in Pocket
Outlook ▪ Synchronizing Email with Pocket Outlook and
Outlook 2000 ▪ How Pocket Outlook Compares to
Palm's Personal Information Management Software

Using Pocket Outlook

Chapter 4

A S YOU KNOW, POCKET PC is an operating system crammed with useful applications right out of the box. These applications are stored in ROM, which means they are permanent and always available for use; you can't uninstall them. Of all the applications that come with a Pocket PC, the one that is likely to see the most use is Pocket Outlook, which is a scaled-down version of the popular desktop information manager, Microsoft Outlook. Pocket Outlook includes basic personal information management features such as the detailed management of contacts, appointments, tasks, email, and support for taking notes.

This chapter introduces you to Pocket Outlook and explores its relationship to its desktop relative, Microsoft Outlook 2000. There is also a primer on performing basic functions with Pocket Outlook, along with a quick comparison of Pocket Outlook to similar software on Palm devices.

Pocket Outlook Versus Outlook 2000

Although Pocket Outlook is likely the application you will use the most on your Pocket PC, you probably wouldn't know it if all you've been doing is tinkering with your device. Because Pocket Outlook isn't implemented as a single Pocket PC application, it doesn't go by the name "Pocket Outlook" in the context of the Pocket PC user interface. Instead, Pocket Outlook is implemented as five different applications that work in concert to carry out roughly the same functionality as Outlook 2000, the desktop version of Outlook. I say "roughly" because Pocket Outlook takes a much leaner approach to personal information management than Outlook 2000; this is a necessity given the resource constraints of mobile devices.

There is no arguing that Pocket Outlook has a smaller feature set than Outlook 2000, but that's not necessarily a bad thing. When using a handheld device such as a Pocket PC, you want a streamlined computing experience. Granted, this should ideally be the same goal for desktop software, but desktop software typically offers such a broad set of features that it's acceptable for the user interface to be a little more complex. Mobile devices have to be much more careful when it comes to balancing features with simplicity and usability, an area in which previous iterations of the Windows CE OS have failed.

Aside from having limited memory, the most dramatic limitation imposed on mobile devices such as Pocket PCs is limited screen real estate. Resolutions upward of 800×600 are now very common on desktop monitors, whereas Pocket PCs are working with a much smaller 240×320 space. More than anything else, limited screen real estate is the most revealing factor in terms of gauging the differences between Pocket Outlook and Outlook 2000. As an example, look at Figure 4.1, which shows Outlook 2000's Calendar feature. Now contrast this with the Pocket PC Calendar application in Figure 4.2.

Undocumented
If you don't already have Outlook 2000 and you'd like to use it on your desktop computer to accompany Pocket Outlook, the ActiveSync CD-ROM that came with your Pocket PC includes a full version of Outlook 2000.

It's obvious from the figures that the Pocket PC Calendar application is significantly slimmer in terms of its user interface than the desktop Calendar.

Aside from the obvious user interface differences, Pocket Outlook is surprisingly similar to Outlook 2000. You can do just about everything in Pocket Outlook that you can in Outlook 2000; perhaps the only significant problem I've encountered is the granularity of synchronized data. More specifically, you are capable of synchronizing Contacts, Calendar, Tasks, Notes, and Inbox data but you can't specifically target subfolders of those applications. For example, I like to keep emails related to my eBay auctions in a special eBay

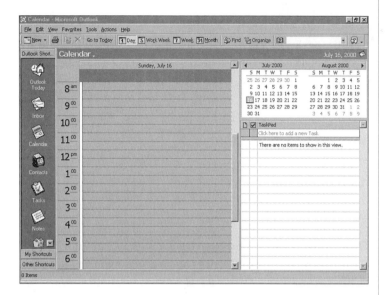

Figure 4.1
The Calendar feature of Outlook 2000 demonstrates how being a desktop application gives Outlook a great deal of flexibility when it comes to a full-featured user interface.

Figure 4.2
The Pocket PC Calendar application takes a minimalist approach to its user interface to help conserve screen real estate.

folder beneath my Inbox folder in Outlook 2000. The subfolder limitation of ActiveSync doesn't allow me to synchronize my eBay email folder with my Pocket PC.

Keep in mind that this limitation has more to do with ActiveSync than it does Pocket Outlook. The Inbox application allows you to create custom subfolders beneath the Inbox folder, but ActiveSync is the culprit because it is responsible for allowing you to configure exactly which subfolders get synchronized. I have to stress again that this "weakness" in Pocket Outlook is not a deal breaker, but it is something I want Microsoft to add to its wish list for a future version of the Pocket PC operating system.

A Pocket Outlook Primer

As you now know, Pocket Outlook is actually implemented in the Pocket PC operating system as five different applications, which are accessible from the Start menu by default:

- Contacts

- Calendar

- Tasks

- Notes

- Inbox

These applications provide a rich suite of personal information management features. The next few sections explore the basics of how to use each of the Pocket Outlook applications. The goal of this portion of the book is to give you enough information to hit the ground running with Pocket Outlook. The next two chapters get into more detail with each Pocket Outlook application, and reveal some interesting tips and tricks. For now, let's spend a few moments getting to know Pocket Outlook.

Contacts

The Contacts application is responsible for managing all your contacts. This can include business associates, relatives, friends, and even enemies if you so desire—basically anyone for whom you want to keep contact information. The Contacts application parallels the Contacts portion of Outlook 2000, and is capable of being synchronized with Outlook 2000 Contacts data. Figure 4.3 shows the Contacts application in action.

In Figure 4.3, you'll notice that the category of the contacts is listed just below the Start menu. Although not strictly required, it is a good idea to categorize your contacts. For example, I have my contacts divided into three categories: Business, Personal, and Family. The Contacts application defaults to showing contacts in all categories. You can filter the view in Contacts to a specific category by following these steps:

Undocumented
The Find feature in the Pocket PC operating system is available for use with all the Pocket Outlook applications. To search for information in any of the Pocket Outlook applications, just tap Find in the Start menu, and then specify the type of information (Contacts, Calendar, Tasks, Notes, or Inbox) in the Find window.

Figure 4.3
The Contacts
application is
responsible for
managing your list
of contacts.

Inside Scoop
You can filter the
view in Contacts
to multiple cate-
gories by select-
ing More in the
drop-down list that
appears when you
tap "All
Categories."

1. Tap All Categories near the top of the screen.

2. Select the category for which you want to see contacts.

Figure 4.4 shows the results of changing the category in my
contact list to Personal.

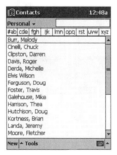

Figure 4.4
You can filter the
contact list in the
Contacts applica-
tion by changing
the category of
contacts
displayed.

In addition to filtering categories via the drop-down list below
the Start menu, you can also select multiple categories and edit
individual categories by tapping More in the list. This results in
the display of a category screen that allows you to select multiple categories to be filtered. This screen also includes an
Add/Delete tab that is used to add and delete categories.

Even though you will probably want to synchronize existing
contacts from your desktop PC, you are still likely to add new
contacts directly into the Contacts application on your device.
Just follow these steps:

1. Tap New near the bottom of the screen.

2. Use the Soft Input Panel to enter relevant contact
   information.

Shortcut
You can quickly
narrow down the
list of contacts by
typing the name of
a contact into the
edit box to the
right of the cate-
gory combo box.
The small box to
the right of the
edit field restores
the complete list
of contacts from
the currently
selected category.

Shortcut
To copy, delete, or send a contact, tap and hold the contact and then select the appropriate command in the pop-up menu that appears.

3. Make sure to scroll down and select a category or categories for the contact.

4. Add additional text, a drawing, or a voice recording by tapping the Notes tab.

5. Tap OK to save the new contact.

After entering a new contact, it appears in the contact list under the appropriate category. To see the details of the contact, just tap it in the list.

Calendar

The Pocket PC Calendar application is used primarily to schedule appointments, and is capable of being synchronized with Outlook 2000 Calendar data. Figure 4.5 shows the Calendar application in its default Agenda view. The Calendar application provides several different views depending on how wide a timeframe you want to see.

Figure 4.5
The Agenda view is the default view in the Calendar application.

Remember
The Agenda view provides the most detail when viewing appointments. At the other end of the spectrum is the Year view, which provides the least detail by not even showing appointments.

It's easy to create new appointments in the Calendar application. Just follow these steps:

1. Tap New near the bottom of the screen.

2. Use the Soft Input Panel to enter relevant appointment information.

3. Select the amount of time before the appointment that you want to be given a reminder.

4. Make sure to scroll down and select any attendees for the appointment.

5. Add additional text, a drawing, or a voice recording by tapping the Notes tab.

6. Tap OK to save the new appointment.

After a new appointment is entered, it appears in the list of appointments under the Agenda view. To see the details of the appointment, just tap it in the list.

Tasks

The Tasks application is used to manage tasks that you are working on or work that must be completed. Similar to Contacts and Calendar, the Tasks application is capable of being synchronized with Outlook 2000 Tasks data. Figure 4.6 shows the Tasks application at work.

Shortcut
To copy, delete, or send an appointment, tap and hold the appointment and then select the appropriate command in the pop-up menu that appears.

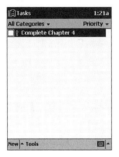

Figure 4.6
The Tasks application organizes your tasks so you can focus on completing them.

As you can see, my only task is completing the writing of this chapter. This is obviously a task that I've already entered. To create new tasks, just follow these steps:

1. Tap New near the bottom of the screen.

2. Use the Soft Input Panel to enter relevant task information.

3. Add additional text, a drawing, or a voice recording by tapping the Notes tab.

4. Tap OK to save the new task.

The new task appears in the task list after you enter it. If you've specified that the task be of a high priority, a small exclamation point appears to the left of the task. To see the details of the task, just tap it in the list.

Shortcut
If you want to quickly create a task with only a subject, tap the Tools menu and then tap Entry Bar. An edit box appears near the top of the screen; you can tap the box and enter new tasks without going through the detailed task creation window.

Shortcut

To copy, delete, or send a task, tap and hold the task and then select the appropriate command in the pop-up menu that appears.

Notes

Notes are the digital equivalent of the ever-popular paper sticky notes. The Pocket Outlook Notes application allows you to enter such notes, which can range from simple reminders to directions to a friend's house. Unlike the other Pocket Outlook applications, which represent a simplified version of an Outlook 2000 equivalent feature, the Notes application is actually a step ahead of Outlook 2000 because it supports ink (hand drawings) and voice recordings. These notes can then be attached to other types of Pocket Outlook data such as contacts and tasks. Figure 4.7 shows the Notes application in action.

Figure 4.7
The Notes application displays a list of notes (just one in this case) that is logically equivalent to a stack of paper sticky notes.

To view the details of a note, you tap it in the note list; Figure 4.8 shows an example of a note containing nothing but text.

Figure 4.8
A simple text note is sufficient for simple reminders and daily to-do lists.

More impressive notes can contain drawings and voice recordings. To create a note, follow these steps:

1. Tap New near the bottom of the screen.

2. Use the Soft Input Panel to enter note information.

3. Draw directly on the screen with the stylus to add drawings or handwritten text to the note.

4. Hold down the hardware voice recorder button to record a voice message and attach it to the note; the voice recording appears as a speaker icon in the note. You can add multiple voice recordings to a note if you so desire.

5. Tap OK to save the new note.

Figure 4.9 shows a note with text, a hand drawing, and a voice recording. This really shows off some of the multimedia capabilities of Pocket PCs.

Shortcut
To copy, delete, send, rename, or move a note, tap and hold the note and then select the appropriate command in the pop-up menu that appears.

Figure 4.9
With support for text, hand drawings, and voice recordings, the Notes application blows away traditional paper sticky notes.

Remember that you view a note by tapping it in the note list. To listen to a voice recording in a note, tap the speaker icon that appears in the note. If multiple voice recordings are included in a note, each is identified by a different speaker icon; tapping the appropriate icon will play that particular voice recording.

Inbox

The Inbox application is undoubtedly the most full-featured Pocket Outlook application because email is a fairly complex feature to support. The Inbox application is a little different from the other Pocket Outlook applications in that it doesn't necessarily require synchronization with Outlook 2000 to be extremely useful. You could make the argument that all the Pocket Outlook applications are useful without Outlook 2000, but I think the Inbox application stands apart in this regard due to the fact that you can use a CompactFlash (CF) modem to send and receive email with no desktop PC in sight. Even so, I still find it very useful to synchronize the Inbox application with Outlook 2000 just as I do the other Pocket Outlook applications.

You learn how to send and receive email with the Inbox application via a CF modem in Chapter 9, "Email and the Pocket Outlook Inbox." For now, let's focus on synchronizing email with Outlook 2000, which is likely the initial usage you'll find for the Inbox application.

The primary step in synchronizing email with Outlook 2000 is to enable Inbox synchronization in ActiveSync on your desktop PC. When you enable Inbox synchronization in ActiveSync, the Inbox folder is synchronized by default but the Outbox folder isn't; you'll need to explicitly enable Outbox synchronization.

→ **See Also** Chapter 9, "Email and the Pocket Outlook Inbox," **p. 139**.

When email is synchronized via ActiveSync, email messages from the Inbox folder of the desktop PC are transferred to the Inbox folder of the Inbox application. On the outgoing side of things, email in the Outbox folder of the Pocket PC is transferred to the Outbox folder of Outlook 2000, where it is ready for delivery.

Figure 4.10 shows the Inbox application with the Inbox folder in view.

Figure 4.10
The Inbox folder of the Inbox application displays received email messages.

To view and read an email message, just tap the specific message in the Inbox list. To create a new email message, follow these steps:

1. Tap New near the bottom of the screen.

2. Tap To to select an email recipient from your contact list, or enter an email address in the edit box.

3. Tap the edit box next to Subj to enter the subject of the email message.

4. Tap the body of the email and enter the message.

5. Tap the Send button to queue the email message for sending; this places the message in the Outbox folder.

6. Synchronize with the ActiveSync software to actually send the email message.

It's important to understand that no email messages are sent until you synchronize with ActiveSync. Of course, by default, your Pocket PC will attempt to synchronize as soon as you place it in its cradle, in which case you won't have to explicitly initiate synchronization.

Shortcut
To copy, move, reply to, forward, or delete an email message, tap and hold the message and then select the appropriate command in the pop-up menu that appears.

Pocket Outlook and Palm

Being the underdog in handheld computing, Pocket PCs still have a long way to go to prove themselves. You're already no doubt aware that its chief competition consists of devices that run the Palm operating system. Unlike Pocket PCs, Palm devices are designed more around being personal digital assistants (PDAs), as opposed to full-featured handheld computers. Nonetheless, this means that Pocket Outlook is the most scrutinized aspect of Pocket PCs because it is competing against Palm's equivalent personal information management (PIM) software, which is immensely popular. Knowing this, I thought it would be helpful to quickly go over some of the main differences between Pocket Outlook and the equivalent Palm software.

Table 4.1 contains some of the more interesting differences between Pocket Outlook and the equivalent PIM software in the Palm IIIxe device, which runs version 3.5 of the Palm operating system. Palm makes other devices but I chose the Palm IIIxe because it is the most popular Palm device as of this writing. It is also very similar to the Palm IIIc, which is currently the only color Palm device available.

TABLE 4.1: MAIN DIFFERENCES BETWEEN POCKET OUTLOOK AND PALM 3.5 PIM SOFTWARE

Feature	Pocket PC	Palm IIIxe
Today at a glance	Yes	No
Calendar length of day	Fixed	User-definable
Email notification of appointments	Yes	No
Alarm sound	User-definable	User-selectable from list of seven
Notes	Text, ink, voice recordings	Text only
Maximum note size	No maximum size	4KB
Email attachments	Yes (including HTML)	No

Remember
Because Handspring Visor handheld devices are based upon the Palm operating system, the comparison between Pocket PCs and Visors is very similar to the previous comparison with Palm devices.

Although the table highlights some of the major differences between Pocket Outlook and the Palm PIM software, it is by no means an exhaustive list. Although I personally find Pocket Outlook to be a better PIM, I encourage those of you still deciding between the two to start with the information in the table and make your own determination of which device you prefer for performing PDA functions.

Essential Information

- The most significant difference between Pocket Outlook and Outlook 2000 is the simplified user interface in Pocket Outlook, which is a result of the limited screen real estate of Pocket PCs.

- The Contacts, Calendar, and Tasks applications are components of Pocket Outlook that allow users to effectively manage their daily schedule.

- The Notes application is the component of Pocket Outlook that allows you to include text, ink (hand drawings), and voice recordings in notes.

- The Inbox application is the component of Pocket Outlook that manages your email, including sending and receiving email messages.

- Pocket Outlook outperforms the PIM software in the Palm 3.5 operating system, but it still faces an uphill battle when it comes to winning over Palm users because of the popularity of Palm devices.

Keeping It Together with Contacts and Calendar

T HE PREVIOUS CHAPTER INTRODUCED Pocket Outlook and covered the basics of using the five Pocket Outlook applications to manage personal information. This chapter continues in the discussion of Pocket Outlook by digging deeper into two of the Pocket Outlook applications, Contacts and Calendar. The Contacts application serves as a high-powered electronic Rolodex, and synchronizes with the Contacts feature in Outlook 2000. The Calendar application is a flexible electronic day planner that allows you to plan your life with as much detail as you desire. Similar to Contacts, the Calendar application synchronizes with Outlook 2000 to allow you to share personal information between your desktop PC and Pocket PC device.

Unlike the previous chapter, which gave you just enough information to begin using the Contacts and Calendar application, this chapter goes into much more detail and reveals some tips and tricks for getting the most out of these applications.

Managing Contacts

Contacts are displayed in the Contacts application as a list of names and related fields of contact information. You learned in the previous chapter that contacts in the contact list can be filtered and displayed according to the category to which they are assigned. This is a convenient way to focus on a group of contacts but it requires you to assign categories to all your contacts for it to be useful. If you want a quicker way to navigate contacts, try clicking the small ABC tabs at the top of the contact list.

The ABC tabs at the top of the contact list allow you to jump to a section of the contact list based upon the names of the contacts. For example, tapping the cde tab jumps to the first contact with a last name beginning with the letter C. To jump to one of the other letters in a tab, just tap the tab again. For example, to jump to contacts with a last name beginning with E, just tap on the cde tab three times. This alphabetic approach to navigating through the contact list works quite well because the contacts are always alphabetically sorted according to the last name of the contact.

Keep in mind that you can also type in the edit box in the upper-right corner of the Contacts application to jump to contacts quickly. The difference between this approach and the ABC tabs approach is that the edit box includes both first and last names that match your criteria, although tabs jump only to contacts with last names that match the letter you select. Another difference between the edit box and ABC tabs navigation approaches is that the tabs are used to move the selection cursor within the list of contacts, although the edit box actually filters the list. Figure 5.1 shows the results of typing "sol" in this edit box to find my imaginary friend, Sol Rosenberg.

Figure 5.1
Entering a name in the edit box near the top of the Contacts screen results in the contact list being filtered for contacts with a similar first or last name.

Speaking of contact names, you can alter the manner in which they are displayed in the contact list. One neat trick you can use is to alter the File As property in Outlook 2000. When you edit a contact in Outlook (right-click the contact and select Properties), you can change the File As property to alter the way in which the contacted is referenced. The significance of this with respect to Pocket Outlook is that the Contacts application uses the File As property as the basis for displaying synchronized contacts. In other words, by altering the File As property for a contact in Outlook 2000, you are affecting the way the contact name is displayed in Pocket Outlook. Figure 5.2 shows how I changed the Outlook 2000 File As property for Sol to display his name as "Sol Rosenberg," as opposed to "Rosenberg, Sol."

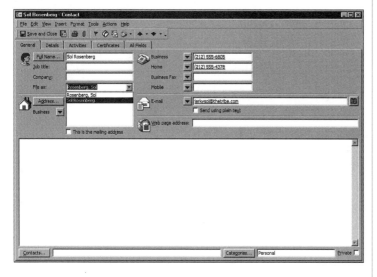

Figure 5.2
The File As property in Outlook 2000 allows you to change the way contact names are displayed in the Pocket Outlook Contacts application.

Remember
You must have Contacts checked for synchronization in the ActiveSync synchronization settings for the contact information to be synchronized between Outlook 2000 and the Contacts application.

After changing the File As property for a contact in Outlook 2000, you'll need to synchronize with your Pocket PC for the changes to be reflected in the Contacts application. Figure 5.3 shows the contact list in the Contacts application with Sol's name changed. This figure also reflects a change in the Contacts setting that enables the display of additional contact information such as phone number, email address, and so on.

We'll get into how this setting is enabled and disabled in a moment.

Figure 5.3
The display format
of the contact is
reflected in the
contact list after
changing the File
As property in
Outlook 2000.

You'll notice that Sol's fictitious email address is displayed to the right of his name, along with a small letter e. The letter e indicates that the extra contact information to the right of his name is in fact his email address. A handy feature of the Contacts application is the ability to change the contact information displayed next to the contact name by tapping the identification letter—in this case, the letter e. When you tap the letter, a drop-down list of relevant contact information is displayed from which you can select (see Figure 5.4).

Tapping a different piece of contact information in the drop-down list results in it being displayed next to the contact name. This is a useful feature because you might want to have the home phone number of close friends readily displayed, although it would probably make more sense to have the work number displayed for business associates.

Inside Scoop
Help is always just
a couple of taps
away while using
the Contacts
application; just
tap Help in the
Start menu, and
then tap Contacts
in the Help
Contents.

Figure 5.4
When you tap the
identification let-
ter on the far
right of the con-
tact entry, you
are presented
with a drop-down
list of available
contact
information.

Navigating Contacts with Hardware Buttons

Pocket PC devices are required to include hardware buttons that make it easy to launch commonly used applications. Although you can custom tailor these hardware buttons to do whatever you want, most are set by default to launch the two most commonly used Pocket Outlook applications, Contacts and Calendar. The Contacts hardware button usually is labeled with a small icon representing a contact card from a Rolodex. Try pressing the Contacts button on your device to quickly launch the Contacts application.

Another hardware button, the Action button, is very useful for navigating contacts. The Action button is designed as a push button that can be rotated up and down, and is useful in scrolling through the contact list and viewing individual contacts. Just roll the Action button up or down to scroll through the contact list. When you arrive at the contact you want to view, push the Action button and you will see the contact details just as if you had tapped it.

Customizing the Contacts Application

The Contacts application is extremely usable with its default settings, which display name, phone number, and email address. Even so, you might find it necessary to customize its functionality a little to suit your own tastes. I've already alluded to one customization, displaying only the names of contacts in the contact list. There are also a few other settings you can tweak to customize the application. To view these settings, tap Tools at the bottom of the screen, and then tap Options to open the Options window, as shown in Figure 5.5.

Show ABC Tabs allows you to disable the ABC tabs that provide quicker navigation in the contact list. Disabling the tabs frees up a little screen space and allows you to see an extra name in the list, which is beneficial if you don't plan on using the tabs. Show Contact Names Only is used to hide the additional contact information displayed to the right of the contact name. I used this setting earlier in the chapter to hide the phone numbers of contacts. Your main motive for using it would be to give the contact list a cleaner look. I think most will find that seeing

Undocumented
If you are already in the Contacts application, pressing the Contacts button changes the currently selected category. You can continue pressing the Contacts button to cycle through the categories of contacts.

Watch Out!
All Pocket PCs are required to have hardware buttons but they are given leeway as to what applications the buttons launch. Most Pocket PCs are set up by default with hardware buttons for the Contacts and Calendar applications, along with a Start menu button, a Record button for recording voice dictations, and an Action button for scrolling and selecting items. Please refer to your device's manual for more information about its default button settings.

the contact information is more useful because it can provide a quick view of someone's phone number or email address. The Use Large Font setting displays the contact list in a large font for easier readability. You won't be able to see as many contacts onscreen at once, but for those of us without 20/20 vision, it can be useful.

Figure 5.5
The Options window in the Contacts application allows you to customize the application to your own preferences.

The Country/Region settings in the Options window of the Contacts application contain information about your geographical location. The area code is your telephone area code, and its purpose is to automatically fill in the area code of phone numbers when entering them for contacts. This is a small timesaving feature, but it can help in terms of minimizing taps for data entry. If you are entering a new contact outside of your default area code, this feature still doesn't slow you down any because the area code is the first highlighted field when you enter a phone number. This means that you can begin entering a different area code and it will automatically overwrite the default. The Country/Region setting contains your country/region, and is used to fill in the country of contact addresses as another timesaving feature.

Beaming Contacts via Infrared

One of the most convenient features of the Contacts application is its support for beaming contacts using the infrared port on your Pocket PC. This establishes a modern alternative for swapping business cards. Instead of trading printed paper, you align your Pocket PC with that of another person and automatically swap contact information electronically. To beam contact information to another Pocket PC via infrared, follow these steps:

1. Navigate to the contact in the contact list.

2. Tap and hold the contact entry.

3. Tap Send via Infrared on the pop-up menu that appears.

4. Line up the two devices and wait for the transfer to complete; keep the devices aligned and within a few inches of each other throughout the transfer.

Figure 5.6 shows the pop-up menu used to initiate the transfer of a contact via infrared.

Figure 5.6
The Send via Infrared command is used to send a contact to another device via infrared.

Receiving contact information via infrared from another Pocket PC is just as simple:

1. Tap Tools near the bottom of the screen.

2. Tap Receive via Infrared on the menu.

3. Line up the two devices and wait for the transfer to complete.

It's hard to say whether infrared contact beaming will ever replace traditional business cards, but it definitely makes for a convenient approach to sharing contact information with other people that use Pocket PCs.

Sharing Contacts with Other Devices

In the previous section you might have been asking yourself what to do when you meet someone who uses a different type

Watch Out!
This is relatively obvious, but keep in mind that you can use Peacemaker only with Palm or Psion devices that have an infrared port. Although most of these devices now have infrared ports, unfortunately, some of the earlier models do not.

of handheld device such as a Palm or Psion device. In this situation, the infrared beaming support in Pocket Outlook won't work, but there is an alternative. Peacemaker, an application by Conduits Technologies Inc., is a third-party utility that allows you to exchange contacts with Palm and Psion device users using the infrared port on your Pocket PC. The neat thing about Peacemaker is that it integrates into the Contacts application by adding new menu items to the Tools menu.

Peacemaker doesn't require any special software to be installed on the other side of the infrared connection. In other words, the Palm/Psion user with which you are communicating doesn't need the Peacemaker software. This is a huge convenience because of the significant market share owned by Palm devices; it is unlikely that Palm users would be too concerned about installing software to share information with Pocket PCs, at least in the near future. A similar situation exists on desktop computers in which there is a lot of support for Macintosh computers that want to access PC data, but not a lot of support for the reverse. When it comes to computers, the market leader (Palm in this case) doesn't have any significant motivation to address compatibility with its competition (Pocket PC).

Getting back to Peacemaker, it offers two approaches to sharing contact information:

- Beam Selected
- Card Exchange

The Beam Selected feature allows you to select one or more contacts in the contact list of the Contacts application and beam them to the other device. Figure 5.7 shows the Beam Selected feature in action.

The Card Exchange feature is designed as a one-to-one business card exchange. In this case, you preselect a single contact entry as your business card. This contact is then swapped with a single contact from the other device when you initiate the Card Exchange transfer. Figure 5.8 shows a Card Exchange transfer taking place.

Figure 5.7
The Beam
Selected feature in
Peacemaker is
used to send one
or more contacts
to another device.

Figure 5.8
The Card
Exchange feature
in Peacemaker is
used to swap busi-
ness cards with
another device.

There are a few limitations with the transfer of contact information using Peacemaker. The limitations have to do with contact fields in Pocket Outlook contacts that aren't supported on
other devices. For example, Palm devices store only one address
per contact, whereas Pocket Outlook contacts
can include both home and work addresses. If you are beaming
a Pocket Outlook contact with both addresses defined, Peacemaker prompts you to select one of them for the transfer.

Peacemaker is freely available for download from the Peacemaker Web site at `http://www.conduits.com/ce/peacemaker`. There
is a more powerful version of Peacemaker called Peacemaker Pro
that you can purchase from the site. Peacemaker Pro supports
the transfer of more types of personal information such as
appointments and tasks.

Getting the Most out of the Calendar

The Calendar application in Pocket Outlook manages all date-
and time-related functions of the Pocket PC. The previous
chapter covered the basics of creating appointments in the
Calendar application but it didn't really get into the practical

nature of having such a powerful application on a mobile device. Although I do give you a few ideas regarding getting the most out of the Calendar application to help organize your life a little better, I'm not a proponent of using gadgets in every facet of life. There's a time and place for everything, so keep in mind that sometimes it's better to do something the old-fashioned way. Regardless, I think you'll find that the Calendar application can be beneficial when used appropriately.

It's obvious that the Calendar is ideal for keeping track of business meetings and engagements. I've also found that it is useful for keeping other types of scheduled commitments such as doctors' appointments in Calendar. On the entertainment side of things, you might want to consider using Calendar to keep track of television shows you don't want to miss. If you participate in chat rooms, you might want to use Calendar to schedule upcoming chats. As an example of another use for Calendar, I play hockey in a league where our games are scheduled in a seemingly random manner, so it helps me to enter them in Calendar and know when I have a game coming up.

It's really up to you how much you want to schedule your life via Calendar. But, after you've determined what events you do want to keep track of, you then need to be able to view the calendar and see what is coming up. The Calendar application supports several views that provide different perspectives on your upcoming appointments:

- **Agenda**—Displays upcoming appointments.

- **Day**—Displays appointments for the selected day.

- **Week**—Displays the current week, including appointments.

- **Month**—Displays the current month, including appointments.

- **Year**—Displays the current year.

The calendar views are very important because they allow you to see what's coming up in the short term, and also keep long-range commitments in sight. All the calendar views have a consistent user interface in terms of calendar navigation buttons that are displayed in the upper-right corner of the window. Figure 5.9 shows the Agenda view.

Figure 5.9
The Agenda view displays upcoming appointments, and includes the calendar navigation buttons in the upper-right corner of the window.

The two navigation buttons on the far right (left and right arrows) are used to move the calendar backward and forward in time. In the Agenda, Day, and Week views, these buttons move the calendar forward or backward a week. In the Month view, the buttons move the calendar forward or backward a month, and so on. The other navigation button appearing to the left of the arrows is used to take you immediately to the current date. Regardless of where you have navigated in the calendar, you can always return to the current date by tapping this button.

Although all the calendar views are useful, the Month view is particularly interesting because it uses visual icons to indicate the time commitment of each day. Figure 5.10 shows a Month view with several appointments that are identified with different icons.

Figure 5.10
The Month view uses small icons to indicate the time commitment of each day.

Following are the meanings of the icons on the Month view:

- A dark triangle in the upper portion of the box indicates a morning appointment.

- A dark triangle in the lower portion of the box indicates an afternoon appointment.

- A solid dark box indicates morning and afternoon appointments.

- A larger hollow outlined box indicates an all-day event.

These icons allow you to see at a glance whether you are committed on a given day. Just to make sure you understand how the icons work, take a look at Figure 5.10 again. The icon on the 19th includes a dark triangle in the lower portion of the box, which means there is an afternoon appointment on that day. The 28th includes an oppositely oriented icon, which means that there is a morning appointment. The solid box on the 26th indicates that there are appointments in the morning and afternoon. The larger hollow box on the 24th identifies an all-day event. Finally, the current date is identified by the highlight around the date, which in this case is the 18th.

The Day view also uses some interesting icons to provide information about the type of appointments scheduled. Instead of communicating information about the time and duration of appointments like the Month view, the Day view uses icons to convey appointment specifics such as whether it has a specified location, whether it has attendees, or whether it is a private appointment. Figure 5.11 shows a Day view with a couple of appointments.

Figure 5.11

The Day view uses icons to provide information about the appointments for the day.

Following are the types of appointments that are identifiable via icons in the Day view:

- Appointments with reminders

- Recurring appointments

- Appointments with notes

- Appointments with a location

- Appointments with attendees

- Private appointments

Figure 5.11 shows the icons that are used to indicate each type of appointment. The 9:00 appointment with Travis includes three icons that identify the appointment as having a reminder, being a recurring appointment, and being a private appointment. The Lunch appointment at 12:00 also has a reminder, but additionally has attendees, attached notes, and a location. Although these icons are very informative, you can turn them off if you find them cluttering the appointment list. You learn how to turn them on and off later in the chapter.

Navigating the Calendar with Hardware Buttons

You learned a little earlier in the chapter that most Pocket PCs have a hardware button that is devoted to launching the Contacts application. There's also usually a hardware button devoted to the Calendar application, making the application a button push away. The Calendar hardware button usually is labeled with a small icon representing a calendar page. Press the Calendar button on your device to quickly launch the Calendar application. Please refer to your device's manual if you don't immediately see a Calendar button.

The Action button provides a quick way to navigate through the Calendar interface. Scrolling the Action button results in the current calendar view incrementing a length of time. For example, in the Agenda and Day views, the Action Button increments the calendar by a day. In the Week and Month views, the Action Button increments the calendar by a week. In the Year view, the Action Button increments the Calendar by three months.

Inside Scoop
Help is always just a couple of taps away while using the Calendar application; just tap Help in the Start menu, and then tap Calendar in the Help Contents.

Inside Scoop
Similar to the Contacts application, the Calendar application allows you to beam appointments to another Pocket PC. To beam an appointment, tap and hold the appointment and then tap Send via Infrared on the pop-up menu that appears.

Undocumented
If you are already in the Calendar application, pressing the Calendar button changes the current view. You can continue pressing the Calendar button to cycle through the different views (Agenda, Day, Week, Month, and Year).

Pressing the Action Button results in the creation of a new appointment if you are in the Day or Week views; otherwise, it does nothing.

Customizing the Calendar Application

The Calendar application can be customized to suit your needs by tapping the Tools menu and then tapping Options. You will see the Options window, which is shown in Figure 5.12.

Figure 5.12
The Options window allows you to customize the Calendar application to your own tastes.

The first setting, 1st Day of Week, establishes the first day of the week as either Sunday or Monday. The Week View setting allows you to view a week as 5, 6, or 7 days; the 5-day view is intended to reflect a business week by excluding weekends. The Show Half Hour Slots setting impacts only the Day and Week views. It adds more granularity to the views by breaking down days into half-hour blocks of time instead of hour blocks. The Show Week Numbers setting applies only to the Week view, and when set it shows the number of the week with respect to the beginning of the year. The Use Large Font setting applies to the Agenda and Day views, and displays appointment information in a larger font.

The Set Reminders for New Items setting results in new appointments automatically defaulting to having a reminder set for a given length of time before the appointment. You can set the amount of time you need. Keep in mind that this setting is just a timesaving feature; you can still individually alter the reminder time for appointments after creating them.

The Show Icons feature enables and disables the display of icons in the Day view. Although the icons take up a little space on the screen, I find them useful enough to keep them enabled. If you aren't sure about using the icons, you can enable them individually or disable all of them. If an icon is surrounded by black, it's enabled; white indicates that the icon is disabled.

The last customization setting within the Calendar application has to do with how meeting requests are sent to attendees. When you schedule an appointment with attendees, Pocket Outlook generates a meeting request, provided that the attendees use Outlook 2000, Pocket Outlook, or Schedule+. This results in each attendee receiving a notification of the meeting when you synchronize the Calendar application with your desktop PC or connect to an email server. The default approach to sending meeting requests is to use ActiveSync, but you can change this to some other service if you so desire. An example of another service is Puma Technology's Intellisync, which is used to synchronize Pocket PCs with Lotus Notes.

One additional customization related to the Calendar application is the capability of changing the alarm sound that is played to signal an upcoming appointment. The following steps explain how this is accomplished:

1. Tap the Start menu, and then tap Settings.

2. Tap the Sounds & Reminders icon, and then tap the Reminders tab.

3. Select an alarm from the drop-down list of sounds.

Applying Recurrence Patterns

When you create an appointment, you have the option of making the appointment recurring, which means that it repeats according to some criteria such as daily, weekly, or monthly. When setting a recurring appointment, the Calendar application includes several default options that are used to establish the recurrence. However, these default options might not always be what you need. In this event, you need to create a recurrence pattern that spells out exactly how your

Undocumented
The sound played to signal an upcoming appointment is stored as a WAV audio file in the Windows folder of your device. You can substitute your own custom alarm by copying a WAV file to the Windows folder and then changing to the new alarm as described.

appointment repeats. The Calendar application includes a wizard to help you create recurrence patterns.

To create a recurrence pattern, follow these steps:

1. While editing an appointment, tap the combo box next to the Occurs field.

2. Tap < Edit pattern... > in the list of options; the Recurrence Pattern Wizard appears.

3. Set the time and duration of the appointment in the first screen of the wizard (Figure 5.13), and then tap Next.

Figure 5.13
The first screen of the Recurrence Pattern Wizard prompts you to set the time and duration of an appointment.

4. Set the day(s) that the appointment occurs, along with the repetition of it in the second screen of the wizard, and then tap Next.

5. Set the start and end of the pattern in the third screen of the wizard (Figure 5.14).

Figure 5.14
The third screen of the Recurrence Pattern Wizard prompts you to set the start and end pattern of the appointment.

6. Tap Finish to complete the recurrence pattern.

Recurrence patterns provide a great deal of flexibility in creating recurring appointments, especially when you have an appointment that doesn't adhere to the default recurrence options in the Calendar application.

Appointments and the Today Screen

As you know, the Today screen is a great starting point for assessing what is going on with the personal information you keep in your Pocket PC. One of the bands of information displayed in the Today screen contains appointments that are managed by the Calendar application. In addition to being able to turn this band on and off, you can alter its position on the Today screen and customize the types of appointments that it displays.

To customize the Calendar band on the Today screen, follow these steps:

1. Tap Start, and then tap Settings.

2. Tap the Today icon.

3. Tap the check box next to the word Calendar to enable/disable the Calendar band, or just tap the word Calendar next to the check box (Figure 5.15).

Figure 5.15
The Today Settings window allows you to enable or disable the Calendar band, as well as change the positioning of the band with respect to other bands.

4. Tap the Move Up and Move Down buttons to move the Calendar band around with respect to the other bands.

5. Tap the Options button.

6. Tap the Next Appointment radio button to display only the next appointment in the Calendar band, or tap

Upcoming Appointments to display upcoming appointments in the Calendar band.

7. Tap the All Day Events check box to include all-day events in the Calendar band.

8. Tap OK in the upper-right corner, and then tap OK again.

You've now customized the Calendar band of the Today screen. To see the changes, return to the Today screen and take a look at the appointments displayed.

Essential Information

- The ABC tabs at the top of the contact list in the Contacts application serve as a great shortcut for jumping to a section of the contact list based upon the names of the contacts.

- The File As property in Outlook 2000 alters the way in which a contact is displayed in Pocket Outlook.

- Pocket Outlook allows you to share contacts with other Pocket PC devices using the infrared ports on each device. You can also share personal information with Palm devices using the infrared port via third-party software.

- The Calendar application supports several views that provide different perspectives on your upcoming appointments.

- The hardware buttons on your Pocket PC provide a convenient means of quickly accessing the Contacts and Calendar applications.

Staying Organized with Tasks and Notes

C HAPTER 4, "USING POCKET OUTLOOK," introduced the basics of using the Pocket Outlook applications to manage personal information, including the Tasks and Notes applications. This chapter explores these two applications a bit further and presents some insights geared toward getting more out of the applications. The Tasks application serves as a means of keeping track of things that you are working on, also known as to-do's, alerting you to deadlines and overdue tasks. Notes is more of an all-purpose application designed to help you keep a log of thoughts you don't want to lose. You can use the Notes application to store a lot of different information including text, ink (handwriting), and voice recordings. Both the Tasks and Notes applications synchronize with Outlook 2000 to share information with a desktop PC.

From Chapter 4, you already have some understanding of what the Tasks and Notes applications can do. This chapter builds on that knowledge by revealing some interesting tips and tricks that will improve the way you use the applications to manage personal information.

Becoming a Task Master

The Tasks application is the component of Pocket Outlook that is responsible for managing and keeping track of things you need to do. In many cases, these tasks are work-related, but not always. If you have a project, chore, or some other under-taking that is currently a goal or work-in-progress, it probably qualifies as a task. When used appropriately, the Tasks application can really help you stay on track with both personal and work projects; just try to keep everything in perspective and remember that your Pocket PC is supposed to make life easier, not more complicated.

Remember
The traditional approach to creating a new task in the Tasks application is to tap New near the bottom of the screen and then use the Soft Input Panel (SIP) to enter relevant task information.

Let's get into some ideas for specific tasks that you might want to manage with the Tasks application. In addition to obvious uses such as work projects, the Tasks application can help you keep up with long-term projects that you don't even intend to start any time soon. Even if the projects are really just ideas, by entering them as tasks you're able to remember later that these are things that you want to work on at some future time. Granted, some of these ideas might fizzle, but the worst-case scenario is that you simply delete them. The powerful thing about managing ideas as tasks is that you can have the Tasks application remind you when it's time to address a project.

Okay, so you want to enter every pipe dream you've ever had as a task in the Tasks application. Now you have a problem with efficiency because it's taking too long to enter all your tasks, especially the ones that don't require any more information than a subject. For these kinds of tasks, it's much quicker to enter them using the Tasks application's entry bar, which is disabled by default. To enable the entry bar, tap the Tools menu and then tap Entry Bar. An edit box appears near the top of the screen, which you can tap and enter new tasks into without going through the detailed task creation window. Figure 6.1 shows the Entry Bar being used to enter a task.

Figure 6.1
The Entry Bar in the Tasks application provides a quick method of creating new tasks.

The two buttons to the left of the Entry Bar allow you to designate the task as being high-priority (the exclamation point) or low-priority (the down arrow); leaving both buttons off results in the task having a normal priority. The task isn't actually created until you tap below the Entry Bar in the main window of the Tasks application (see Figure 6.2). Keep in mind that you can still edit the newly created task if you want to alter the details. However, if you intend to create a detailed task from the start, you might as well forgo the Entry Bar and just use the New menu in the lower-left corner of the screen instead.

Tasks can be set up based upon recurrence patterns, which are used to determine how a task repeats. Repetitive tasks might not be common for you, but if you ever need to manage one, you'll find recurrence patterns to be a big help. Please refer to the discussion of recurrence patterns in Chapter 5, "Keeping It Together with Contacts and Calendar," for more information on how they are created and used.

→ **See Also** Chapter 5, "Applying Recurrence Patterns," **p. 93**.

Remember
To create a recurrence pattern for a task, tap the combo box next to the Occurs field while editing the task. Tap "< Edit pattern... >" in the list of options, and then follow the steps presented in the Recurrence Pattern Wizard.

Figure 6.2
After tapping off of the Entry Bar, a newly created task is displayed in the task list.

Remember
Just like you can with Contacts, you can share tasks with other Pocket PC users via the infrared port by tapping and holding the task, and then tapping Send via Infrared.

After you've entered some tasks and you have a task list to manage, you're ready to investigate the different navigational tools used to display the tasks. Keep in mind that tasks can be assigned to specific categories such as Business, Personal, and so on. You can control the tasks that are displayed in the list by tapping and selecting a category in the upper-left corner of the screen (see Figure 6.3). By default, the Tasks application displays tasks in all categories, but you can select a different category to limit the tasks displayed. You can also filter the task list by distinguishing between active and completed tasks. By checking Active Tasks or Completed Tasks in the list, you limit the task list to one or the other.

Figure 6.3
Tapping the task category in the upper-left corner of the screen reveals a drop-down list from which you can filter the task list.

Inside Scoop
Help is always just a couple of taps away while using the Tasks application; just tap Help in the Start menu, and then tap Tasks in the Help Contents.

The other way to alter the display of tasks is to tap on the sort method near the upper-right corner of the screen, which displays a drop-down list of methods to use for sorting the task list (see Figure 6.4). By selecting a different sort method, you alter the order of the task list, which can be useful in determining the order in which you work on a given task. For example, I typically use the Priority and Due Date sort methods because they tell me which tasks are most important and which tasks are due or overdue.

Figure 6.4
Tapping the sort method in the upper-right corner of the screen reveals a drop-down list from which you can sort the task list.

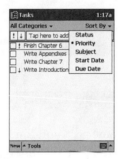

Navigating Tasks with Hardware Buttons

Unlike the Contacts and Calendar applications, which are usually accessible from a conveniently labeled hardware button, the Tasks application is a little less obvious to launch, unless you're using the familiar Start menu. The Tasks application can be launched from hardware buttons on most devices, but it's different because it requires a button combination. The combination usually involves holding down the Action button and pressing one of the other hardware buttons. For example, the Casio E-115 requires you to use the Action button in conjunction with the Menu (Launch) button to bring up the Tasks application. A similar approach is employed to access the Notes application, which you learn about a little later in the chapter. Consult your specific Pocket PC manual to find out what works with your particular device.

Speaking of the Action button, it also provides a way to navigate through the Tasks interface. Scrolling the Action button moves up and down the task list, and pressing the Action Button is the same as tapping the currently selected task. Although this isn't necessarily an easier (or more difficult) method of navigation, it does give different users more choices in how they use their device.

Customizing the Tasks Application

Like all the other Pocket Outlook applications, the Tasks application is customizable via the Tools menu. To customize the application, tap the Tools menu and then tap Options. You will see the Options window, which is shown in Figure 6.5.

Figure 6.5
The Options window in the Tasks application allows you to customize the application.

Set Reminders for New Items automatically sets a reminder for new tasks after you enter the due date for the task. You should probably keep this setting enabled because reminders are helpful for most tasks. The Show Start and Due Date setting displays the start and due date for a task in the task list just below the subject of the task. Although this setting takes up more screen space, you might find it useful if you want to see more information about each task in the task list. The Use Large Font setting displays task information in a large font.

Tasks and the Today Screen

Similar to the appointments created in the Calendar application, tasks can be displayed as an information band on the Today screen. Along with being able to turn the Tasks band on and off, you can alter its position on the Today screen and customize the types of tasks that it displays.

To customize the Tasks band on the Today screen, follow these steps:

1. Tap Start, and then tap Settings.

2. Tap the Today icon.

3. Tap the check box next to the word Tasks to enable/disable the Tasks band.

4. Tap the Move Up and Move Down buttons to move the Tasks band around with respect to the other bands.

5. Tap the Options button.

6. Tap the High Priority Tasks, Tasks Due Today, or Overdue Tasks check boxes to display the number of each task in the Tasks band.

7. Tap the Category combo box to select a category that is used to filter the tasks displayed in the Tasks band.

8. Tap OK in the upper-right corner, and then tap OK again.

You've now customized the Tasks band of the Today screen. To see the changes, return to the Today screen and take a look at the tasks displayed.

Expressing Yourself with Notes

Notes is probably the most flexible application included in the Pocket Outlook family of applications mainly because the notes you create can be used to store all kinds of different information. The idea behind notes is to provide an electronic equivalent of the popular sticky paper notes that you often see stuck to monitors in offices. Pocket PC notes are much more advanced than their paper counterparts in that they can include text, ink (handwriting), and voice recordings. The Notes application is responsible for supporting these different media types and providing a user interface for inputting each of them.

The interesting thing about the Notes application is that each user is likely to use it in a unique manner. Whereas I might use notes to jot down a quick materials list for a run to the hardware store, some other user might take it a step further and include a drawing of the project to accompany the materials list just in case a substitution becomes necessary after you get to the store. You also might be on the road and have an idea you want to document and share with an associate at work. By making a voice recording in a note and synchronizing with a dial-up connection, you can share your idea with ease.

Remember
Notes entered in the Notes application are synchronized with the Notes portion of Outlook 2000.

The Notes application does away with the need to have a microrecorder to record dictations or voice notes. You are literally a button push away from making your own voice recordings that coexist with other information within the context of a note. Pocket PC supports various audio formats for making voice recordings, which allow you to strike a balance between audio quality and storage space. To change the audio format used for voice recordings, you must go to the Options window for the Soft Input Panel. For more information about how to do this, please refer to Chapter 3, "Setting Up Your Pocket PC."

→ **See Also** Chapter 3, "Tweaking the Soft Input Panel," **p. 44**.

Notes are different from other types of Pocket Outlook data because they are stored in individual files, as opposed to being stored in a database for a given application. This makes notes somewhat more flexible because you can access and manipulate them individually from File Explorer. By default, notes are created in the My Documents folder, but you can store them in any folder you want. The Notes application is capable of listing

Remember
You can share notes with other Pocket PC users via the infrared port by tapping and holding the note, and then tapping Send via Infrared. Or you can send notes as email attachments by tapping Send via E-Mail instead.

all the notes stored on your device regardless of the folder in which they are located. I use the word "capable" because it is possible to limit the list of notes to a specific folder. To do so, tap the folder in the upper-left corner of the Notes screen. A drop-down list appears that allows you to select the folder whose notes are displayed (see Figure 6.6).

Figure 6.6
Tapping the note folder in the upper-left corner of the screen reveals a drop-down list that allows you to set the folders for which notes are displayed.

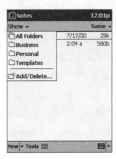

You might find it useful to create a special folder to store notes to keep your My Documents folder from getting cluttered. To create a new folder for storing notes, just select Add/Delete from the drop-down list shown in Figure 6.6. The Add/Delete Folders window appears as shown in Figure 6.7.

Figure 6.7
The Add/Delete Folders window allows you to create, rename, and delete folders that are used to store notes.

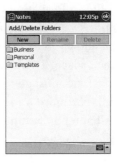

After creating any new folders that you want to use to store notes, you can easily move notes between the folders by tapping and holding the note and then tapping Rename/Move. This results in the Rename/Move window being displayed, which allows you to select a folder for the note, as well as decide whether you want to store the note in the main system memory or in a CF storage card (see Figure 6.8).

Figure 6.8
The Rename/Move window allows you to move notes between folders, as well as between system memory and a CF storage card.

Navigating Notes with Hardware Buttons

Similar to the Tasks application, the Notes application usually doesn't have a dedicated hardware button associated with it. Instead, you have to use a combination of the Action button and one of the other hardware buttons. As an example, the Casio E-115 requires you to use the Action button in conjunction with the Contacts button to bring up the Notes application.

One hardware button that is particularly useful with the Notes application is the Record button, which is usually located on the side of a device near the Action button. The Record button is used to initiate voice recordings, and is the easiest way to include voice recordings as part of a note. Your device has a microphone that is readily accessible somewhere on the device. The microphone on the Casio E-115 is located on the lower front of the device, the microphone on the HP Jornada 540 series Pocket PC is located on the top-left side of the device, and the Compaq iPAQ H3600 series Pocket PC has its microphone near the top of the device.

When you make a voice recording using the Record button, the recording is stored as a wave audio file in the My Documents folder. You can access voice recordings from the Notes application or by opening the My Documents folder in the File Explorer application.

Customizing the Notes Application

As you might have guessed, the Notes application is customizable via the Tools menu. To customize the application, tap the Tools menu and then tap Options. You will see the Options window, which is shown in Figure 6.9.

Shortcut
You can move multiple notes at once by tapping and dragging the stylus over the notes to select them, lifting the stylus, tapping and holding over the selected notes, and selecting Rename/Move from the pop-up menu that appears.

Undocumented
When you move a note to a folder other than My Documents, the folder name appears in front of the filename when the note is synchronized and displayed in Outlook 2000.

Figure 6.9
The Options win-
dow in the Notes
application allows
you to customize
the application.

Inside Scoop
Help is always
just a couple of
taps away while
using the Notes
application; just
tap Help in the
Start menu, and
then tap Notes in
the Help
Contents.

Inside Scoop
When recording
voice, you should
speak with your
mouth about four
inches from the
microphone on
your device.

The Default Mode setting determines the input mode, which can be either writing or typing. Set this according to whether you prefer creating notes by hand writing with the stylus or pecking keys on the SIP keyboard. The Default Template setting determines the type of note created by default. In addition to creating blank notes, the Notes application includes standard templates to help in creating commonly used notes. The default template can be set to one of these templates:

- Meeting Notes

- Memo

- Phone Memo

- To Do

Figure 6.10 displays a newly created note that uses the Phone Memo template. This gives you an idea of how templates can be useful for determining the structure of notes.

Figure 6.10
The Phone Memo
note template pro-
vides a standard
format for enter-
ing phone memos
as notes.

The Save To option allows you to change the location to which notes are saved. You can choose between main system memory and a CF Storage Card. If you choose the Main Memory option, which is the default option, then all notes are stored in the My Documents folder. The Record Button Action setting determines what happens when the Record button is pressed to make a voice recording. The default setting is for the Notes application to appear when you make a recording. This makes sense because you will likely use the Notes application to play and manage voice recordings. However, if you want to stay in the current application when you make voice recordings, you can change the setting accordingly.

Editing Notes

The note list is displayed as the main window in the Notes application, and has the familiar New and Tools menus. You might have noticed an icon to the right of the Tools menu that looks like a small cassette tape. This button allows you to enable and disable the Voice Bar, which is displayed near the bottom of the screen and provides a user interface for handling voice recordings. The Voice Bar serves as an alternative to the Record button, and is ultimately more flexible because it allows you to stop and play recordings, as well as change the volume of the device (see Figure 6.11). The Voice Bar is automatically displayed if you use the Record button, so you have access to it without having to use the icon next to the menus.

Figure 6.11
The Voice Bar provides a user interface for working with voice recordings.

While editing a note, you might notice an additional icon next to the Voice Bar button. The button looks like a small pencil, and is used to change the input mode for entering note data. When enabled, the pencil button sets the input mode to

Remember
While they both are a form of handwriting recognition, keep in mind that the Recognize feature for Notes is a separate program from the more powerful Transcriber utility covered in Chapter 12, "Transcriber: Handwriting Recognition That Works."

writing, while a disabled setting results in a typing input mode. You might find yourself turning the setting on and off to switch between writing and typing while editing a note.

If you like to hand write information into notes but would prefer having the end result stored as text, you should try the Recognize feature in the Tools menu. To use this feature, hand write text into a note and then tap Recognize in the Tools menu. Figure 6.12 shows some handwritten text I entered into a Memorandum note.

Figure 6.13 shows the results of using the Recognize feature to convert my handwritten text to simple text.

As you can see, the capitalization was interpreted slightly differently than I had intended, but overall the Recognize feature did a great job. This is a powerful feature that you will likely start using a great deal if you like to hand write text in notes.

Figure 6.12
Text that is handwritten in a note can be converted using the Recognize feature.

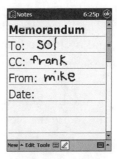

Figure 6.13
The end result of using the Recognize feature might not be exactly what you expected, but If your handwriting is decent it will be surprisingly close.

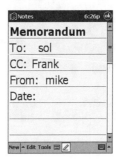

Essential Information

- When used appropriately, the Tasks application can be beneficial in helping you stay on track with both personal and work projects.

- The entry bar in the Tasks application provides a convenient way to enter tasks quickly.

- You can use the Action button in conjunction with other hardware buttons to launch the Tasks and Notes applications.

- Notes are different from other types of Pocket Outlook data because they are stored in individual files, as opposed to being stored in a database.

- The Recognize feature in the Notes application allows you to hand write information and then have it converted to simple text.

GET THE SCOOP ON...
The Role of the File Explorer Application ▪
Manipulating Files in File Explorer ▪ Using CF
(CompactFlash) Storage Cards for Extra
Storage Space ▪ Different Approaches to Installing
Pocket PC Software

Managing Files with File Explorer

E XCEPT FOR MAYBE MICROSOFT OUTLOOK and Microsoft Word, Windows Explorer is without a doubt the most used application on my desktop PC. It serves such a vital role in providing a view to the file system and a means of manipulating it that I would feel helpless trying to use my computer without it. Pocket PC includes a similar application called File Explorer that allows you to view and manipulate the file system of your Pocket PC. Although file management is somewhat less critical on a handheld device because a lot of the data you enter is stored in databases instead of files, the File Explorer application nonetheless serves a vital purpose. As you learn a little later in the chapter, one area in which the File Explorer application is a necessity is copying and moving files back and forth between system memory and CF storage cards.

In addition to putting File Explorer through its paces, this chapter tackles the subject of CF storage cards and how they impact file management. You also learn about Pocket PC software installation, which is closely related to file management because installing software mainly involves moving files around.

Using the File Explorer Application

Unlike most of the standard applications that permanently reside in your Pocket PC's ROM, the File Explorer application isn't available from the Start menu by default. However, you can certainly add it to the menu if you find yourself using it a lot. Refer to Chapter 3, "Setting Up Your Pocket PC," for details on how this is done. To run File Explorer, tap the Start menu and then tap Programs. In the Programs window, tap the File Explorer icon to launch the File Explorer application. The application opens, displaying the contents of the My Documents folder, as shown in Figure 7.1.

→ **See Also** Chapter 3, "Customizing the Start Menu," **p. 40**.

Figure 7.1
The File Explorer application begins with the My Documents folder in view.

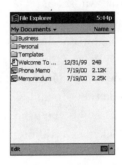

You can change the current folder being displayed by tapping the folder near the upper-left corner of the screen. This results in the display of a drop-down list from which you can select a different folder. Tapping My Device reveals the top-level folder structure of your device, which consists of the following folders by default:

- **My Documents**—Application data and related documents.

- **Program Files**—Installed programs and settings.

- **Temp**—Temporary files.

- **Windows**—Windows settings and support files.

Of these standard folders, the one with which you are most concerned is My Documents, where you will store any files or documents that you create. You can create subfolders of the My

Documents folder, but it's important to keep any data files that you create in this folder or beneath it. This is necessary so that the files will be accessible from Pocket PC applications.

The upper-right corner of the File Explorer screen includes a sort method drop-down list that allows you to sort the files and folders by name, date, size, or type. I prefer to set File Explorer so that it sorts by type, which keeps files of the same type together visually. This can be helpful if you're looking for a certain type of file like a specific image. Even so, the File Explorer sort method is a preference that can be set to suit your needs.

When viewing files in the file list of File Explorer, make sure you pay close attention to the file size displayed to the right of the file entry. Unlike Windows Explorer, which uses the word "bytes" to identify file sizes under 1KB, File Explorer uses the letter B. It also uses the letter K to signify kilobytes (KB) and M for megabytes (MB). Even though these letters are easily distinguishable, it's a slightly different look from Windows Explorer that can go unnoticed.

File Explorer always opens the My Documents folder when you launch it; it does not return you to the folder you were last in before you closed File Explorer. Theoretically, if you leave File Explorer and return to it before Pocket PC has time to remove it from memory, you should be able to remain in the last folder you were viewing. However, this is not the case—the My Documents folder is always displayed upon revisiting File Explorer.

Copying and Moving Files

File Explorer makes it easy to copy and move files from one folder to another, between your device and desktop PC, between your device and another device, or between your device and a CF storage card. However, because Pocket PC doesn't support drag and drop, you must always use the familiar tap and hold technique to manipulate files. To copy or move a file from one folder to another, follow these steps:

1. Tap and hold on the file to display a menu of file options.

2. Tap Copy to copy the file, or Cut to move the file.

Watch Out!
For some reason, the standard Pocket PC applications recognize files up to only one folder level beneath the My Documents folder. For example, if you place a note in the Personal subfolder beneath the My Documents folder, the Notes application will display it in the note list when you select All Folders. However, if you create a subfolder named More Personal beneath the Personal folder and place files in it, Notes will not be able to access the files. This rule applies to any Pocket PC application that stores files in the My Documents folder.

Undocumented
The File Explorer application doesn't allow you to view or edit the file extension of a file. This means that you can't change the type of a file by changing its file extension, which is a common practice in Windows Explorer on desktop PCs. If you need to change the type of a file on your Pocket PC, you have to copy the file to your desktop, rename the file, and then copy it back. Optionally, you can use the Explore feature in ActiveSync to rename Pocket PC files from your desktop PC.

3. Navigate to the folder in which you want the file placed.

4. Tap Edit in the lower-left corner of the screen, and then tap Paste. You can also tap and hold in the File Explorer window, and then tap Paste on the pop-up menu.

In addition to copying and moving individual files, you can also work with groups of files. To do this, you must tap on the first file and drag the stylus down to select additional files. Of course, this requires the files to appear next to each other in the file list. After you've selected a group of files, tap and hold on any of the files and follow the same series of steps that were just explained for copying and moving them .

Renaming and Deleting Files

Renaming files in File Explorer also involves the popular tap-and-hold technique, and is a straightforward process. Just tap and hold on the file that you want to rename, and then tap Rename on the pop-up menu that appears. The name of the file turns into an edit box, and you use the SIP to enter the new filename. Tapping off the edit box commits the name change.

Deleting files is similar to renaming them; you tap and hold on the file and then tap Delete on the pop-up menu. File Explorer presents you with a confirmation box to make sure that you want to delete the file (see Figure 7.2). If you haven't changed your mind, just tap OK and the file is deleted.

Figure 7.2
A confirmation box is displayed to make sure that you want to delete a file; tapping OK follows through with the deletion.

Sending Files

In addition to copying, moving, renaming, and deleting files, you can also send files in File Explorer. There are two different ways you can send files via File Explorer:

- **Email**—Files are sent as email attachments.

- **Infrared**—Files are sent to another device via the infrared port.

Both of these sending options are available from the pop-up menu that appears when you tap and hold over a file in File Explorer. If you elect to send a file via email, an email message is created with the file attached to it. You are then responsible for filling in the details of the message, such as the recipient(s), the subject, and any message to accompany the attachment. Sending a file via infrared requires you to align your device with the infrared port of another device, after which the file will be sent. Sending files via infrared is handy if you are in physical proximity to another user who has a Pocket PC; the email approach is a necessity if you are sending files to remote locations.

Taking Advantage of CF Storage Cards

It's hard to discuss files and file storage without addressing CF storage cards and how they fit into the picture. If you have a CF storage card installed in your Pocket PC, it appears as a folder named Storage Card in File Explorer beneath the My Device root folder, as shown in Figure 7.3.

Undocumented
File Explorer doesn't have a Find Files feature; to find files or other information on your device, you must use the Find application that is accessible from the Start menu.

Inside Scoop
To select multiple files that aren't adjacent to each other, tap the Ctl key (Control) on the SIP Keyboard. With this key selected, you can select and deselect individual files as part of a group.

Figure 7.3
A CF storage card is represented by a folder named Storage Card that appears beneath the My Device root folder.

Undocumented
If you want to delete (uninstall) an application, tap the System menu, and then tap Settings. From there you must tap the System tab, followed by the Remove Programs icon. You can then select the application(s) you want to uninstall.

The Storage Card acts just like any other folder on your device, with the exception that files stored in the folder actually reside on the storage card instead of in main system memory. If you have several storage cards or remove your card often for any reason, then you must be careful about what kind of files you store on it. This caution is necessary because you don't want to miss files that are on the card if you forget to carry the card with you. Many users have a single storage card that is kept in the device as long as they don't need to use a modem or some other CF peripheral. In this case, you must still be careful about what you put on the card because it won't be accessible while using a modem or other CF card.

If you plan on using a CF card to store data files for Pocket PC applications such as Pocket Word, Pocket Excel, or Windows Media Player, you'll need to create a folder named My Documents on the card. This is necessary because Pocket PC applications are specifically designed to store files in the My Documents folder, and will not see files stored elsewhere on the device. To create the My Documents folder on a storage card, follow these steps:

1. Tap the folder in the upper-left corner of the screen, and then tap My Device.

2. Tap the Storage Card folder in the file list.

3. Tap Edit in the lower-left corner of the screen, and then tap New Folder. You can also tap and hold in the File Explorer window, and then tap New Folder on the pop-up menu.

4. Enter the name "My Documents" as the folder name using the SIP.

5. Tap off the folder name to create the new folder.

The My Documents folder on the storage card can be thought of as an extension to the My Documents folder in main memory. In fact, if you use the Save Document As function in Pocket Word or the Save Workbook As function in Pocket Excel, you will have the opportunity to specify the main memory or the CF card to store the file, in which case it will be stored in the respective My Documents folder.

If you don't like the idea of having all your documents and data files stored in one folder, you can create subfolders beneath the My Documents folder. For example, you could create a Pocket Word folder for Word files and a Pocket Excel folder for Excel files. Actually, the My Documents folder in main memory already includes Business and Personal folders for one possible schema of organization. In fact, it's not a bad idea to use these same names on your CF memory card so the folders blend with those in main memory.

Installing Pocket PC Software

A discussion of Pocket PC file management wouldn't be complete without tackling the issue of installing Pocket PC software, which basically boils down to installing a bunch of files. Fortunately, most Pocket PC applications include installation programs that handle the details of putting files in the right place and taking care of any appropriate settings. Software installation is important because there are all kinds of interesting applications that you can download or purchase to expand your Pocket PC's capabilities.

Before getting into the details of how Pocket PC software is installed, I want to caution you that storage is a valuable and limited commodity on your Pocket PC, which usually means that you have to pick and choose the software that you install on the device. The massive size of desktop hard drives has spoiled many of us into installing as much software as we want with no concern about how much space it eats up. You can't get away with this when it comes to your Pocket PC, unless you've sprung for one of IBM's expensive 1GB Microdrive CF cards (covered in Appendix A, "A Guide to Pocket PC Accessories"). You should take stock of how much space you have available on your device before installing additional software.

Watch Out!
Although you are free to name subfolders of the My Documents folder anything you choose, you must create a My Documents folder on your CF storage card to access files from a Pocket PC application such as Pocket Word, Pocket Excel, or Windows Media Player. Otherwise, the applications won't see any files on the card.

Watch Out!
Regardless of how you install Pocket PC software, it is extremely important that you install the correct version of the software. Unlike desktop PCs, Pocket PCs use different processors across different manufacturers, which usually results in a different executable file for each device. As of this writing, the Casio, Symbol, and Compaq Aero 1550 devices use NEC MIPS processors, the HP Jornada devices use SH3 processors, and the Compaq iPAQ H3600 devices use Intel StrongARM processors. Some software includes "smart" installers that detect your processor and install the correct version automatically. There is also a new executable format coming called CEF (Common Executable Format) that alleviates this problem at the expense of slightly diminished performance and a larger executable file size.

→ **See Also** Appendix A, "IBM Microdrive Cards," **p. 367**.

Software is installed onto a Pocket PC in one of three ways, which is largely dependent on where the software originates:

- The software is on a CD-ROM and is installed from a setup program that runs on a desktop PC.

- The software is downloaded onto the device or located on a CF card and the setup program runs from the device.

- There is no setup program; the software is downloaded straight from the Web or from a desktop PC to the device.

The next few sections address the details of each of these installation approaches.

Installing Software from a Desktop PC

The smoothest way to install software is to run an installation program on your desktop PC and let it do all the work. Of course, this requires you to have your device connected to the desktop PC via a cradle or some other (serial/USB) cable connection. You'll also need to establish a connection via the ActiveSync software because ActiveSync is what actually allows the communication to take place between the desktop PC and the device.

With an ActiveSync connection established, the only thing left to do is run the setup program on the desktop PC. Every setup program is different so I won't try to generalize the process other than to say that you'll be presented with a series of steps that outline the different options available for installing the software. After you've gone through the steps, the installation should proceed, resulting in a new icon in the Programs folder of the device. To run the newly installed program, tap Programs in the Start menu, look for the new icon, and then tap it.

Installing Software Directly from the Pocket PC

The decision to install Pocket PC software from a desktop PC or directly from the device is not in your hands. The software publisher makes this decision when it packages the software for installation. Software designed for installation directly from your device is packaged in a file with a .cab extension. These CAB files are special compressed files similar to ZIP files that are designed specifically for software distribution. You could obtain software in CAB form by downloading it off the Web or copying it straight off a CD-ROM, but the distinction is that CAB files install themselves directly on your device.

To install software from a CAB file, copy or download the CAB file to your device and use File Explorer to open the folder in which the file is located. Tap the file and follow the installation instructions to install the software. Similar to the desktop installation process, the CAB installation finishes by placing a new icon in the Programs folder of the device. To run the newly installed program, tap Programs in the Start menu, look for the new icon, and then tap it.

Installing by Copying an Application File

The final approach to installing Pocket PC software is a more hands-on approach and doesn't involve any special setup programs. In this case, you basically are working with an executable application with an .exe or .cef file extension that you place in a folder on your device. You could obtain the file by downloading it off the Web, copying it from a CD-ROM, or transferring it from the hard disk on your desktop PC.

The drawback to software installed in this manner is that no icon is automatically placed in the Programs folder, which means you'll have to navigate to the file location and tap the file to run the application. Another option is to move the application to the Programs folder, which will make it more accessible. To do so, follow these steps:

1. Run File Explorer and navigate to the location of the application's executable file.

2. Tap and hold on the file, and then tap Cut.

3. Navigate to the My Device root folder.

4. Tap the Windows folder, and then tap the Start Menu folder.

Remember
While an ActiveSync partnership is absolutely essential when synchronizing data between your desktop and your Pocket PC, it is not necessary when just installing software.

Remember
If you are installing software from a CF card, the setup program runs directly on your Pocket PC. Typically, the setup program runs automatically when you insert the CF card.

5. Tap Programs to open the Programs folder.

6. Tap Edit in the lower-left corner of the screen, and then tap Paste.

Because you've moved the application file to the Programs folder, an icon for it appears next to other installed applications when you view the Programs folder via the Start menu. Keep in mind that unlike desktop Windows, which allows shortcuts to applications, you moved the application file itself.

Essential Information

- The My Documents folder is an important folder in the Pocket PC file system because it is designated as the storage location for Pocket PC application data files.

- Files can be copied, moved, renamed, and deleted in File Explorer by using the tap-and-hold technique.

- File Explorer supports sending files as email attachments or using the infrared port.

- CF storage cards seamlessly integrate into the Pocket PC file system and are accessible from File Explorer just as if they were folders in main memory.

- Pocket PC software installation is usually straightforward provided that you install a version of the software appropriate for the processor in your device.

PART III

Pocket PC: The Network Appliance

GET THE SCOOP ON...
■ Modem Networking with Your Pocket PC ■
The Types of CompactFlash Modems Available
■ Establishing a Dial-Up Modem Connection
■ Establishing an Ethernet Connection ■ Using an
Ethernet Connection to Speed Up ActiveSync
Synchronization

Getting Online

P RIOR TO THE INTERNET, most computers were islands unto themselves that had little interaction with one another. More importantly, computer users viewed computers as standalone tools that were entirely dependent on installing new software to access new information. Software still undergoes changes and requires upgrades, but information is no longer dependent on the software itself. The Internet has, in many ways, severed the dependency between software updates and information access. You can now install a Web browser, throw away the CD-ROM, and access limitless information with nothing more than a phone line and a modem. This same capability applies to Pocket PCs.

Like desktop computers, Pocket PCs require networking hardware to connect to a remote network such as the Internet. Options include a CompactFlash (CF) modem card that connects to a phone line or a CF Ethernet card that connects to an existing Local Area Network (LAN) with Internet access. This chapter explores these different wired approaches to getting online with your Pocket PC; wireless options are covered in Chapter 11, "Wireless Communications."

Modem Networking

The most common and inexpensive approach (at least at the moment) used to connect a Pocket PC to the Internet is a CF modem card, which requires a phone line and a dial-up Internet service. With this approach, a phone cord is plugged into the CF modem card to establish the wired network connection. You then dial up an Internet service provider (ISP) on your Pocket PC much as you would on a desktop computer. Aside from the miniature hardware, connecting a Pocket PC to the Internet isn't really any different from connecting a desktop computer via a dial-up Internet service.

CF Modem Cards

Several CF modem cards are available for dial-up Pocket PC networking. These cards are all 56Kbps CF cards that include tiny 56Kbps (kilobits per second) embedded modems. CF modem cards are relatively power efficient, which results in minimal battery drain on your Pocket PC. Following are the most popular CF modem cards available as of this writing:

- Casio Cassiopeia CompactFlash Modem

- Compaq 56K CompactFlash Fax Modem

- Kingston Technology Compact I/O 56K Modem

- Pretec 56K CompactModem

- Xircom CompactCard Modem 56

There are some variations in each of these modems, but they are all suitable for getting your Pocket PC online with a dial-up Internet service. The only significant difference between the modems is whether they include a jack for a phone line directly on the modem, or whether they use an additional connector for the phone line. Modems that include the phone jack are larger (to accommodate the jack) but they don't require you to keep track of an extra piece of hardware (the phone line connector). Modems that use a connector are the same size as Type I CF cards, which is beneficial because they don't stick out of your device, but you have to make sure you don't forget or lose the plug.

→ **See Also** Appendix A, "A Guide to Pocket PC Accessories," **p. 361**.

Regardless of which modem you use, they all function similarly after you get them installed and configured for your device.

Configuring a Modem Connection

Installing a modem is very straightforward when you consider that drivers are already included on your device for most of the popular modems. Because the drivers are already in place, the modem is recognized the moment you plug it into your device. Because there is no hardware installation involved other than plugging in your modem, establishing a modem connection primarily consists of entering information about your dial-up Internet service. If you purchase a modem whose drivers aren't already included on your device, then you'll need to follow the modem manufacturer's installation instructions, which will likely involve installing a driver from a CD-ROM inserted in your desktop computer.

To set up a modem connection on your device, you first need to tap Settings in the Start menu to go to the Device Settings screen. Tapping the Connections tab in this screen displays a screen with different types of connections. To view the modem connections, tap the Modem icon, which displays the Modem Connections screen as shown in Figure 8.1.

There are no modem connections in the list; the New Connection item in the list is used to create new connections. To create a new connection, tap New Connection in the list. This displays the Make New Connection screen shown in Figure 8.2.

Remember
The special plug on CF modems that don't include a built-in phone line connector is also known as a dongle. An unfortunate name, yes, but it's the truth.

Remember
Be sure to plug your modem into your Pocket PC before setting up a modem connection.

Figure 8.1
The Modem Connections screen includes a list of all the modem connections set up for the device, which in this case is empty.

Figure 8.2
The Make New
Connection screen
gets you started
creating a new
modem connec-
tion.

Shortcut
The Connections
link near the bot-
tom of the Modem
Connections
screen allows you
to establish a
modem connec-
tion that has been
created.

Inside Scoop
Obviously, not all
modems have
built-in drivers that
are included in the
Pocket PC operat-
ing system. If your
Pocket PC doesn't
automatically
recognize your
modem when you
attempt to estab-
lish a modem con-
nection, you'll
need to install
software drivers;
these drivers
should be included
with the modem
when you pur-
chase it.

The Make New Connection screen is where you identify the type of modem you are using; in this case, I'm using a Pretec 56K CompactModem. Because the Pretec modem driver is built into the Pocket PC operating system, I didn't have to install any drivers. In fact, the Make New Connection screen automatically recognized the modem and selected it for me. My responsibilities in this screen include entering the name of the connection and setting the baud rate. The connection name is for identification purposes and can be anything you want.

You might notice an Advanced button in the Make New Connection screen that is used to enter advanced modem con- nection details. In most cases, you won't have to worry about the advanced settings, but if for some reason you need to alter the default port settings or set a specific IP address or Domain Name Server (DNS), you'll want to take a look at the Advanced settings. The Advanced Modem Connection screen has three tabs: Port Settings, TCP/IP, and Name Servers. Figures 8.3 through 8.5 show each of these tabs, which you can use to change advanced modem connection settings.

The Port Settings tab includes options for changing the data bits, stop bits, parity, and flow control of the connection. There are also options for terminal settings such as using a terminal window before or after the connection, or manually entering dialing commands. Unless you know for certain that you need to change these settings, you'll probably want to keep the defaults.

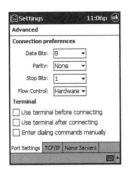

Figure 8.3
The Port Settings tab of the Advanced Modem Connection screen allows you to fine-tune the port settings for the connection.

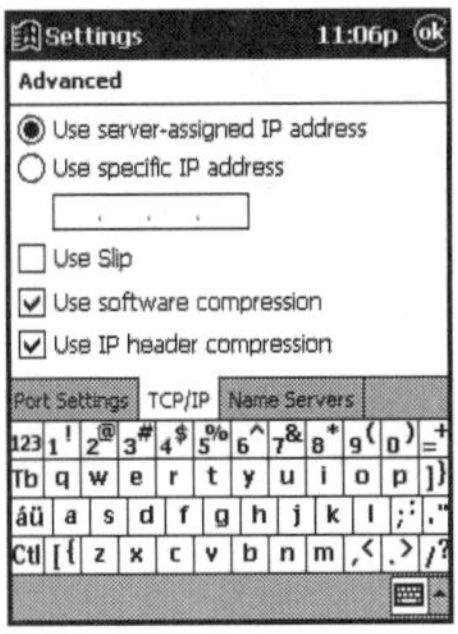

Figure 8.4
The TCP/IP tab of the Advanced Modem Connection screen allows you to fine-tune the TCP/IP settings for the connection.

The TCP/IP tab allows you to change settings related to the TCP/IP address for the connection. You can elect to have your Internet service provider assign an address for you or use a specific address. Unless your Internet service provider specifically mentions setting the IP address, set the first radio button so that the server assigns the address. The remaining options in the TCP/IP tab allow you to enable or disable compression.

Figure 8.5
The Name Servers tab of the Advanced Modem Connection screen allows you to fine-tune the name server settings for the connection.

Undocumented
If you have prob-
lems with your
modem connec-
tion after com-
pleting the
connection setup
process, you
might want to
consider turning
off software com-
pression and IP
header compres-
sion in the
TCP/IP tab of the
Advanced Modem
Connection
screen (refer to
Figure 8.4).

Remember
If your ISP's
access number is
a local number,
go ahead and
enter the area
code in the Phone
Number screen so
that the Pocket
PC dialer will
know whether the
call is a local or
long distance call.
This is important
because you can
set up multiple
locations from
which you estab-
lish a modem con-
nection, and
these locations
might have differ-
ent area codes.

The Name Servers tab includes settings for explicitly specifying domain name server addresses. You can also set the first radio button to have the server assign the address automatically.

It's probably best not to change the advanced modem connection settings unless you know for certain that your dial-up service requires a special setting. Some dial-up Internet services automatically assign advanced properties such as the IP address and domain name server addresses, whereas others require you to enter the address of a domain name server (which they must provide). I encourage you to use the connection settings recommended by your specific Internet service provider. When you are finished tinkering with advanced modem connection settings, tap OK in the upper-right corner of the screen to return to the Make New Connection screen (refer to Figure 8.2).

To continue creating the new modem connection, tap Next in the Make New Connection screen. This displays the Phone Number screen where you can enter the phone number for your dial-up ISP. After entering the access phone number for your ISP, tap the Next button to continue along with the modem connection setup process. Figure 8.6 shows the Dialing Details screen, in which you enter details about the dial settings for the modem connection.

For most purposes, the default settings in the Dialing Details screen are acceptable. However, you can use this screen to shorten the timeout period for canceling a call if a connection isn't established or to wait for a dial tone before attempting a call. This second option can be useful if you use your phone line for both voice and data. Nothing can pop an eardrum when you're on the phone like a modem trying to dial out. The remaining two options allow you to specify a timeout period for a credit card dial tone and enter modem commands that are executed during dial-up.

More than likely, you'll probably be able to keep the default settings, in which case you tap the Finish button to complete the creation of the modem connection. The Modem Connections screen shown earlier in Figure 8.1 displays the new modem connection added to the list. Tap OK in the Modem Connections screen to return to the Device Settings.

Figure 8.6
The Dialing Details screen is used to customize the dialing options for your dial-up modem connection.

Establishing a Modem Connection

With the modem connection created, you are ready to go online. All network connections for your Pocket PC are accessed from the Connections folder, which you can find by tapping Programs in the Start menu, and then tapping the Connections icon. The contents of the Connections folder include icons for all the connections that are set up for the device.

To establish a connection, tap an icon in the Connections folder. In this case, you want to tap the modem connection icon, which has whatever name you assigned it in Figure 8.2. This displays the Connect To screen, which is where you actually initiate a modem connection (see Figure 8.7).

Figure 8.7
The Connect To screen is used to initiate a dial-up modem connection.

The first time you make a connection, you must enter the usual account information (password and username) for your dial-up Internet account on the Connect To screen. To avoid having to enter your password every time you connect to the service, check the Save password check box. This displays a warning message reminding you that anyone using your device can access your dial-up account if you choose to save the password.

Watch Out!
Even if your ISP provides you with a domain name for use in establishing a dial-up connection, don't enter it in the Domain field on the Connect To screen. This domain name is required only for connecting to Windows NT servers, typically corporate networks, and causes problems if entered for most ISPs. As an example, my ISP would consistently drop the connection after a few seconds when I had the domain name entered.

Although security is an ever-increasing issue in our online culture, your dial-up password is probably not as sensitive as other information that you would protect. Besides, as the warning message points out, you can always password protect the device itself, in which case no one will be able to get in your Pocket PC to use your dial-up account.

On the Connect To screen, there is a Dialing Options button that is used to set information about the location from which you are dialing. Notice in the Connect To screen that there is a Dial From field set to Home. This is where you specify the location from which you are dialing, which impacts whether the call is a local or long distance call. To set up the specifics of each location where you expect to dial out from, tap the Dialing Options button. This displays the Dialing Options screen shown in Figure 8.8.

Two locations (Home and Work) are automatically included in the Dialing Options screen, but you can create more if you want. It is a good idea to provide dialing details for all the locations that you plan to use. Creating a new location is as simple as tapping the New button and entering the name of the location. You can also remove the currently selected location by tapping the Remove button. Figure 8.8 shows the dialing details for my Home location. Notice that the call-waiting feature of the phone service is disabled so that incoming calls don't disrupt the connection. Use the Dialing Patterns button to alter dialing patterns such as whether it is necessary to dial a 9 before the phone number. When you're finished entering information for the dialing locations, tap OK in the upper-right corner of the screen to return to the Connect To screen.

You're now ready to go online with your modem connection. Tap the Connect button in the Connect To window to dial your ISP.

Figure 8.8
The Dialing Options screen allows you to set dialing information about dialing locations.

A pop-window appears as the modem dials in. If all goes well, after a few moments the screen will indicate that the device is connected, as shown in Figure 8.9. You are now online and ready to surf the Web, check email, and perform any other online tasks.

Figure 8.9
The device is successfully connected to the Internet via a modem connection.

If for some reason the dial-up connection fails, you should double-check the dial-up settings such as your ISP username and password. Also, make sure you have a dial tone on the phone line that you're using, and that the access number for your ISP is correct. If you're still having trouble, check to make sure that the Domain field on the Connect To screen isn't set. This domain name is required only for connecting to Windows NT servers, and can cause problems for ISPs. If you still can't get a connection established, you probably should contact your ISP and clarify the settings required to connect through its network.

Ethernet Networking

Another Pocket PC networking option that you might not have considered is Ethernet networking, which involves connecting your device to a desktop computer or LAN to synchronize and connect to the Internet. Ethernet networking is primarily useful for synchronizing as opposed to connecting to the Internet because you would likely just use a desktop computer for Internet access if you have access to a LAN. In terms of synchronization, Ethernet networking is quite powerful for Pocket PCs because of the sheer speed. An Ethernet connection is significantly faster than a serial or USB connection, and keeps your device in sync with a desktop computer in a seamless fashion.

With an Ethernet connection, using ActiveSync to back up your device becomes much easier to perform on a regular basis because of the speed at which it is carried out. It is also much quicker to install software and copy files back and forth between a desktop computer and your Pocket PC. Basically anything that you do with your device via ActiveSync will be sped up with an Ethernet network connection.

CF Ethernet Cards

CF Ethernet cards allow you to connect a Pocket PC to a computer or LAN for quick synchronization and Internet access. CF Ethernet cards are similar to CF modem cards in that they plug into the CF slot of a Pocket PC and require a wired cable connection to function. Following are the most popular CF Ethernet cards available as of this writing:

- Pretec CompactLan Card

- Socket Communications Low-Power Ethernet CF+ Card

- Xircom CompactCard Ethernet 10

These cards are all similar in the Ethernet networking support that they provide. All the cards are Type I CF cards, which means they will work with all Pocket PCs that have a CF slot.

→ **See Also** Appendix A, "A Guide to Pocket PC Accessories," p. 361.

Watch Out!
When you install a CF Ethernet card in your Pocket PC with an active network connection, your Pocket PC might not power down automatically if left idle. Be sure to manually turn off the device if you don't plan on using it for a while.

Establishing an Ethernet Connection

Unlike a dial-up modem connection, which is temporary because of its dependence on a phone call, an Ethernet connection is permanent to the extent that the physical network connection is still active. In other words, there is no special dialing or anything required to initiate an Ethernet connection; after it is properly set up and configured, you are connected. Although this aspect of an Ethernet connection is beneficial, an aspect that isn't so good is the specifics of how an Ethernet connection is configured. I say this because many of the Ethernet settings are dependent upon the specific network you are accessing.

Because there are some variations in how an Ethernet connection is established, I'm going to outline the general steps required to establish a connection with a desktop PC on a network. You'll need to obtain specific configuration information about the network to which you are connecting to carry out your own configuration.

Before you get started setting up an Ethernet connection with your Pocket PC, it is important to clarify a few hardware and software requirements. Following is a list of requirements that must be met before creating the connection:

- You must have an Ethernet card in your desktop computer.

- The desktop computer must be configured to use TCP/IP and the Client for Microsoft Networks.

- You must have an Ethernet hub or a crossover cable in which to plug your Pocket PC.

- You must have a CF Ethernet card for your Pocket PC.

If you meet all the previous requirements, you're ready to begin creating an Ethernet connection for your Pocket PC. At this point, I have to share the good news that it is quite possible that you can establish an Ethernet connection with little to no work. If you have a Dynamic Host Configuration Protocol (DHCP) server installed on the network to which you are

Inside Scoop
If your CF Ethernet card is compatible with NE2000, a generic network adapter driver, you won't have to install drivers because the Pocket PC operating system includes NE2000 drivers. Otherwise, you'll need to install the appropriate drivers that came with the card. Source: U.S. Census Bureau

connecting, the Ethernet card installation is pretty much automatic. When you insert the card into your device, the DHCP server automatically detects the card and allocates an IP address for it. The Ethernet connection will immediately become established and you can begin synchronizing your device and connecting to the Internet via the connection.

If there isn't a DHCP server on the network to which you are connecting (check with your network administrator), all is not lost; you'll just have to configure the connection yourself. The first step in establishing the Ethernet connection is setting an IP address and subnet mask for the desktop computer, which will identify it as a domain name server for the Pocket PC device. To enter these settings, click the Network icon in the Control Panel of the desktop computer. The Configuration tab of the Network window includes a list of all the installed network components. Click the TCP/IP component and then click the Properties button to edit its properties. This displays the TCP/IP Properties window, which is shown in Figure 8.10.

Figure 8.10
The TCP/IP Properties window in Windows 98/NT/2000 allows you to alter TCP/IP network settings.

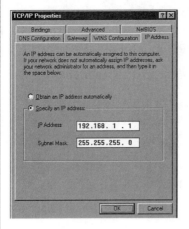

In the TCP/IP Properties window, you need to specify an IP address to identify the computer for the Pocket PC connection, along with a subnet mask. Following are some suitable settings for these properties, which are reflected in Figure 8.10:

- IP Address - 192.168.1.1

- Subnet Mask - 255.255.255.0

These two settings are all that are required on the desktop side of the Ethernet connection. To get your Pocket PC ready for the connection, tap Settings on the Start menu, and then tap the Connections tab. Tap the Network icon to access the installed network drivers. Figure 8.11 shows the Network Connections screen, which lists the installed network drivers.

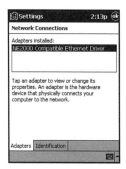

Figure 8.11
The Network Connections screen contains a list of the network drivers installed on your device.

To alter the properties of a driver, tap the driver name in the list. This displays the Driver Settings screen shown in Figure 8.12. The Network Connections screen includes an Identification tab that allows you to enter network credentials for accessing remote network resources. These credentials consist of a user name, password, and domain, and may or may not be necessary for your specific network.

Figure 8.12
The Driver Settings screen allows you to change settings related to the IP address of the Ethernet driver.

Change the settings in the IP Address tab of the Driver Settings screen so that a specific IP address is used. Use the following IP address and subnet mask settings, which are shown in Figure 8.12:

- IP Address - 192.168.1.2

- Subnet Mask - 255.255.255.0

After entering these settings, tap the Name Servers tab to edit the name servers for the driver. Figure 8.13 shows the proper setting for the name server settings, which is to set the Alt DNS property to 192.168.1.1. This is the setting that identifies the desktop computer for connection purposes.

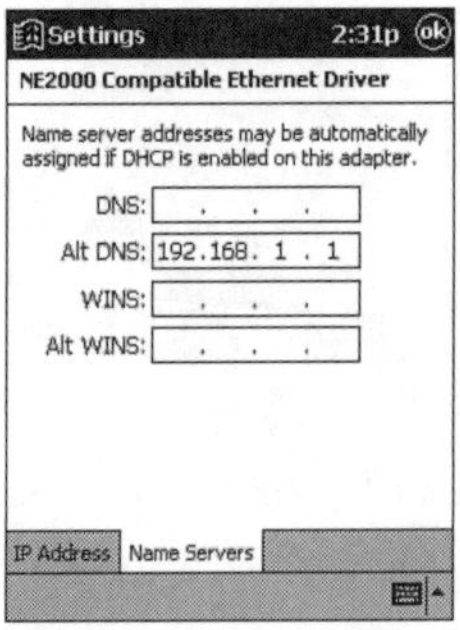

Figure 8.13
The Name Servers tab on the Driver Settings screen allows you to change name servers of the Ethernet driver.

This completes the network settings required to establish an Ethernet connection between your Pocket PC and desktop PC. To activate the connection, plug both machines into the network hub or connect them via a crossover cable. The connection should immediately activate, allowing you to synchronize and connect to the Internet on the Pocket PC through the desktop computer.

Ethernet Synchronization with ActiveSync

ActiveSync typically uses a USB or serial connection to synchronize a Pocket PC device through a cradle that holds the device. To synchronize via an Ethernet connection, you must change a setting in ActiveSync so that it knows to use Ethernet instead of a USB or serial connection. Even though the

Inside Scoop
After configuring the network settings on your Pocket PC, you might want to remove the CF Ethernet card and reinsert it to ensure that the new settings go into effect.

ActiveSync application runs on the desktop computer, you find this setting on your Pocket PC.

To change ActiveSync so that it uses an Ethernet network connection for synchronization, tap Programs on the Start menu, and then tap Connections to open the Connections folder. Tap the ActiveSync icon to alter the method used to connect to ActiveSync (see Figure 8.14).

The connection method needs to be changed to Network Connection for ActiveSync to use the Ethernet connection. You should also make sure that the name specified in the Connect To field is set to the desktop computer name. After the settings are made, tap Connect to connect to ActiveSync via the Ethernet connection.

Remember
Your desktop computer's Ethernet card has a link light on it that is lit if everything is okay with the network connection. Checking this light is one way to tell whether there is a problem with your Ethernet connection.

Figure 8.14
To synchronize with ActiveSync using an Ethernet connection, change the ActiveSync connection method to Network Connection.

Essential Information

- The most common and inexpensive approach (at least at the moment) used to connect a Pocket PC to the Internet is a CF modem card, which requires a phone line and a dial-up Internet service.

- The drivers for most CF modem cards are included in the Pocket PC operating system, which means the modem is recognized the moment you plug it into your device.

- The dialing options for your device allow you to specify multiple dialing locations, which help smooth over the details of whether a call to an ISP's access number needs to be dialed as local or long distance.

Watch Out!
If the Pocket PC is in its cradle when you tap ActiveSync in the Connections folder, a USB or serial connection is automatically made. To select a different connection method, you must remove the device from the cradle.

- CF Ethernet cards allow you to connect your Pocket PC to a desktop computer or LAN via an Ethernet connection, which greatly improves the synchronization speed of ActiveSync.

- Unlike a dial-up modem connection, which is temporary because of its dependence on a phone call, an Ethernet connection is permanent as long as the physical network connection is still active.

GET THE SCOOP ON...

• Email Protocols and Why They Matter • Connecting Your Pocket PC to an Email Server • Accessing Email on the Microsoft Network • Synchronizing Email with a Desktop PC • Working with Email Attachments • Managing and Organizing Email Messages

Email and the Pocket Outlook Inbox

O NE OF THE MOST EXCITING uses of Pocket PCs is being able to read and write email messages when you're not near a desktop computer. Those of us who live and die by email communication can really appreciate the capability of staying in touch via email while on the go. Even if you aren't an email addict, you might still find it empowering to be able to receive email messages while away from home. The Pocket PC application that facilitates email is Inbox, which is part of the Pocket Outlook application suite. The Pocket Outlook application suite is covered in Chapter 4, "Using Pocket Outlook." The Inbox application allows you to synchronize with Outlook 2000 to share email with your desktop computer, or connect directly with an email server.

This chapter explores the Inbox application and how it is used to send, receive, and manage email. The different email protocols are examined, along with their role with Inbox. You also learn how to manage and organize email messages.

Understanding Email Protocols

Like most information capable of being sent and received over a network, email adheres to very specific protocols that govern the structure of messages and how they are delivered.

139

Although there is a set protocol used for sending email messages, you have a couple of options for receiving email messages from a mail server. Following are the email protocols supported by the Inbox application:

- SMTP (Simple Mail Transfer Protocol)

- POP3 (Post Office Protocol version 3)

- IMAP4 (Internet Message Access Protocol version 4)

Remember
Email protocols impact only the Inbox application when you connect directly to a mail server to send and receive email messages. When you synchronize email with the ActiveSync application, no protocols are required.

The SMTP protocol is used to send email messages from the Inbox, and is the only protocol available for this purpose. In other words, learn to love the SMTP protocol because it is your only option. Fortunately, SMTP is a capable protocol and will serve your email sending needs just fine.

The POP3 and IMAP4 protocols are both used to retrieve email messages from a mail server. These protocols handle the details of downloading email messages from a mail server and making them available to the Inbox. There are some differences between the protocols that will likely impact your choice of which protocol to use. However, the ultimate decision as to which protocol you use might come down to which one your mail server supports. Most ISPs support POP3, so it is likely the protocol you will be forced to use unless you're connecting to a corporate mail server that supports IMAP4.

The IMAP4 email protocol is more powerful than POP3 in that it provides a finer level of control over how email messages are retrieved from a server and stored on your device. IMAP4 allows you to synchronize the Inbox directly with a mail server, which alleviates the issue of deciding to leave a copy of messages on the server or removing them after they've been retrieved. IMAP4 also supports multiple mail folders for organizing incoming email automatically.

Before you get the idea that IMAP4 is the ultimate email protocol, let me back up and say that POP3 is a perfectly good protocol for retrieving email with the Inbox. POP3 is very popular and is quite likely the email protocol you will find yourself using because it is the only option for retrieving email from your mail server. The point to take from this discussion is that, should you have the option, IMAP4 is a more powerful protocol, and you should consider using it. However, in the absence of IMAP4, the POP3 protocol will likely serve your needs just fine.

Sending and Receiving Email

The two primary actions taken with email are sending and receiving email messages. These are simple concepts, but there are a couple of different approaches available for carrying out the specific transport of the messages:

- Send and receive email messages by connecting the Inbox to a remote email server.

- Send and receive email messages by synchronizing the Inbox with a desktop computer using the ActiveSync application.

The neat thing about the Inbox in Pocket Outlook is that you can use both approaches to manage email messages. Of course, trying to use both approaches at the same time would prove problematic because of synchronization problems, among others. However, it is totally feasible to use a remote mail server to send and receive messages while you're away from your desktop computer, and then synchronize messages via ActiveSync when you're at home or work and have access to a desktop computer.

Regardless of how you actually transport email messages, the task of creating a new message is pretty simple:

1. Launch the Inbox application from the Start menu.

2. Tap New near the bottom of the screen to open a blank message (Figure 9.1).

3. Tap To to select an email recipient from your contact list, or enter an email address in the edit box.

4. Tap the edit box next to Subj to enter the subject of the email message.

5. Tap the body of the email and enter the message.

6. Tap the Send button to queue the email message for sending; this places the message in the Outbox folder.

Figure 9.1
A blank email message is created when you tap the New command in the Inbox application.

At this point, the new message is in the Outbox, which means that it is queued to be sent as soon as an opportunity arises. This opportunity is either a connection to a mail server or a synchronization with a desktop mail client such as Outlook 2000. The next few sections explore the details of transporting email messages using these two approaches.

Connecting to an Email Server

Connecting to an email server to send and receive email implies that you have some kind of network connection that makes the server accessible. This network connection will likely be a wired connection via a phone line and modem, or possibly a wireless connection using a wireless network card or mobile phone. The specifics of the network connection aren't important; for the purposes of this discussion, let's just assume that you've used a CF modem card to connect to an ISP. In reality, any Internet connection will work when it comes to connecting to an email server to send and receive email messages.

After you've established an Internet connection, you're ready to configure the email settings in the Inbox to communicate with a mail server. Although the process for IMAP4 isn't much different, I'm going to assume that you're using the POP3 incoming mail protocol because it is the most commonly supported protocol. Following are the pieces of information you need to configure the Inbox to connect to a mail server:

- Email user ID

- Email password

- POP3 mail server IP address

- SMTP mail server IP address

The email user ID and password should have been provided to you by your ISP when you signed up for the service; they are often the same as your login user ID and password used to get online. The POP3 and SMTP mail server IP addresses are very important because they identify the actual servers used to send and receive email messages. These server addresses should be easy to find in the documentation for your ISP service, or with a quick call to the ISP's technical support. If you are already using a desktop email application to access the same account, you can check the settings in it because the same server addresses had to be set up there.

Now that you know what information is required, you need to fill in the blanks in the Inbox to get it ready to connect to a mail server. Launch the Inbox and tap the Services menu, followed by New Service. This displays the Service Name screen, which is shown in Figure 9.2.

Inside Scoop
The POP3 and
SMTP mail server
IP addresses are
often the same,
but you should
check with your
ISP to make sure.
Source: U.S.
Census Bureau

Figure 9.2
The Service Name
screen prompts
you to specify the
service type
(incoming email
protocol) and the
email service
name.

In the Service Name screen, select POP3 Mail as the email protocol, and then type a service name that identifies the email service to you. The service name is purely descriptive, so you can enter any name you want. After entering the name, tap

Inside Scoop

If you already use an email client on your desktop computer such as Outlook or Outlook Express, you should be able to quickly obtain all of the information required to configure the email settings in the Pocket PC Inbox application. In Outlook 2000, this information is available by selecting Accounts from the Tools menu, highlighting the email account, and then clicking the Properties button. You will be able to ascertain your user name as well as mail server IP addresses from the Properties window that appears. Of course, your email password will be masked out so you'll have to remember it on your own or request it from your ISP.

Next to continue to the first POP3 Service screen, which is shown in Figure 9.3.

Select the service you want to use to connect to the mail server. I elected to use a dial-up connection through a CF modem card; this connection was created in Chapter 8, "Getting Online." The POP3 mail server IP address that you acquired earlier is entered in the Server field. Your email user ID and password are then entered in the remaining fields. If you don't want to enter the password every time you check your email, check the Save password check box. Tapping Next takes you to the second POP3 Service screen, shown in Figure 9.4.

The Domain property for your email service should be left blank unless you are accessing a mail server on a corporate network that is running on Windows NT. The next property in the second POP3 Service screen is where you enter the SMTP server's IP address. The third property is the return email address that you want to include on all email messages sent from the Inbox. You can enter any address you want, but keep in mind that anyone replying to your messages will be replying to this address. When you're finished with these settings, tap Next to continue along to page three of the POP3 Service settings (see Figure 9.5).

The third POP3 Service screen presents options related to how email is delivered. These options are all highly dependent on your personal tastes. The default settings will do fine for most users if you don't have strong opinions about how email is delivered. If you're connecting to the Internet only to download email, the first option will automatically disconnect for you after it's finished sending and receiving mail. However, it's very inconvenient if you have more to do online. Some people don't want messages automatically sent or downloaded, or like to alter the frequency between checking for new messages, which is set at 15 minutes by default. The MIME format option specifies that email messages are to be sent using the MIME (Multipurpose Internet Mail Extensions) format, which is the most common format used to encode email messages sent across the Internet. You might also want to consider the last setting, which determines the messages that are displayed based upon how old they are; you might decide to uncheck this option to see all messages. Tap Next when you're finished making decisions to move to the last screen of the POP3 Service settings (see Figure 9.6).

Figure 9.3
The first POP3 Service screen prompts you to specify the connection, POP3 mail server, user ID, and password for the service.

Figure 9.4
The second POP3 Service screen prompts you to enter the domain, SMTP mail server, and return mail address for the service.

Figure 9.5
The third POP3 Service screen contains settings specific to the delivery of mail.

Figure 9.6
The fourth POP3 Service screen contains settings that determine how email is retrieved.

Undocumented
I recommend starting out with the Domain property blank and going back and entering a domain address only if you have problems connecting with the mail server. On the other hand, if you are accessing a corporate mail server and the Domain property is necessary, you need to get that information from your network administrator.

Inside Scoop
Although you can enter any email address you want as the return address in the POP3 Service settings, it is possible to run into a problem if your ISP compares the return address with the email address that they have on record for you. Although restrictive to users, some ISPs do this to catch junk mail (spam) senders.

The final screen in the POP3 Service settings includes options that determine how email is retrieved. The first setting allows you to either obtain full email messages or just message headers. Obtaining only message headers makes message retrieval much faster. If you receive a lot of messages, you can sift through the headers and download full messages for only the most important ones. If you don't have a problem with the download of email messages taking a little longer, you might want to set this option to get a full copy of messages because this allows you to read the messages immediately.

The Include check box allows you to specify the maximum lines of text retrieved for an email message. Because the Inbox already has a 5KB maximum size for email messages, you might not want to fool with this setting. On the other hand, if you want to keep your messages extremely lean, then by all means check the box and set the number of lines to your liking. Keep in mind that the 5KB limitation applies only to the text making up the body of an email message, and not any attachments that may be included in the message.

The Get meeting requests check box allows you to retrieve and respond to meeting requests, which are email notifications sent out to appointment attendees. If you don't use email for managing meeting requests, you can probably leave this box unchecked. The final option determines whether file attachments are retrieved with messages. As you probably know, file attachments are files that accompany an email message. File attachments can be any kind of file such as a Word document, an Excel workbook, a JPEG image, or even a WAV audio clip. File attachments can get quite large, so I recommend enabling attachments only if you plan on getting important files as attachments. Later in the chapter, you learn more about handling email attachments.

Tap the Finish button to finish with the POP3 Service settings. You're now ready to connect with an email server to send and receive email messages. Launch Inbox from the Start menu and tap the Services menu, and then tap Connect. If automatic sending and receiving is enabled, any messages in the Outbox folder will be delivered, whereas any new messages will be delivered to the Inbox folder.

One potential problem that might arise when you first attempt to send and receive email through a mail server is a warning that you can receive email messages but not send them. This is a common problem that is somewhat tricky to understand and fix. Unlike most email clients, the Pocket PC Inbox attempts to access the outgoing SMTP port before it logs in to the POP3 port to see whether any email messages are queued for delivery. The problem arises when your ISP performs a POP authentication, which involves checking the POP3 user ID and password before allowing access to the SMTP port. Because the Inbox attempts to access the SMTP port prior to sending the POP3 user ID and password, the authentication fails and you get the warning about not being able to send email.

The good news is that after the POP3 port is accessed and the logon information (user ID and password) is sent, the SMTP port can be accessed without a problem. So, if you attempt to send and receive email after the initial attempt, you will suddenly be able to do so with no problems or warnings. As described on the Pocket PC Web site, this email port problem is a "chicken before the egg" dilemma in that POP3 logon information is needed to verify access to the SMTP server.

Accessing MSN Email

Speaking of authentication and mail servers, the Microsoft Network's (MSN) email server uses a special security feature that makes its email a little tricky to receive using Pocket Inbox. The security feature is called Secure Password Authentication (SPA), and it requires the installation of an add-on for the Inbox to access MSN email. The MSN E-Mail for Pocket PC add-on is freely available for download from the Pocket PC Web site at `http://www.microsoft.com/POCKETPC/downloads/msnsspc.asp`.

After downloading the add-on, execute the setup program to install it on your Pocket PC. The setup program will handle the details of copying the appropriate files to the proper

Remember
To download the full copy of a message when viewing the message header, tap Get Full Copy on the Edit menu. Optionally, you can tap Get Full Copy from the Services menu while viewing the list of message headers.

Inside Scoop
A 5KB email message contains roughly 16,000 characters, which is a pretty sizable message by most standards. Source: U.S. Census Bureau

Inside Scoop
Although POP3 email servers support only the complete enabling or disabling of attachments, IMAP4 mail servers allow you to specify a maximum attachment file size, which gives you more control. Source: U.S. Census Bureau

Inside Scoop
The only real workaround to the "chicken before the egg" email port problem is to use a different SMTP server that doesn't use POP authentication. Keep in mind, however, that the problem doesn't keep you from being able to send email, it just adds an extra step to receiving it.

Undocumented
To reverse the sorting of messages, tap the same sorting option again. For example, the first time you tap From, the messages will be sorted alphabetically (from A to Z) by the sender's name. Tapping From again reverses the alphabetical sort so that it goes from Z to A.

locations. After installing the add-on, you'll need to create a new email service for MSN email. The steps for setting up this service are identical to the earlier steps you followed to set up an ISP email service, except that you'll be entering information pertinent to MSN. Following are the different mail server settings required for MSN:

- POP3 mail server IP address - `pop3.email.msn.com`

- SMTP mail server IP address - `secure.smtp.email.msn.com`

After creating and configuring the MSN email service in the Inbox, you can go about sending and receiving email just as you would with any other email service.

Synchronizing with Outlook 2000

Earlier in the chapter, I mentioned that the two main approaches to sending and receiving email are connecting to an email server and synchronizing with a desktop computer via ActiveSync. The synchronization approach requires that you have Microsoft Outlook 2000 installed and configured on a desktop computer. The ActiveSync application is then used to synchronize email messages between Outlook 2000 and Pocket Inbox. During the synchronization process, email messages from the Inbox folder of Outlook 2000 are transferred to the Inbox folder of the Inbox application. Additionally, email messages in the Outbox folder of Pocket Inbox are transferred to the Outbox folder of Outlook 2000, where they await delivery.

Email synchronization is set up in ActiveSync because ActiveSync is responsible for carrying out the transfer of messages between the desktop PC and Pocket PC email applications. Launch ActiveSync and click the Options button in the main toolbar. This displays the Options window, which is shown in Figure 9.7.

To enable email synchronization, click the check box next to Inbox in the list of information types in the Options window. To fine-tune the email synchronization settings, click the Settings button, which displays the Inbox Synchronization Settings window (see Figure 9.8).

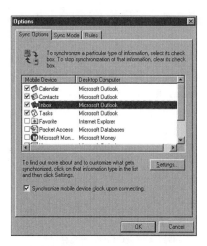

Figure 9.7
The ActiveSync
Options window
allows you to spec-
ify the types of
information that
are synchronized
via ActiveSync.

Figure 9.8
The Inbox
Synchronization
Settings window
allows you to
change the email
synchronization
settings for
ActiveSync.

You'll notice that the synchronization settings in the Inbox
Synchronization Settings window are very similar to the settings associated with Inbox email services, which you saw earlier in the chapter when you created an email service. Because
most of these settings are self-explanatory and are up to your
individual tastes (and available Pocket PC storage space), I
won't go into any detail regarding suggested settings. The only
setting worth a closer look is the last one, which determines
what email services are used to send mail via a synchronized
connection. You will probably want to check the ActiveSync
check box so that messages created in the ActiveSync Outbox
on your Pocket PC will be synchronized and delivered by
Outlook 2000 on your desktop computer.

Undocumented
When you create a new email message on your Pocket PC, its method of delivery is determined by the service to whose Outbox it belongs. Each email service that you create has an Inbox and Outbox, so you need to make sure new messages are placed in the appropriate Outbox for the type of delivery you desire.

Each email service that you have configured on your Pocket PC has its own Inbox and Outbox. For this reason, there is a special ActiveSync Outbox in which new messages should be placed if you want them to be delivered via an ActiveSync connection to your desktop computer. If you plan on sending mail via a dial-up modem connection with an ISP, then you'll want to make sure the messages are created in the Outbox for the ISP mail service. The current mail service appears just below the list of messages in the Inbox application next to the folder name, and can be changed by tapping the drop-down list just beneath the Inbox application name near the top of the screen.

Handling Email Attachments

Email attachments provide a powerful means of sharing files with people. It is obvious that an email message has an attachment because the envelope icon next to the message header has a small paper clip attached to it. The first message in Figure 9.9 has an attachment, whereas the remaining two messages do not.

Figure 9.9
Email messages with attachments include a small paper clip in the icon next to their header.

To read an email message and access its attachment, tap the message in the Inbox message list. The header and body of the message are then displayed, along with a bar along the bottom of the screen that includes the attachment (see Figure 9.10).

To open the attachment, tap the attachment icon in the bar along the bottom of the screen. If the attachment had already been downloaded, it will be opened in the appropriate application suitable for viewing and/or editing it (if a suitable application is not find, the file does not open). If not, Pocket

Outlook begins downloading the attachment. After the download is complete, the attachment is opened in an application. If you are not connected, the attachment is flagged so that it's downloaded the next time you connect. The status of an attachment is shown by a graphical indicator that appears to the left of the attachment; no indicator means the attachment has been downloaded.

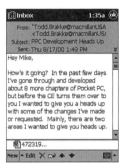

Figure 9.10
When reading an email message with an attachment, the attachment is accessible in a bar along the bottom of the screen.

Receiving and opening attachments is easy enough, and so is creating an email message with an attachment. To attach a file to an email message, open the outgoing message and tap the Insert File button on the Inbox toolbar, and then select the file using the Open window that appears. Another option for sending attached files is to use the File Explorer application to find a file you want to send, and then tap and hold on the file. Select Send via E-Mail in the pop-up menu that appears, and a blank email message is created with the file attached to it. Fill out whom the email is to and send it away.

Managing Email Messages

The Inbox application is a full-featured email client that includes standard features for managing email messages. Most of the email management commands are accessible from the pop-up menu that appears when you tap and hold an email message (see Figure 9.11).

Undocumented
If you have a POP3 email account, the paper clip next to the mail message indicates that the attachment has already been downloaded to your device, whereas in an IMAP4 account it means that the message has an attachment but it has yet to be downloaded. When you open a message with an attachment, the icon next to the attached file or files indicates whether the file is still being downloaded.

Figure 9.11
Tapping and holding an email message results in the display of a pop-up menu full of useful email commands.

Following are the commands accessible from the email pop-up menu, along with a brief description of what they do:

Inside Scoop
Although I describe the email commands in terms of acting upon a single message, all the commands will work with multiple messages if you tap and drag to select the messages, and then tap and hold to access the pop-up menu.

- **Mark As Unread**—Marks a read message as unread so that it stands out.

- **Copy to**—Copies a message to a different folder (preserves the original message).

- **Move to**—Moves a message to a different folder (deletes the original message).

- **Get Full Copy**—Retrieves a full copy of a message that was only partially retrieved.

- **Reply**—Replies to a message (only the sender of the message is replied to).

- **Reply All**—Replies to a message (all addresses on the message are replied to).

- **Forward**—Forwards a message to a different email address.

- **Delete**—Deletes a message by moving it to the Deleted folder.

Aside from issuing commands to manage email messages, you can also alter the manner in which messages are displayed in the Inbox. More specifically, there is a drop-down list in the upper-right corner of the Inbox screen that allows you to alter the sort order of email messages. Following are the different sorting options available:

- **From**—Sorts messages alphabetically by the sender's name.

- **Received Date**—Sorts messages by the received date, with newest messages appearing first (this is the default sorting option).

- **Subject**—Sorts messages alphabetically by the subject.

Essential Information

- Similar to most network data, email adheres to specific protocols that govern the structure of messages and how they are delivered.

- The IMAP4 email protocol is a more powerful and flexible protocol, but the POP3 protocol is much more widely used.

- Connecting directly to an email server allows you to send and receive email from your Pocket PC without the need for a desktop PC.

- To access MSN email using the Inbox application, you must download and install a special security add-on that supports Secure Password Authentication (SPA).

- Synchronizing the Inbox application with a desktop PC allows you to share email with the desktop PC's email client and use it as a means for sending mail from your Pocket PC.

- A paper clip icon next to a mail message in the Inbox indicates that the message has an attachment.

- The Deleted folder in the Inbox application functions like the Windows Recycle Bin in that it must be emptied from time to time to conserve space.

Undocumented

The Deleted folder in the Inbox application functions like the Windows Recycle Bin in that it must be emptied from time to time to conserve space. You can easily empty the contents of the Deleted folder by selecting Empty Deleted Items from the Inbox Tools menu. You can also have the Deleted Items folder emptied automatically by setting the "Empty deleted items" option in the Inbox Message Options screen, which is accessible by selecting Options in the Tools menu, followed by tapping the Message tab.

GET THE SCOOP ON...
- The Differences Between Pocket Internet Explorer and Internet Explorer - Browsing Web Sites Online
- Using Mobile Favorites to Browse Web Sites Offline
- Using the AvantGo Information Service to Browse Content Tailored for Handheld Devices
- Getting the Most out of Pocket Internet Explorer

Using Pocket Internet Explorer

The Web browser is without a doubt the killer application of the Internet. Web browsing has done more to change the public perception of computers than any other software application to date. Although I don't consider the Web browser to be the killer application for Pocket PCs, it is an extremely valuable asset to pocket computing. The ability to synchronize Web content to a Pocket PC and then view it away from an Internet connection is appealing. Even more alluring is the ability to connect to the Internet directly and browse the Web live on your Pocket PC. Both of these approaches to Web browsing are supported by Pocket Internet Explorer, the Pocket PC version of Microsoft's popular Internet Explorer Web browser.

This chapter examines the capabilities of Pocket Internet Explorer and how it is used to put the Web in your pocket. There are several different ways to use Pocket Internet Explorer, and I attempt to highlight the strengths and weaknesses of each. You learn how to browse Web content online and offline with Pocket Internet Explorer, as well as subscribe to Web channels.

Chapter 10

The Ups and Downs of Pocket Internet Explorer

As a pocket version of Internet Explorer, you might expect Pocket Internet Explorer to cut a lot of corners and support only the most basic of Web technologies. Although there are a few important technologies not supported in Pocket Internet Explorer, it fully supports several critical technologies, including some advanced security features. Let's start with the bad news because you are probably more interested in learning how Pocket Internet Explorer is different from its desktop counterpart. The primary Web technologies that aren't supported in Pocket Internet Explorer are

- Java applets

- HTML 4.0

- Dynamic HTML (Web scripting)

- Animated GIF images

Java applets are special programs that run within the confines of a Web page. Although Java has become very popular and is used widely across the Web, it requires Web browsers to have a significant functional component called a runtime engine. Because the Java runtime engine incurs a fair amount of overhead, Microsoft elected to leave it out of Pocket Internet Explorer in favor of a more streamlined application. The end result is that you will find some Web sites that don't function properly in Pocket Internet Explorer because of their usage of Java applets.

Although this might not be a huge issue to the average Web user, Web developers care a lot about which browsers adopt the latest Web development standards. As you might know, HTML (Hypertext Markup Language) is the markup language used to describe the structure of Web pages. As of this writing, HTML 4.0 is the latest version of HTML supported in the major desktop Web browsers, including Internet Explorer. Pocket Internet Explorer supports only HTML 3.2, which puts it a little behind its desktop counterparts. Although it would be nice for Pocket Internet Explorer to support HTML 4.0, keep in mind that even Internet Explorer 5.0 didn't include complete support for HTML 4.0. Because of this, Web developers have been hesitant to build pages around the latest and greatest HTML features. For this reason, the support for HTML 3.2 isn't too big of a drawback when it comes to browsing the vast majority of Web sites with Pocket Internet Explorer.

Dynamic HTML (DHTML) is a fancy term used to describe the scripting of HTML with a scripting language such as JavaScript. JavaScript provides a means of embedding program code directly in a Web page so that you can perform interactive tasks such as processing input from forms or performing calculations. You will likely find more Web sites that use DHTML than you will those that use Java applets, so the lack of DHTML support is somewhat more significant to Pocket Internet Explorer.

The least of the missing ingredients in Pocket Internet Explorer is animated GIF images, which are special GIF images consisting of multiple frames that are displayed in rapid succession to give the effect of animation. In Internet Explorer, animated GIF images are responsible for adding a little pizzazz to Web pages. In Pocket Internet Explorer, the animated portion of these images is ignored; instead of displaying an animation, just the first frame of the animated image is displayed.

Aside from these technological differences between Pocket Internet Explorer and Internet Explorer, the other huge difference between the two browsers is the limited screen space of Pocket Internet Explorer. This might not seem like a big deal, but keep in mind that Web designers specifically target certain screen sizes when designing Web pages. The absolute minimum screen size that Web designers concern themselves with is 640×480, which is four times the size of a Pocket PC screen. Most Web pages are now designed around an 800×600 screen, which is even larger. There are a couple of ways to deal with the screen size issue, which you learn about in the section titled "Pocket Internet Explorer Tips and Tricks," later in this chapter.

Now that you understand the main areas in which Pocket Internet Explorer is weak, let's focus on some of its strengths. One of the most interesting technologies supported in Pocket Internet Explorer is XML (Extensible Markup Language), which is a meta-language used to describe specific markup languages such as HTML. XML is quickly gaining acceptance among Web developers and is considered by some to be the technology that will ultimately provide structure and context to Web data. A technology closely tied to XML and supported by Pocket Internet Explorer is XSL (Extensible Stylesheet Language), which is a special language used to transform and render XML data for display purposes. XSL is important because it provides a means of stylizing and displaying XML data, which otherwise wouldn't be very pretty to view.

Inside Scoop
Warning, shameless plug coming up! To learn more about XML, check out my book *XML Unleashed,* published by Sams.

Perhaps the most significant asset of Pocket Internet Explorer is its support for security features. Security is a big concern for practically all Web users because there is so much at stake in terms of personal information, credit card numbers, and so on. There are two mains types of security employed by Web sites:

- Secure authorization based upon a user logon

- Encrypted data transfer via Secure Socket Layer (SSL)

The first security approach involves you logging into a Web site to have access to it. This security approach is designed primarily to protect a Web site from unwanted users, as opposed to protecting users from giving up sensitive information. The second approach is the one with which you are probably more familiar, because it is used by practically all e-commerce Web sites. This type of security is designed to protect users who are transmitting sensitive data such as personal information or credit card numbers to Web sites. The sensitive information is encrypted before being transmitted, and then decrypted at the other end of the connection. This keeps the information safe should someone gain access to it while it is in transit.

Pocket Internet Explorer supports both security approaches with a small limitation on the secure authorization security approach. The limitation comes into play if a Web site is protected using the Windows NT Challenging Protocol. As of this writing, Pocket Internet Explorer doesn't support the Challenging Protocol, so you won't be able to access sites protected by it. You also won't be able to access sites that use Java applets to implement security, because Pocket Internet Explorer doesn't currently support Java. Pocket Internet Explorer does support SSL security, which allows you to access sites protected for e-commerce such as Amazon.com and other popular shopping sites.

The SSL support built into Pocket Internet Explorer when you buy a Pocket PC isn't quite as advanced as the latest encryption used in Internet Explorer. More specifically, the standard version of Pocket Internet Explorer doesn't support 128-bit encryption, which provides the highest level of encryption currently available in a Web browser. The good news is that Microsoft offers a High Encryption Pack for Pocket Internet Explorer that is freely available for download from the Pocket PC Web site at `http://www.microsoft.com/POCKETPC/downloads/ssl128.asp`. This expansion pack adds 128-bit encryption support to Pocket Internet Explorer.

Unlike Internet Explorer, Pocket Internet Explorer doesn't provide any visual indication regarding the security of a site. In Internet Explorer, a small padlock icon is displayed in the status bar to let you know that a page is a secure page. Pocket Internet Explorer doesn't provide any indication of this. Fortunately, there is a quick way to determine whether a page is secure: Tap the View menu in Pocket Internet Explorer, and then tap Properties to find out the security settings for the page (Figure 10.1).

Pocket Internet Explorer Essentials

Unlike Internet Explorer on the desktop, which is used primarily to view Web pages while you're directly connected to the Internet, Pocket Internet Explorer is designed with offline browsing in mind. Don't get me wrong—Internet Explorer includes support for online browsing, but offline browsing is much more of a necessity for Pocket PC users than for desktop Internet Explorer users.

Inside Scoop
Because Windows NT Challenging Protocol is typically employed only on corporate intranets, Pocket Internet Explorer's lack of support for it is not a tremendous loss.
Source: U.S. Census Bureau

Inside Scoop
Although it might sound like overkill, 128-bit encryption provides a maximum level of security over the transmission of sensitive information through a Web browser. I would encourage you to download the High Encryption Pack for Pocket Internet Explorer if you think you'll be doing any online shopping with your Pocket PC or otherwise providing sensitive information to a Web site.
Source: U.S. Census Bureau

To summarize, the following two approaches are available for browsing in Pocket Internet Explorer:

- Online browsing of live Web content through an Internet connection

- Offline browsing of synchronized Web content

The next couple of sections explore these browsing approaches in more detail.

Browsing Online with an Internet Connection

Browsing online with Pocket Internet Explorer requires an Internet connection. You can either establish the connection prior to launching Pocket Internet Explorer or you can connect from within Pocket Internet Explorer. To launch Pocket Internet Explorer, tap Programs on the Start menu, and then tap the Internet Explorer icon. The initial page displayed in Internet Explorer is shown in Figure 10.2, and is actually stored on your Pocket PC.

To establish an Internet connection from within Pocket Internet Explorer, tap the Tools menu and then Tap Options, which displays the Options screen. The Connections tab on the Options screen allows you to select a connection from a combo box of choices. Figure 10.3 shows a dial-up modem connection selected in this screen.

→ **See Also** Chapter 8, "Getting Online," **p. 123**.

Figure 10.3
The Connection Options screen in Pocket Internet Explorer allows you to specify an Internet connection to use for browsing Web content.

Along with selecting an Internet connection, the Connection Options screen allows you to specify whether Pocket Internet Explorer should automatically connect when you attempt to access a Web page that isn't stored locally. Tap the Access remote content automatically check box to enable this option. The Proxy options in the Connection Options screen allow you to configure a proxy server for the connection. Proxy servers are typically necessary only when accessing corporate networks, in which case you may want to find out proxy server settings from the network's adminstrator.

After you've set a service, you can connect to the Internet by tapping Connect in the Tools menu. The device establishes a connection and returns you to Pocket Internet Explorer, where you can browse the Web live. To go to a specific Web page, tap Address Bar in the View menu to display the address bar. You can type a Web page address (URL) in the address bar and then tap the Go button to go to the site (see Figure 10.4).

Figure 10.4
The Address Bar
allows you to enter
the address (URL)
of a Web site you
want to visit.

Back ———┐   ┌——— Favorites
Refresh ————┘   └——— Home

Another option for navigating to a Web site is to select the site from the list of favorites; this is accomplished by tapping the Favorites button on the right end of the toolbar.

The Favorites screen is relatively empty to start with, but you can add the current Web site to the Favorites list by tapping the Add/Delete tab on the Favorites screen, and then tapping the Add button. This displays the Add Favorite screen, shown in Figure 10.5. When adding a new Web site to the Favorites list, you can enter a different name for the site if you want.

Figure 10.5
The Add Favorite
screen allows you
to add the current
Web site to the
Favorites list.

When you're finished browsing in Pocket Internet Explorer, tap Disconnect on the Tools menu and the connection is terminated.

Browsing Offline with Mobile Favorites

When you don't have the luxury of a live Internet connection in which to browse Web content, you can browse such content offline by downloading it to your device from your desktop PC as part of the synchronization process. This feature requires the ActiveSync application, which oversees all synchronization between your device and a desktop PC. It also requires that you know ahead of time which sites you want to browse and to then set them up in Internet Explorer on your desktop PC.

Normally, Internet Explorer favorites on your desktop are stored in the Favorites folder of Internet Explorer. When you install ActiveSync, an additional folder named Mobile Favorites is created in Internet Explorer. This folder is used to store the addresses (URLs) of Web sites that you want to browse offline on your Pocket PC. A new button named Create Mobile Favorite is also added to the Internet Explorer toolbar. To add a site to the Mobile Favorites folder, navigate to it in Internet Explorer and click the Create Mobile Favorite button in the toolbar. This results in the display of a window that prompts you for the name of the Web site and the update options for the site (see Figure 10.6).

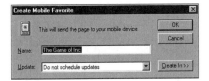

Figure 10.6
The Create Mobile Favorite window in Internet Explorer prompts you to enter the name and update options for a mobile favorite.

The update schedule for a mobile favorite applies only if the site changes fairly often and you want to have it updated regularly. You can have the site updated daily in the morning or afternoon, or weekly. There is no need to provide update information if you don't plan on regularly retrieving site updates. The Create In button allows you to change the folder in which the site is stored. The default location is Mobile Favorites, which is where you should probably keep it unless you've created subfolders within Mobile Favorites.

When you add a Web site to the Mobile Favorites folder, ActiveSync should begin synchronizing with your Pocket PC to copy the site to the device. However, you have to enable the Favorite information type in ActiveSync. To enable it, launch ActiveSync and click the Options button on the toolbar. Click the check box next to Favorite in the list to enable the synchronization of mobile favorites. You can also click the Settings button to alter the settings associated with Favorite synchronization. The Favorite Synchronization Options window is then displayed, as shown in Figure 10.7.

Figure 10.7
The Favorite Synchronization Options window in ActiveSync enables you to enable and disable mobile favorites.

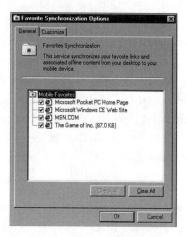

This window allows you to enable and disable mobile favorites. The Customize tab allows you to further control the synchronization of all mobile Web content by enabling and disabling the synchronization of specific types of content (see Figure 10.8).

Figure 10.8
The Customize tab of the Favorite Synchronization Options window enables you to control the types of content synchronized.

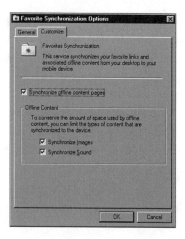

The primary purpose of the Customize tab is to optimize offline Web content for space. When you consider that images and sounds can be quite large in terms of file sizes, you might want to disable one or both of them by clearing the appropriate check box to conserve memory space on your device. This is a personal choice, and is ultimately dependent on how much Web content you synchronize and the degree to which they use images and sounds.

After you click OK in the ActiveSync Options window, ActiveSync immediately starts synchronizing the Web sites located in the Mobile Favorites folder. After synchronization is complete, you can begin browsing the sites on your device. Just tap the Favorites button on the toolbar in Pocket Internet Explorer. Figure 10.9 shows the Favorites screen in Pocket Internet Explorer, which includes the synchronized mobile favorites.

Figure 10.9
The synchronized mobile favorites appear in the Favorites screen in Pocket Internet Explorer after being synchronized.

You might be wondering why most of the mobile favorites are grayed out. These Web sites were included in Mobile Favorites by default when you installed ActiveSync, but they are disabled for synchronization purposes. You can easily enable them, which you learn how to do in a moment. For the time being, let's look at how to browse a site offline. Tapping the The Game of Inc. mobile favorite displays it in Pocket Internet Explorer, as shown in Figure 10.10.

Inside Scoop
The Web site shown in Figure 10.10 is for a board game produced by my game company, Gas Hound Games. The game is called Inc. The Game of Business, and is quite fun!

It's important to understand that by default ActiveSync doesn't attempt to synchronize links to other pages from a mobile favorite. For this reason, if you tap a hyperlink in an offline Web site, Pocket Internet Explorer will inform you that the page is unavailable. Of course, if you view a synchronized Web site and establish an Internet connection, the hyperlinks will work just fine. In a moment, you learn how to tweak the settings for a mobile favorite so that linked pages are also synchronized.

Mobile favorites are managed on the Internet Explorer side of the synchronization equation. To organize mobile favorites, click Organize Favorites in the Favorites menu in Internet Explorer. The Organize Favorites window appears, which contains a list of all the favorites for Internet Explorer. Click Mobile Favorites in the list to focus on mobile favorites. A list of mobile favorites appears below the Mobile Favorites folder, in which you can select and modify individual favorites. This is where you enable and disable mobile favorites for synchronization. Figure 10.11 shows how I've enabled the MSN Web site mobile favorite.

After you enable a mobile favorite, a Properties button appears that allows you to further customize the favorite. Clicking the Properties button results in the display of the Properties window, shown in Figure 10.12.

Figure 10.12
The Properties window in Internet Explorer allows you to customize the details of a mobile favorite.

You'll notice that the Properties window includes several tabs for customizing the details of a mobile favorite. The last two tabs, Schedule and Download, are the most important because they have the biggest impact on how the Web site is synchronized. The Schedule tab allows you to customize the specifics of how a site is updated; this is the same update information you select for a mobile favorite when you first add it to the Mobile Favorites folder. The Download tab is much more interesting in that it allows you to carefully control the amount of content synchronized for the Web site (see Figure 10.13).

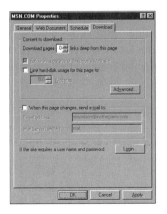

Figure 10.13
The Download tab in the Properties window allows you to carefully control the amount of content synchronized for a mobile favorite.

Watch Out!
Although it might be tempting, I don't recommend setting the depth of links in the Download tab to more than one or two. You could easily create a domino effect that results in the synchronization of loads of files.

Inside Scoop
If you set the link depth to more than one in the Download tab, I recommend limiting the hard-disk usage for the site so that you don't risk being overwhelmed by linked content.

The Download tab includes some powerful options for controlling the amount and types of content that are synchronized. The first option is the most dramatic in that it allows you to set the link depth of synchronized pages. A link depth of one means that Web pages directly linked from the synchronized page are synchronized as well. A link depth of two means that pages linked from the linked pages are synchronized, too. As you might be thinking, the link depth can dramatically impact the amount of content synchronized for a site.

This brings us to another important option, which allows you to limit the hard disk space for a synchronized site. This option is important because it allows you to place a cap on the size of the content synchronized for a Web site. This can be a valuable option when used in conjunction with the link depth. The default value of 500KB is a decent value to use for this setting for most Web sites.

The Advanced button is used to further customize the types of content synchronized for the Web site. More specifically, you can individually enable and disable images, sound, video, ActiveX controls, and Java applets, as well as hyperlinks to content other than HTML Web pages. The Java option in this case reflects the fact that Internet Explorer is designed to support several lightweight versions of Internet Explorer, including some that may support Java. The end result is that the Java setting has no impact on Pocket Internet Explorer because Pocket Internet Explorer doesn't support Java.

Using the AvantGo Information Service

In addition to traditional Web sites that are designed for viewing on desktop computers with full-size monitors, there is Web content available that is designed for viewing on handheld devices. AvantGo is a free information service that specializes in offering Web content in a form that is easily viewed on handheld devices such as Pocket PCs. AvantGo content is synchronized with your Pocket PC much like mobile favorites.

To enable AvantGo for synchronization, launch ActiveSync and click the Options button. In the Options window, click the check box next to AvantGo to enable the synchronization of

AvantGo content. There are no settings available in ActiveSync for AvantGo, so after you enable the information type you can click OK to accept it and synchronize. When the synchronization finishes, launch Pocket Internet Explorer and tap More Web sites near the lower-right corner of the screen to set up AvantGo. The AvantGo home page is displayed, which contains a list of AvantGo channels (see Figure 10.14).

The channels shown in the figure are the default channels configured for synchronization with AvantGo. You can begin viewing their content by tapping any of them. However, you'll probably want to choose your own AvantGo Web sites, which requires you to register with AvantGo. To register, tap the "personalize this account" hyperlink on the AvantGo home page. This displays a page that prompts you to enter an email address to begin the registration process. Enter your email address and then scroll down and tap the My Channels button. This will return you to the AvantGo home page.

Remember
The default values set in the Download tab are designed to include a minimal amount of content while providing a reasonable browsing experience.

Figure 10.14
The AvantGo home page contains a list of hyperlinks for the AvantGo channels that are synchronized on your device.

At this point, you need to retrieve the email from AvantGo that was automatically sent to the email client you entered on AvantGo's registration page. This email includes details about how you use a Web browser on your desktop computer to manage AvantGo channels for your device. It also includes a hyperlink that you must follow to activate your AvantGo account. Figure 10.15 shows the registration Web page that you use to register with AvantGo.

Figure 10.15
Registering with
AvantGo is as easy
is filling out a form
on the AvantGo
Web site in
Internet Explorer.

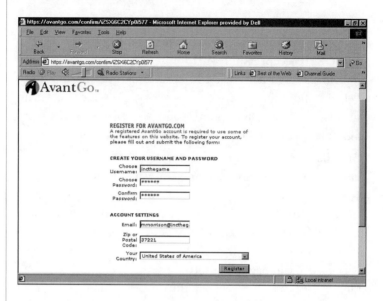

After you register with AvantGo, you'll be prompted to configure your handheld device profile for use in connecting with
the AvantGo server. Go ahead and follow the directions to configure the profile. After this is finished, you will be logged on
to the AvantGo Web site where you can start selecting channels
for synchronization with your device. You add channels by
clicking the plus sign next to each one as if you were adding it
to a shopping cart. To remove channels, click The Edit button
in the My Account window. Figure 10.16 shows the My
Channels page, which displays a list of the selected channels,
along with the respective sizes of their content. Keep in mind
that the selection and configuration of AvantGo channels take
place within Internet Explorer on your desktop computer.

When you are finished setting up AvantGo channels, you can
exit Internet Explorer. To have the new AvantGo channels synchronized with your device, open ActiveSync and click the
Sync button on the toolbar. The AvantGo content will then be
synchronized with your device, after which you need to refresh
the AvantGo home page in Pocket Internet Explorer. You're
now ready to browse the new AvantGo content in Pocket
Internet Explorer. Figure 10.17 shows The New York Times
AvantGo channel as it is viewed in Pocket Internet Explorer.

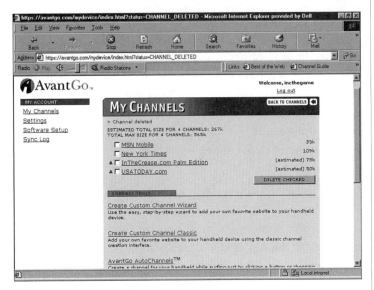

Figure 10.16
The My Channels
page includes a
list of the AvantGo
channels selected
for synchroniza-
tion.

Figure 10.17
AvantGo content is
tailored to the
small screens of
handheld devices,
as The New York
Times channel
reveals.

Pocket Internet Explorer Tips and Tricks

There are several tips and tricks that you might find useful
while browsing Web sites with Pocket Internet Explorer. One
of the most important tips is to make use of the Fit to Screen
option, which scales Web pages so they fit within the Pocket PC
screen a little better. The Fit to Screen option is enabled by
default, but if for some reason you don't have it turned on, be
sure to tap Fit to Screen in the View menu to enable it. The
advantage of the Fit to Screen feature is that it reformats a Web
page and resizes its images so more of the page is visible on the
Pocket PC's small screen. Of course, this might not always be a
good thing, especially when it comes to sites that use a lot of
tricky formatting. For this reason, you might find yourself turn-

ing Fit to Screen on and off depending on the specific page you are viewing.

Another handy feature similar to Fit to Screen is Text Size, which is also located in the View menu. The Text Size feature controls the size of the text on a Web page, and can be used to decrease the text size and fit more text on the screen. Of course, the default text isn't all that large to begin with, so if you have a hard time reading small text, this option might not be too appealing.

Remember
Even with careful use of the Fit to Screen and Text Size features, you are unlikely to get most Web pages to completely fit within the confines of the Pocket PC screen. Don't forget that you can use the scrollbars to move around the page.

Like in Internet Explorer, you can change the home page of Pocket Internet Explorer. Navigate to the page that you want to use as the home page, and then tap Options in the Tools menu. Near the top of the screen, you'll see a button named Use Current; tap this button to set the current Web page as the home page. Figure 10.18 shows how I've set the eBay auction site as the home page for Pocket Internet Explorer. The remainder of the General tab in the Options screen allows you to adjust the amount of time recently visited URLs are stored, as well as manually clear the history list and temporary Internet files. The Advanced tab in the Options screen allows you to enable and disable cookies, images, sounds, and security warnings, as well as establish the language used in the browser.

Figure 10.18
The Options window in Pocket Internet Explorer allows you to change the home page.

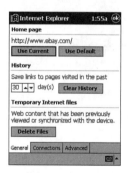

Speaking of eBay, I regularly find items on eBay that I think friends and family might be interested in. Most of the time I'm on my desktop computer, so I just create an email and copy and paste the address of the page containing the item into the email message. A quick way to send a hyperlink via email in Pocket Internet Explorer is to tap Send Link via E-mail in the Tools menu. This results in the address of the current Web page being pasted into a new email message as a hyperlink. It is up to you to fill out the To and Subject parts of the email and make sure it gets sent.

Essential Information

- Pocket Internet Explorer doesn't support Java applets, Dynamic HTML, or animated GIF images, although it does have support for XML and common advanced security methods.

- Pocket Internet Explorer allows you to browse live Web content online or browse synchronized content offline.

- Offline Web content is selected and stored in the Mobile Favorites folder in Internet Explorer, and then synchronized with a Pocket PC via ActiveSync for browsing in Pocket Internet Explorer.

- AvantGo is a free information service that specializes in offering Web content in a form that is easily viewed on handheld devices such as Pocket PCs.

- The Fit to Screen and Text Size features in Pocket Internet Explorer allow you to help fit full-size Web pages to the Pocket PC screen.

Wireless Communications

Chapter 11

AS POWERFUL AND CONVENIENT as it might be to plug your Pocket PC into a cradle and synchronize with a desktop computer, it requires a wired connection to the computer. Similarly, a dial-up modem connection on a Pocket PC requires a wired phone line connection. Although there is nothing wrong with wires, for a mobile device such as the Pocket PC, wires tend not to be very useful when you are away from a desktop PC or phone line. The solution is wireless communications, which allows you to connect a Pocket PC to individual computers and networks without any physical wires. Wireless communication options for Pocket PCs range from infrared connections between devices and other computers to dial-up connections involving mobile phones.

This chapter tackles the topic of Pocket PC wireless communications, and introduces you to the main options available for establishing and using wireless connections. You find out how the infrared port on your device provides many options for performing tasks without wires, as well as how to use wireless network cards and mobile phones to establish wireless Internet connections.

Communicating via Infrared

As you might know, all Pocket PC devices include an infrared port that uses a beam of infrared light to communicate with other devices and computers. Infrared light isn't visible to the

Inside Scoop
Infrared communications on a Pocket PC is sometimes referred to as IrDA, which stands for Infrared Data Association. IrDA is a standard to which infrared hardware must adhere to be compatible. Virtually all computer infrared ports adhere to the IrDA standard.

human eye, so you can't see anything when data is being transmitted and received using the infrared port. However, a clear line of sight is still necessary between the infrared ports on the machines that are communicating via infrared. Although the infrared port doesn't solve the problem of wireless Internet connectivity, it does play an important role in helping you share information between two devices or a device and a computer.

Most laptops these days include an infrared port that can be used to communicate with your Pocket PC. Additionally, you can purchase an infrared port adapter for your desktop computer that effectively turns a USB or serial port into an infrared port. With a suitable infrared port on your desktop or laptop computer, you can synchronize your Pocket PC without having to plug it into a cradle or use any wires.

Synchronizing with ActiveSync

Infrared synchronization with ActiveSync is extremely painless. In fact, all you must do is initiate the connection on your Pocket PC and the rest is automatic. To initiate an infrared ActiveSync connection from your device, tap Programs on the Start menu, and then tap the Connections icon to open the Connections folder (see Figure 11.1).

Figure 11.1
The Connections folder contains all the connections setup for use with your device, including the IR ActiveSync connection.

Tap the IR ActiveSync icon in the Connections folder to establish an infrared connection with ActiveSync. Be sure to line up the infrared ports so a clear line of sight is visible. After the infrared connection is established, ActiveSync synchronizes your device just as if it were resting in its wired cradle.

If, for some reason, ActiveSync doesn't start synchronizing via the infrared connection, you should make sure infrared is enabled in ActiveSync. Select Connection Settings from the File menu in ActiveSync to view the connection settings, as shown in Figure 11.2.

In the Connection Settings window, make sure the first or second check box is checked, depending on whether you are using a built-in infrared port or a serial/USB infrared port adapter. In reality, you might as well have all the check boxes checked (the default), because ActiveSync automatically looks for a suitable connection across all enabled connection types.

Inside Scoop
The XTNDAccess infrared adapter by Extended Systems allows you to turn a USB or serial port on a desktop computer into an infrared port that can communicate with your Pocket PC's infrared port.

Sharing Information with Other Devices

In addition to performing synchronization with ActiveSync, infrared communication can be extremely valuable when used to share information with other handheld computer users. Pocket PCs include built-in support for exchanging data with other Pocket PCs via the infrared port. There is also third-party software for using the infrared port to share data with other devices such as the popular Palm devices. Chapter 5, "Keeping It Together with Contacts and Calendar," covered the Peacemaker application and how it beams contacts between a Pocket PC and Palm device using the infrared port.

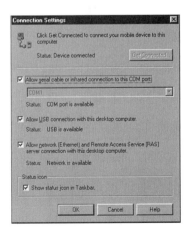

Figure 11.2
The Connection Settings window in ActiveSync contains settings that determine what types of connections are allowed for synchronization.

→ **See Also** in Chapter 5, the section "Sharing Contacts with Other Devices," **p. 85**.

Inside Scoop
A software package called bPrint by BSQUARE allows you to print from a Windows CE device to any printer compatible with Hewlett-Packard (HP-PCL) or Epson (ESC/P2) printers. The interesting thing about bPrint is that it takes advantage of the infrared ports found on many popular printers such as HP's LaserJet series of printers. This allows you to print from a handheld device to a printer without wires by lining up the infrared ports. Unfortunately, as of this writing the bPrint application hasn't been upgraded to specifically target the Pocket PC operating system, although I would expect BSQUARE to remedy this situation soon.

Contacts are a particularly useful type of information to exchange with other Pocket PC users via infrared. Exchanging contact information with someone using infrared ports is the high-tech equivalent of exchanging business cards. Of course, you can also exchange other Pocket PC data, including tasks, notes, appointments, and files. Pocket PC applications that support infrared data exchange include a Send via Infrared command on the pop-up menus that appear when you tap and hold on a piece of information. For example, to send a contact, tap and hold on a contact in the Contacts application, and then tap Send via Infrared in the pop-up menu that appears. Line up your device's infrared port with the receiving device's port and your device attempts to establish an infrared connection.

On the other end of the exchange, the other user needs to tap the Tools menu in the Contacts application, and then tap the Receive via Infrared command. This causes the device to look for the infrared connection and get ready to receive the data. After the data is successfully beamed across, the contact is automatically added to the device's contact list.

Infrared and Your Mobile Phone

Another usage of the infrared port on Pocket PCs is to connect to mobile phones to establish a wireless dial-up Internet connection. Some high-end mobile phones include infrared ports that can be used for this purpose providing the phone also includes a built-in modem. In this scenario, the mobile phone does all the networking work and shuttles data back and forth with the Pocket PC via infrared.

The downside to an infrared connection with a mobile phone is the obvious requirement that the ports maintain a line of sight within a close proximity to each other. Although this might not be a problem on a flat surface, it can be much tougher if you're accustomed to holding your Pocket PC in your hand while working.

Pocket PCs and the Wireless Internet

Earlier in the chapter, I mentioned that it is possible to use an infrared connection between a Pocket PC and a mobile phone to establish a wireless Internet connection. This is one of several options available for getting a Pocket PC online without wires. These options essentially boil down to the type of network being accessed to provide Internet access. Following are the different options currently available to Pocket PC users when it comes to accessing the wireless Internet:

- Wide Area Network (WAN)

- Local Area Network (LAN)

- Personal Area Network (PAN)

Keep in mind that these are general terms used to describe networks with which you are probably already familiar. WANs are distributed networks that connect computers over a wide area; the Internet is itself a WAN. WANs also include traditional mobile phone networks that are capable of carrying data along with the voice data they are already shuttling around. WANs provide the most flexibility in connecting to the Internet wirelessly because you can establish a connection anywhere that a mobile phone has service. In fact, familiar mobile phone service providers are often the same companies you use as your ISP when connecting a Pocket PC to a WAN for Internet service.

There are several products already on the market that allow you to connect to a WAN using your Pocket PC. Some of these products require a mobile phone to facilitate a dial-up connection, whereas others serve more as wireless network cards. The mobile phone option typically consists of a CompactFlash (CF) card that is connected to a mobile phone by a short cable. This is a more flexible approach than the infrared mobile phone approach discussed earlier because it doesn't require you to maintain a clear line of sight (usually keeping both devices on a flat surface) between the infrared ports of the devices.

Watch Out!
There is a limit on the distance between which infrared ports can communicate. The Pocket PC infrared port is rated at a maximum distance of about 30cm, which is a little under 12 inches. So, don't expect to be beaming infrared data across rooms!

Inside Scoop
Small automotive computers known as Auto PCs are being developed that are based on the Pocket PC operating system. Auto PCs look like high-end car stereos, and are capable of performing some interesting functions within an automobile, including infrared communications with Pocket PCs. This makes it possible to transfer Pocket Streets maps via infrared for navigational purposes. Source: U.S. Census Bureau

Inside Scoop
Setting up an infrared mobile phone connection on your Pocket PC isn't difficult at all. In fact, you create the connection in very much the same way as you created a modem connection in Chapter 8, "Getting Online."

Remember
If you don't like the idea of using an infrared link with a mobile phone to establish a wireless Internet connection, then read on because later in the chapter I explain how you can use a wired connection with a mobile phone to establish a wireless Internet connection.

Inside Scoop
Bluetooth-compatible devices might actually be available as you are reading this.

The wireless network cards available for Pocket PCs are CF cards that have small antennas sticking out of them. These cards are quite amazing when you consider that they are capable of doing the job of a mobile phone within the confines of a CF card. Several Pocket PC manufacturers are preparing to offer wireless device bundles that include a Pocket PC and a wireless network card. Of course, wireless network cards require a wireless network service, which can be an ISP or a corporate network. Wireless internet access via an ISP is more expensive than its wired counterpart, but the flexibility is well worth it to users who need Internet access while on the go.

The LAN approach to wireless Pocket PC connectivity involves hardware that is capable of accessing a LAN via a wireless connection. This technology is very similar to the Apple AirPort network hub, which allows laptop users to move around an office or home and still maintain a wireless connection to their LAN. Compaq also has a similar wireless networking technology in the works. Of course, you can only access a wireless LAN only within a reasonably close proximity of the network, typically a few hundred feet. This makes wireless LANs feasibly only for users who plan to work close to the network to which they are connecting.

Even though it suffers from the same limitations as wireless LAN networking, the PAN approach to wireless connectivity is pretty exciting because of the manner in which it aims to change office connectivity. You might not have heard of a PAN, and that's because they currently don't exist. A much-anticipated technology called Bluetooth is attempting to redefine the way in which computing devices communicate with each other. More specifically, Bluetooth establishes a standard by which computers, peripherals, and office devices can communicate with one another via a wireless network.

One of the huge benefits of Bluetooth is that it will get rid of a lot of the wires that are strewn around offices connecting peripherals to computers. It will also alleviate the need to plug in a device such as a digital camera when you need to interface it with your computer. The idea behind Bluetooth is that there is a specified range of communication, and when a compatible device enters that range, it is immediately identified and added to the network. You can think of it as the ultimate form of plug and play. Bluetooth utilizes radio signals that alleviate the line-of-sight requirement of wireless infrared communication.

In terms of Pocket PCs, Bluetooth will hopefully make it possible to both synchronize and connect to the Internet via a wireless connection that goes live the moment you walk into range carrying your device. Bluetooth and PANs have a lot of potential and are being eagerly anticipated, but it isn't too clear how fast or widespread support for them will be.

Essential Information

- A clear line of sight is necessary between the infrared ports of Pocket PCs that are communicating via infrared.

- Most laptops manufactured in the last few years include an infrared port that can be used to communicate with your Pocket PC.

- You can use ActiveSync to synchronize via infrared just as you would through a cradle or wired connection.

- Most standard Pocket PC applications support the Send via Infrared command, which allows you to send information over the infrared port.

- Some high-end mobile phones include infrared ports that can be used to establish a wireless Internet connection on your Pocket PC.

- The most flexible option for wireless Internet access involves using a Wide Area Network (WAN), which is typically a network designed to carry mobile phone data.

- An interesting technology that will likely impact Pocket PCs in the near future is Bluetooth, which makes it possible to establish a wireless Personal Area Network (PAN).

Pocket PC: The Portable Office

PART IV

GET THE SCOOP ON...

Using Transcriber to Recognize Handwriting ▪ Installing Transcriber ▪ Using Transcriber Gestures to Optimize the Entry of Handwritten Text ▪ Customizing Transcriber to Fit Your Writing Style

Transcriber: Handwriting Recognition That Works

Chapter 12

O NE OF THE MOST INTERESTING Pocket PC software features is included when you buy a Pocket PC but is not installed by default. I'm referring to Transcriber, an incredibly powerful utility that is included on the ActiveSync CD-ROM that ships with all Pocket PCs. Transcriber is a handwriting recognition utility that is installed as another input method within the SIP (Soft Input Panel). Unlike the built-in Character Recognizer input method, Transcriber allows you to write complete words anywhere on the screen and automatically convert them to text. It also supports cursive handwriting, and can be customized to fit your writing style.

This chapter introduces you to Transcriber and examines some of the ways that it is used to enter text via handwriting. In addition to getting a feel for how Transcriber is used, you also learn how to tweak Transcriber to do a better job of accurately recognizing your handwriting.

What Is Transcriber?

As you might already know, Microsoft has a strong track record for either acquiring or licensing powerful technologies and incorporating them into its products. One such technology that made its way into Pocket PC via a licensing deal is Transcriber, which is based on the Calligrapher handwriting recognition software by ParaGraph (http://www.paragraph.com). Calligrapher made its mark as the only handwriting recognition software for handheld devices that could recognize both cursive and printed text. Transcriber uses similar technology found in Calligrapher to bring advanced handwriting recognition to Pocket PCs.

Transcriber is surprisingly accurate at recognizing handwriting, and will change the way you use your Pocket PC. The interesting thing about Transcriber is how you can customize it to suit your personal writing style. I use a lot of capital letters and tend to print everything I write, as opposed to using cursive writing. I can customize Transcriber so that it expects me to write in printed uppercase, and doesn't look for cursive writing. Customizing Transcriber in this way can improve the accuracy and speed of the handwriting recognition.

In addition to recognizing handwritten text, numbers, and symbols, Transcriber also supports several gestures, which simulate control keys such as Space and Enter, and perform common tasks such as cut, copy, and paste. Transcriber gestures are very similar to the gestures that are part of the Keyboard input method. Like the Keyboard gestures, Transcriber gestures are easy to learn and significantly speed up the entry of text information.

Installing Transcriber

Although Transcriber is a Microsoft product, it isn't part of the standard Pocket PC applications that are burned in the ROM of your Pocket PC device. Instead, Transcriber is included on the ActiveSync CD-ROM that accompanies Pocket PC devices. To use Transcriber on your device, you must first install it by running a setup program from the CD-ROM on your desktop computer.

To install Transcriber from the ActiveSync CD-ROM, you need to connect your device to the desktop PC via a cradle or some other (serial/USB) cable connection. You'll also need to establish a connection via the ActiveSync software because ActiveSync is responsible for handling communication

Inside Scoop
If you happen to have an electronics background, you might appreciate knowing that Transcriber uses advanced fuzzy logic and neural network techniques in its algorithms for handwriting recognition. This basically means that Transcriber takes a sophisticated approach to handwriting recognition, which is reflected in its accuracy.

between the desktop PC and the device. With an ActiveSync connection established, you must navigate to the Extras\TScribe folder on the ActiveSync CD-ROM using Windows Explorer on the desktop PC. You'll see a file named setup.exe, which is the setup program for Transcriber. Double-click this file to launch the Transcriber setup program.

Upon running the setup program, Transcriber opens a Welcome window with some basic information about the program. To get the setup process going, click the Continue button, which displays the standard Windows warning about closing all Windows programs before continuing with the setup of Transcriber. This is a good idea to avoid any potential conflicts with shared DLLs (Dynamic Link Libraries) used by open applications. Clicking the Next button takes you to the Software License Agreement, which you must accept, by clicking Yes, before installation can continue. The next window displayed is the User Information window, shown in Figure 12.1.

After entering your name and company name, click the Next button to continue to the Choose Destination Location window. This destination location is the location on your desktop PC where Transcriber files are to be installed. This might seem strange because Transcriber will actually reside on your Pocket PC, but in this case, the installation files are first placed on your desktop PC's hard drive. This also installs a very useful User's Guide on the desktop PC that is helpful in getting the most out of Transcriber. The default destination location is fine unless you have a specific place you want to see Transcriber installed. Clicking the Next button accepts the destination location and moves along to the Select Program Folder window, where you confirm the program folder on your desktop PC to which the Transcriber files are installed.

You are free to select any program folder that you want, but I recommend just keeping the default setting. Clicking the Next button displays the Start Copying Files window, which summarizes your setup instructions and prepares to start copying Transcriber files.

Watch Out!
Some users have experienced errors while trying to install Transcriber with a serial connection speed greater than 57,600Kbps. Although I recommend using a speed setting of 115,200Kbps for faster data transfers between your device and desktop PC, you might want to try dropping the speed down to 57,600Kbps if you experience problems installing Transcriber via a serial connection.

Remember
DLLs are software components that are typically shared by multiple applications. You can think of a DLL as housing a particular application feature such as a spell checker or graphing tool. If two applications both utilize a spell checker, then they might share the DLL and eliminate duplicate code.

Figure 12.1
The User
Information
window in the
Transcriber setup
program prompts
you to enter your
name and com-
pany name, if
applicable.

Figure 12.1
The User
Information
window in the
Transcriber setup
program prompts
you to enter your
name and com-
pany name, if
applicable.

After the setup program churns away for a few moments at installing Transcriber files to your desktop PC, the Pocket PC side of the installation takes place. This is evident by a small window that prompts to see whether you want Transcriber installed to the default application directory on your Pocket PC (Figure 12.2).

Figure 12.2
The Installing
Applications win-
dow in the
Transcriber setup
program prompts
you to confirm the
Pocket PC appli-
cation install
directory.

Clicking the Yes button accepts the default application install directory, which I recommend you use. If you want to change the default application install directory, simply click No and enter the new directory. After clarifying the install directory, the setup program begins installing files to your Pocket PC. This part of the setup process might take a couple of minutes, depending on the speed of your device's connection.

After the setup program finishes copying files, you're ready to complete the Transcriber installation by resetting your device. First remove the device from its cradle, and then perform a soft reset. Please refer to Appendix C, "Resetting Your Pocket PC," for more details on performing a soft reset.

→ **See Also** Appendix C, "Performing a Soft Reset," **p. 380**.

After resetting your device, Transcriber appears as a third input method in the Soft Input Panel (SIP) alongside the built-in Character Recognizer and Keyboard input methods. Because Transcriber is integrated into the SIP, it is available for use in any application that supports data entry via the SIP. You might want to check out the Transcriber Help, which is also installed on the device. To access Transcriber Help, tap Help at the bottom of the Start menu. You'll see Transcriber Help as one of the types of help available within the Help application; tap it to view help on how to use and customize Transcriber.

Using Transcriber

Because Transcriber is integrated into the Pocket PC SIP, you will always access it as part of the SIP; you never run it as a standalone Pocket PC application. Getting started with Transcriber is surprisingly simple considering how powerful it is. To take it for a spin, first launch the Notes application by tapping Notes in the Start menu. Locate the SIP near the lower-right part of the screen, and tap on the up arrow to the right of the SIP icon. A drop-down list appears, from which you need to tap Transcriber to select Transcriber as the input method (Figure 12.3).

Remember
Although the Notes application is used to demonstrate how to use Transcriber, you'll find that Transcriber works equally well with all Pocket PC applications. This is due to the fact that Transcriber integrates directly into the SIP.

Figure 12.3
The SIP contains a drop-down list from which you can select Transcriber as the input method.

Upon selecting Transcriber as the input method, you will see an introduction screen that provides some tips about how to use Transcriber (see Figure 12.4); tap Close to close this screen. If you don't want it to appear each time you select Transcriber from the SIP, check the Don't Show This check box.

You're now ready to begin learning how powerful a utility Transcriber is. In Notes, try hand writing a sentence on the screen using the stylus. Figure 12.5 shows a sentence that I wrote by hand.

Figure 12.4
The Transcriber introduction screen displays tips about how to use Transcriber.

Figure 12.5
Transcriber allows you to write any-where on the screen and have it recognized as text.

When you finish writing, Transcriber kicks in and attempts to recognize the handwriting and convert it to text. The converted text is inserted into the current application at the insertion point, which in this case is the start of a note. Figure 12.6 shows the resulting text that Transcriber successfully recognized. It's important to understand that Transcriber begins recognizing your handwriting when you pause long enough to indicate that you are finished writing a particular word or phrase; as long as you keep writing, Transcriber will wait. This period of time in which Transcriber waits before recognizing the handwriting is known as the "recognition delay," and can be adjusted. You learn how to adjust the recognition delay a little later in the chapter in the section titled "Customizing Transcriber."

As good at handwriting recognition as Transcriber is, it's still common for it to make mistakes. More accurately, unavoidable inconsistencies in our handwriting is what actually results in the mistakes. If you see a mistake or decide to change a portion of the text recognized by Transcriber, you can easily block off the text and try again. For example, if I decide I want to change the sentence so my name is Michael instead of Mike, I can tap and hold briefly just in front of the word Mike. After about a second you will hear a beep, and can then drag the stylus to select the whole word. With text selected, you can write on the screen again and the writing will be recognized and replace the selected text. Figure 12.7 shows how I changed my name using this technique.

Figure 12.6
I got a little lucky because Transcriber perfectly recognized my handwritten sentence on the first try.

Figure 12.7
Writing on the screen while text is selected results in the newly recognized text replacing the selection.

One other Transcriber feature that you'll find useful is the selection stroke. The selection stroke allows you to select text by drawing a line through the text. For example, Figure 12.8 shows how I'm selecting the word hungry by drawing a line through it.

Although Transcriber's handwriting recognition capabilities are impressive, you have to start using gestures to really appreciate its power. Gestures are special strokes you make with the stylus that are interpreted as commands rather than characters or words. Transcriber supports the following commands via gestures:

Watch Out!
If you wait too long while tapping to select text, the Notes application will interpret the tap as a tap and hold, and display a pop-up menu. Hold the tap just long enough to hear the beep, and then quickly drag to select the text you want.

Figure 12.8
The selection
stroke is applied
by drawing a line
through a word or
group of words.

Shortcut
Another good way
to select text
while using
Transcriber is to
double-tap the
text with the sty-
lus. You can even
triple-tap a word
to select an entire
paragraph of text.

- **Enter**—Inserts a carriage return.

- **Space**—Inserts a space.

- **Tab**—Inserts a tab.

- **Backspace**—Deletes the selected text or the character to the left of the insertion point.

- **Quick Correct**—Suggests a correction for a word or opens the Transcriber keyboard.

- **Case Change**—Changes a letter's case.

- **Undo**—Undoes the previous action.

- **Copy**—Copies the selected text to the Clipboard (equivalent to Ctrl+C).

- **Cut**—Cuts the selected text to the Clipboard (equivalent to Ctrl+X).

- **Paste**—Pastes the text on the Clipboard over the selected text or at the current insertion point (equivalent to Ctrl+V).

Each of these gestures has a unique stroke that is used to enter the gesture. Figure 12.9 shows what the different strokes look like; you can also view them in Transcriber Help in the section titled "Microsoft Transcriber Gestures." The arrows in the gesture strokes indicate the direction in which the stroke must be performed. As an example, the Enter stroke requires you to tap, drag the stylus down, drag it to the left, and then release. I've found that the gestures are recognized better if you make large strokes. It takes a little practice, but the gestures provide an incredibly powerful and efficient way to perform common editing tasks.

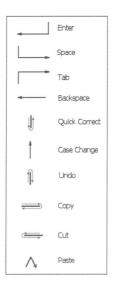

Figure 12.9
Transcriber gestures involve the use of special strokes that are made with the stylus.

Inside Scoop
Transcriber uses a dictionary to suggest words when using the Quick Correct gesture. You can add a word to the dictionary by selecting the word, making the Quick Correct gesture, and tapping Add to Dictionary in the pop-up menu that appears.

The only gesture whose function isn't immediately obvious is the Quick Correct gesture, which suggests a correction for the currently selected text. As an example, check out Figure 12.10, which shows the Quick Correct gesture in action. In this figure, Transcriber has incorrectly recognized the word "hungri," so I used the Quick Correct gesture to display a list of possible corrections. Tapping the word "hungry" quickly solves the problem.

Figure 12.10
The Quick Correct gesture provides a convenient technique for correcting words that are incorrectly recognized.

The Quick Correct gesture actually has another use in addition to correcting words; if you make the Quick Correct gesture with nothing selected, the Transcriber keyboard is displayed. This keyboard contains punctuation characters that are difficult to make using strokes. Figure 12.11 shows how I used the Transcriber keyboard to change a period to a comma.

Figure 12.11
The Transcriber keyboard provides a user interface for entering punctuation characters that are difficult to make using strokes.

Customizing Transcriber

The Transcriber input method is capable of being customized to a considerable degree. Some of the customizations involve the user interface, while others are more significant and impact the manner in which handwriting is recognized. To customize Transcriber, tap the up arrow to the right of the SIP icon, and then tap Options. You will see the Input Settings window, which is shown in Figure 12.12.

Figure 12.12
The Input Settings window allows you to customize input methods, including Transcriber.

With Transcriber selected as the input method, tapping the Option button in the Input Settings window takes you to the Transcriber Options window shown in Figure 12.13.

Figure 12.13
The Transcriber Options window allows you to customize Transcriber settings.

The first setting, Sound On, determines whether Transcriber makes sounds as you write and make gesture strokes. You can obviously use Transcriber effectively without sound, but the subtle cues it provides, such as the sound played when you've performed an undo action, help ensure you don't make errors. The Show Intro Screen setting determines whether the introduction screen is displayed when you select Transcriber as the input method. The Show Iconbar determines whether the Transcriber Iconbar is displayed; this bar is displayed near the bottom of the screen and provides access to some interesting Transcriber features, as well as Transcriber Help. You learn more about the iconbar in a moment.

The other settings in the Transcriber Options window allow you to customize the look of the ink displayed when you draw strokes. More specifically, you can change the color and width of the ink to suit your personal preferences. It's important that the ink stand out, so don't set it to black or make it any narrower than the default width. Keep in mind that this setting affects only the ink that is displayed when you draw in Transcriber, not the resulting text that is recognized.

You might have noticed an additional tab named Recognizer at the bottom of the Transcriber Options window. The Recognizer tab allows you to customize the manner in which handwriting is recognized. Figure 12.14 shows the options that are available under this tab.

Figure 12.14
The Recognizer
tab within the
Transcriber
Options window
provides a means
of customizing
how handwriting
is recognized.

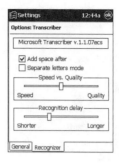

Inside Scoop
The speed of
Transcriber's
recognition is
dependent on sev-
eral factors, the
most important
being the proces-
sor speed of your
device. A good
way to find the
best setting is to
start out with the
slider pegged on
the Quality end. If
the delay is unac-
ceptable, inch the
slider back toward
Speed and con-
tinue testing until
you find a suitable
compromise.

The first setting, Add Space After, determines whether a space is inserted after each word or fragment recognized by Transcriber. I find that keeping this setting activated is very helpful because it keeps you from having to manually add spaces when writing one word at a time. The Separate Letters Mode setting instructs Transcriber to recognize words that are written with letters that aren't connected. In other words, it instructs Transcriber to accept only printed words, as opposed to words written in cursive. You might wonder why you would want to enable such a seemingly limiting option. The reason is because it significantly improves the performance of Transcriber. So, if you're like me and your natural writing style is printing, you will definitely want to set this option to speed up Transcriber. Of course, many people use all cursive or a mixture of print and cursive writing, in which case the perfor- mance improvement won't be worth the limitations in Transcriber's handwriting recognition.

The Speed vs. Quality setting is another performance-related customization. This setting basically allows you to set the accu- racy of Transcriber; of course, accuracy comes at the expense of decreased speed. If you find that Transcriber is making a lot of mistakes, you might want to consider inching the slider toward Quality. On the other hand, you might lean toward Speed if you think Transcriber is taking too long to recognize your writing.

The Recognition Delay setting determines how long it takes Transcriber to begin recognizing text after you finish writing. Keep in mind that you sometimes pause while writing multiple words, which impacts the delay in which you want Transcriber to jump into action. If you move the slider all the way to the left, you will probably not have enough time to accurately write multiple words. On the other hand, the right end of the delay spectrum is probably too slow for most users. I've found that, to start, it's best that you keep the default value for this setting. But if you are a slow or speedy writer, then by all means change the delay to suit your style.

A little earlier, I mentioned the Transcriber iconbar as an option you could turn on or off in the General Tab of the Transcriber Options window. The Transcriber iconbar is a user interface that includes several icons for fine-tuning the entry and recognition of text in Transcriber. The recognition settings available for customization via the Transcriber iconbar are incredibly detailed and allow you to really dial Transcriber into your writing style. You can see the Transcriber iconbar near the bottom of Figure 12.15.

Figure 12.15
The Transcriber iconbar provides access to several interesting features, as well as Transcriber Help.

Remember
The Transcriber icon bar appears only when Transcriber is actually being used as an input method. This occurs when Transcriber is selected as the input method in the SIP and you are in an application that is expecting text entry.

Following are the meanings of the four icons displayed in the Transcriber iconbar, from left to right:

- **Control of Writing Orientation**—Changes the screen orientation to allow you to write at different angles.

- **Recognition Mode**—Changes the recognition mode used to recognize handwriting (uppercase, lowercase, or numerical).

- **Transcriber Keyboard**—Shows/hides the Transcriber keyboard.

■ **Letter Shape Selector**—Changes the stroke shapes expected for letters and symbols.

The Control of Writing Orientation icon allows you to change the screen orientation so you can write at different angles. Maybe you like to rotate your Pocket PC to the left at a 45-degree angle for optimal writing comfort. If so, tap the Control of Writing Orientation icon once and Transcriber factors the angle of the device into the recognition.

The Recognition Mode icon allows you to change the recognition mode used to recognize handwriting, which can be one of the following modes: lowercase, uppercase, and numerical. Lowercase mode actually recognizes both lower- and uppercase text, whereas uppercase mode is exclusively for writing uppercase text. When writing in uppercase mode, everything that you write is automatically capitalized regardless of case. Numerical mode is used to enter numbers, and is handy if you need to enter mathematical information such as equations or fractions. You can still enter numbers in the two text modes, but you won't be able to enter equations, fractions, or other mathematical information.

The Transcriber Keyboard icon shows and hides the Transcriber keyboard, which you learned about a little earlier in the chapter. If you recall, the keyboard provides access to punctuation characters that are difficult to enter using strokes.

The Letter Shape Selector icon is the most interesting of all the icons on the iconbar, and is where you can really customize Transcriber to fit your personal writing style. Tapping this icon opens the Letter Shape Selector, which allows you to customize the strokes used to write individual letters and symbols. Figure 12.16 shows the Letter Shape Selector with the letter A selected for customization.

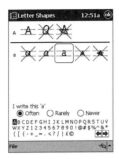

Figure 12.16
The Letter Shape Selector allows you to customize the strokes used to write individual letters and symbols.

As the figure shows, the Letter Shape application shows different ways in which a letter can be written, and allows you to set whether you use a certain stroke Often, Rarely, or Never. In the figure I've already customized the A letter to suit my writing style. By default all the strokes are set to Often, which means that Transcriber attempts to recognize a wide range of writing styles. By fine-tuning each letter and symbol to your own personal style and eliminating as many unused strokes as possible, you improve both the accuracy and speed of Transcriber.

Some of the strokes shown in the Letter Shape Selector might look similar to you. That's because the application is showing you the finished stroke, which can sometimes be the same for different strokes. To really be able to distinguish between strokes, you must see an animation of how they are made. To do this, double-tap the stroke in the Letter Shape Selector.

A good practical example of how to use the Letter Shape Selector is shown in Figure 12.17. In this figure, I've customized the lowercase letter e to suit my personal writing style, which some people consider strange. I write lowercase e's starting at the bottom of the e and circling back around clockwise; most people start on the inside of the letter and circle around counterclockwise. Fortunately, the Letter Shape Selector includes a stroke for my style of e, which works out great.

Remember
The reason for the similar-looking strokes in Transcriber's Letter Shape Selector is because Transcriber takes into account the specific direction the stylus travels when making a stroke that forms a letter. So, even though two letters might look the same, the stylus was moved in different directions to perform the stroke and arrive at the finished shape.

Figure 12.17
I write lowercase
e's a little
strangely but the
Letter Shape
Selector allows
me to customize
Transcriber to
adjust to my writ-
ing style.

Inside Scoop
The File menu in
the Letter Shape
Selector allows
you to set the let-
ter shape settings
as either Master
or Guest. You will
want to set your
letter shape set-
tings to Master,
and leave the
Guest settings as
an option if you
should allow
someone else to
use your device.

Although setting letter shapes can be a tedious and time-consuming process, if you use Transcriber often enough you will appreciate the effort in the long term.

Essential Information

- Transcriber is a utility included on the ActiveSync CD-ROM that allows you to write complete words anywhere on the screen and automatically convert them to text.

- Transcriber gestures provide a powerful and efficient means of manipulating handwritten text.

- Transcriber Help is a great resource for learning Transcriber gestures and other tips for getting the most out of Transcriber.

- You can customize Transcriber to your personal writing style, which results in more accurate and efficient handwriting recognition.

- The Transcriber iconbar allows you to alter the screen orientation and recognition mode, as well as display the Transcriber keyboard and run the Letter Shape Selector.

- The Letter Shape Selector provides incredibly detailed control over how handwriting strokes are recognized, and allows you to account for personal writing styles.

GET THE SCOOP ON...
The Relationship Between Pocket Word and Word ▪
Limitations of Pocket Word ▪ Entering Information in Pocket
Word Using a Variety of Different Input Methods ▪ Managing
Pocket Word Documents ▪ Customizing Pocket Word ▪
Synchronizing Documents Between Pocket Word and Word

Using Pocket Word

Chapter 13

I
F YOU'VE NEVER PONDERED BECOMING a writer and spending
your days traveling around the world recording your
exploits, then you might want to consider it now. Pocket
PC includes an application that makes it easier than ever to
flex your literary muscles while on the go. I'm referring to
Pocket Word, which is the compact version of the industry-
standard Microsoft Word word processor. Pocket Word is
designed specifically for the Pocket PC operating system, and
retains a core set of Word's features in a streamlined application. Don't expect all the fancy tools and extras found in Word,
but do appreciate the fact that you can now pen formatted documents in the palm of your hand.

This chapter explores Pocket Word and what it has to offer in
terms of mobile writing. I examine the relationship between
Pocket Word and its full-grown desktop uncle. I also reveal
some tips and tricks for getting the most out of Pocket Word.

Pocket Word Versus Word

Pocket Word is a significantly scaled-down version of the
immensely popular desktop word processor, Microsoft Word.
Although smaller than Word in both scale and function,
Pocket Word is still a powerful application and is ideal for performing writing tasks on your Pocket PC. Perhaps the biggest
feature of Pocket Word is that it recognizes the Word document format (.doc files), which forms the basis for countless

documents floating around homes and offices everywhere. Even if you don't plan on using Pocket Word for writing, the capability of reading Word documents on your Pocket PC is enough to warrant learning more about Pocket Word.

As a scaled-down version of Word, Pocket Word obviously relies on a significantly smaller set of features. In fact, Pocket Word is more akin to WordPad than it is to Word. If you are a Microsoft Office user, you probably don't pay WordPad much attention, but now might be a good time to start because it provides a similar feature set as Pocket Word. I suggest this because Pocket Word doesn't support all Word's document attributes, so it is possible to lose document information when editing Word documents in Pocket Word. You learn more about the specific Word document attributes that are supported in Pocket Word in a moment.

When a Word document is transferred to the Pocket PC for use in Pocket Word, it undergoes a conversion process. Word documents are actually converted to a special Pocket Word format that has a .psw file extension, as compared to Word's .doc file extension. Word documents are converted to Pocket Word when any of the following things takes place:

- A Word document is synchronized with Pocket Word

- A Word document is manually copied from a desktop PC to a Pocket PC device

- A Word document is opened as an email attachment using Pocket Outlook

When a Word document is converted to Pocket Word, it retains most of its formatting but loses some important attributes. It is critical to understand exactly which document attributes are retained and lost because you don't want to move files back and forth between your desktop PC and Pocket PC and unknowingly lose information. The safest way to preserve the formatting of synchronized Word documents is to use Pocket Word as a document viewer, which involves not saving a document after opening it. This obviously doesn't work for

Remember
In case you aren't familiar with WordPad, it is a basic word processor that ships with Windows and provides support for Word documents.

Undocumented
Pocket Word documents are automatically converted back to Word documents when they are transferred back to a desktop computer. The conversion of Word documents is actually handled by ActiveSync, which is why no conversion takes place if you transfer Pocket Word documents between two Pocket PC devices.

documents that you would like to edit in Pocket Word. To safely edit documents in Pocket Word, you need to become acquainted with its limitations.

Let's start with the Word document attributes that are fully supported in Pocket Word, which follow:

- TrueType fonts (fonts must be installed on Pocket PC)

- Bold

- Underline

- Italic

- Strikethrough

- Bullets

- Paragraph spacing

- Paragraph alignment

In addition to these fully supported document attributes, a few things are retained in the conversion to Pocket Word, but may be slightly altered:

- **Images**—Color depth is reduced to 256 colors.

- **Indentation**—Altered to improve readability.

- **Tables**—Formatting is lost but text is preserved.

- **Table of contents**—Formatting is lost but text is preserved.

- **Index formatting**—Formatting is lost but text is preserved.

- **OLE objects**—Objects are lost and replaced by bitmap placeholders.

Although text is retained for document attributes, such as tables and table of contents, keep in mind that the formatting will be lost. This means that a document converted to Pocket Word, saved, and then moved back to Word will retain table data but won't keep the table formatting. In addition to these Word attributes that are altered in Pocket Word, there is a Pocket Word document attribute that is altered when

Inside Scoop
Documents stored in either Rich Text Format (.rtf files) or simple text format (.txt files) do not have to be converted to work with Pocket Word. For rich text files, this means that no formatting information is lost; text files don't include formatting information.

Shortcut
A good way to avoid the risk of losing document attributes when working with a Word document in Pocket Word is to make a copy of the document file on your desktop PC before copying/synchronizing with your Pocket PC. You can then compare the modified file when it is converted back to Word and correct or reject any unwanted modifications. Word 2000 includes a Merge Documents utility within the Tools menu that assists in merging similar documents.

Undocumented

If you don't mind dealing with the limitations of the document format, another option to avoid losing document attributes when working with a document in both Word and Pocket Word is to use Rich Text Format (RTF), which doesn't require any conversion.

Remember

OLE (Object Linking and Embedding) are software components used throughout Windows to provide special functionality to applications.

Watch Out!

Password-protected Word documents cannot be converted for use with Pocket Word; you must turn off password protection to convert such documents.

converted back to Word. I'm referring to notes and drawings that are created in Pocket Word, which are converted to Windows metafiles when a Pocket Word document is converted to a Word document.

At this point, you understand that some Word document attributes are fully supported, while some are supported with modification. To add to the confusion of this seemingly mixed support for Word document attributes, following are some attributes that are not supported in Pocket Word, but that are restored when you convert a document back to Word:

- Margins

- Gutter size

- Paper size

- Header/footer vertical location

How can an attribute not be supported in Pocket Word yet still be retained when a document is converted back to Word? It's pretty simple—even though Pocket Word doesn't support the functionality of these attributes, it retains them as part of the document structure. So, you wouldn't know that the attributes are there when viewing a document in Pocket Word, but they lurk just below the surface, and therefore are retained when you convert a Pocket Word document back to Word.

The most important Word document attributes with respect to Pocket Word are probably those that aren't supported at all, in which case they are actually lost when converting documents. These attributes follow:

- Borders

- Shading

- Columns

- Numbered lists

- Headers/footers

- Annotations

- Footnotes

- Comments

- Revision marks

- Page setup information

- Frames

- Style sheets

You should be particularly careful when converting and editing files in Pocket Word that use any of these document attributes, because they will be lost during conversion.

Pocket Word Essentials

Like all the standard Pocket PC applications, Pocket Word is very easy to get started. To start Pocket Word, tap Programs from the Start menu and then tap the Pocket Word icon. Pocket Word first appears with a list of Pocket Word documents that can be opened for viewing and editing. If you're using Pocket Word for the first time, you probably won't have any documents in the list. In this case, you'll probably want to create a new one. To create a new document, just tap New in the lower-left corner of the screen.

When you create a new document or open an existing document, the menu at the bottom of the screen changes to reflect commands and options available for Pocket Word. The Edit menu contains commands used to alter the content and appearance of document data. The View menu allows you to enable or disable the Pocket Word toolbar, as well as set the input mode and the zoom level of the document. The Tools menu includes a variety of commands for manipulating documents, such as recognizing handwritten text, sending the document via infrared or email, and setting Pocket Word options. A particularly interesting command on the Tools menu is Save Document As, which allows you to save a Pocket Word document in a variety of different formats including Rich Text Format (RTF), plain text, Word 97/2000, and Word 6.0/95. The last two formats support saving as either a document or a template.

Inside Scoop
Pocket Word, Pocket Excel, and Pocket Outlook are currently the only components of Microsoft Office that are part of the standard Pocket PC platform. There is much interest among users for Pocket PowerPoint and Pocket Access so it is possible, but by no means definite, that we'll see them in the future.

Shortcut
I recommend adding Pocket Word to the Start menu if you plan on using it a lot. Please refer to "Customizing the Start Menu" in Chapter 3, "Setting Up Your Pocket PC," if you aren't sure how to do this.

Watch Out!
For some reason, the standard Pocket PC applications (including Pocket Word) only recognize files up to one folder level beneath the My Documents folder. For example, if you place a Pocket Word file in the Personal subfolder beneath the My Documents folder, Pocket Word displays it in the document list when you select All Folders. However, if you create a subfolder named More Personal beneath the Personal folder and place files in it, Pocket Word will not be able to access the files.

The input mode of Pocket Word is extremely important in learning to use the application effectively. Following are the input modes supported in Pocket Word, which are accessible via the View menu:

- **Typing**—Use the SIP (Soft Input Panel) to enter typed text.

- **Writing**—Use the stylus to write handwritten text.

- **Drawing**—Use the stylus to draw graphics.

- **Recording**—Use the Record button or Voice Bar to enter voice recordings.

The next few sections explore each of these modes in more detail.

Typing Mode

Typing input mode is probably the mode you will rely on the most, as it is very similar to the manner in which text is entered in other Pocket PC applications such as Notes. In this mode, you enter text via the SIP (Character Recognizer, Keyboard, or Transcriber); the significance of this mode is that all data entry results in text, even if you use handwriting to arrive at the text. To try out Typing mode, tap New in the lower-left corner of the screen to create a new document, and then tap Writing in the View menu. Pocket Word displays a blank document ready for you to enter text into.

Entering information in Typing mode involves using the SIP to either hand write characters (Character Recognizer), type characters (Keyboard), or hand write words and sentences (Transcriber). Figure 13.1 shows some text entered into Pocket Word via the SIP.

Although you can use the Edit menu to access formatting functions for formatting text that you've entered, the most convenient way to format text is through the Pocket Word toolbar; tapping Toolbar in the Views menu accesses the Pocket Word toolbar. Alternatively, next to the Tools menu you'll notice an icon with two arrows pointing up and down; tapping this icon also shows the Pocket Word toolbar. Figure 13.2 shows Pocket Word with the toolbar displayed.

→ **See Also** Chapter 12, "Transcriber: Handwriting Recognition That Works," **p. 185**.

Figure 13.1
Typing mode allows you to enter text via the Soft Input Panel (SIP).

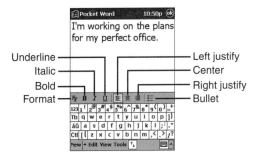

Underline
Italic
Bold
Format

Left justify
Center
Right justify
Bullet

Figure 13.2
The toolbar in Pocket Word provides convenient access to document formatting options.

The first button on the toolbar is the Format button, which displays a window containing a variety of formatting options for use in formatting selected text. To use the Format window, select a word or group of words and then tap the Format button on the toolbar. Figure 13.3 shows the Format window and the different options that are present within it.

Remember
You can find and replace text in Typing mode by tapping Find/Replace on the Edit menu.

Figure 13.3
The Pocket Word Format window provides a means of formatting text.

As you can see in the figure, the Format window allows you to alter the font, font size, font weight, font color, and fill color, as well as other formatting options such as italic, underline, highlight, and strikethrough. Figure 13.4 shows how the formatting of a word is changed using the Format window.

Figure 13.4
Just as with Word on the desktop, Pocket Word allows you to format individual words and sentences for impact.

In addition to formatting text in Typing mode, you can also alter paragraph properties. This is accomplished by tapping Paragraph in the Edit menu. This results in the Paragraph window being displayed, which provides access to paragraph settings such as the alignment and indentation of the selected paragraph or paragraphs (see Figure 13.5). The paragraph settings apply to the paragraph in which the edit cursor is currently located, regardless of whether any text is actually selected.

Figure 13.5
The Pocket Word Paragraph window provides a means of altering paragraph properties.

Getting back to the Pocket Word toolbar, you'll notice that to the right of the Format button are buttons for applying the bold, italic, and underline formatting properties, as well as justifying text to be either left-justified, centered, or right-justified. On the far right of the toolbar is the Bullet button, which creates a bulleted list out of a list of selected text. The interesting thing about the Pocket Word toolbar is that it changes to reflect the current input mode. The toolbar you've seen thus far applies only to Typing mode.

Writing Mode

Writing input mode is different from the Typing mode in that handwriting is not converted to text. This mode is similar to the way drawings are entered in Notes; you write on the screen with the stylus and the writing is retained. Lines are displayed on the screen to aid in writing text. To write text in writing mode, select Writing from the View menu and start writing the text. Figure 13.6 shows how I wrote text in addition to the typed text that was entered via Typing mode.

Inside Scoop
Although the Bullet button provides a convenient way to create bulleted lists, Pocket Word doesn't support numbered lists.

Figure 13.6
Writing mode allows you to enter handwritten text alongside typed text.

You might notice in the figure that the toolbar has changed to reflect a different set of features for Writing mode. The button to the far left of the toolbar is the Pen button, which enables and disables the pen for writing; disabling the pen allows you to select and manipulate text. The button to the right of the Pen button is the Pen Weight button, which allows you to alter the weight (thickness) of written text. To change the weight of written text, you must disable the pen, select the text by double-tapping or dragging across it, and then tap the Pen Weight button and select a new weight. Figure 13.7 shows how the word "very" is made thicker by changing its weight.

Figure 13.7
The Pen Weight
button allows you
to alter the
weight of written
text.

Inside Scoop
If your writing
crosses three
ruled lines in a
single stroke,
Pocket Word auto-
matically inter-
prets the writing
as a drawing.

The next button on the toolbar is the Insert/Remove Space button, which is used to alter the spacing between written words. Next to that button is the Undo button, which is handy for removing poorly written text. The familiar Format button is next, which displays the Format window you saw earlier in Figure 13.3. In Writing mode, the options in the Format window impact only the weight and color of the text; fonts obviously don't apply to handwritten text.

To the right of the Format button are the familiar Bold, Italic, and Underline buttons. It is interesting that these buttons work with handwritten text. The last button on the Writing toolbar is the Highlight button, which draws a colored highlight behind the currently selected text. This feature has a very similar effect as highlighting text on paper with a yellow highlighter pen.

Drawing Mode

Drawing input mode is similar to Writing mode except that the emphasis is on drawing graphics. Pocket Word doesn't display vertical and horizontal lines in Drawing mode, and it interprets strokes as discrete drawings as opposed to characters and words. The other thing that distinguishes Drawing mode from other modes is the graying of any text in the document, which is a clear indication that Drawing mode isn't about entering text information.

The toolbar in Drawing mode includes some powerful drawing-related features (see Figure 13.8). The first two buttons (Pen and Pen Weight) are familiar from Writing mode, while the third and fourth buttons allow you to alter the line color and fill color, respectively. The Undo button is up next, followed by the Format button, which is similar to the text-based Format button you learned about earlier. The remaining buttons are used to align, group, and ungroup drawing objects.

Figure 13.8
The Drawing mode toolbar provides convenient access to drawing-related functions.

To draw graphics objects in Drawing mode, just start drawing with the stylus. You can change the thickness and color of the drawing strokes by using the Pen Weight and Line Color buttons. You can also set the fill color of graphics using the Fill Color button; this button sets the fill color of closed graphics strokes. Figure 13.9 shows a sketch of an office layout that I drew in Drawing mode.

Figure 13.9
You can draw useful pictures using Draw input mode of Pocket Word.

If you tap the Pen button to turn the pen off, you can select individual strokes within the graphic image you've drawn. As an example, Figure 13.10 shows how I've selected the right arm of the chair in the office layout as an individual graphic object, which is indicated by the small group of squares and circles bounding the object.

You can combine individual strokes together to form a single graphic object by using the group function. You can select multiple graphic strokes by tapping and dragging the stylus to enclose the strokes within a selection box. If you want to group all the strokes in a drawing, just tap Select All in the Edit menu. After you've selected the strokes that you want to group, tap the Group button on the toolbar.

You can move and resize graphic objects in Drawing mode by tapping on the object to reveal a bounding box. Tap and drag in the middle of the box to move the object. Tap and drag one of the corners of the box to resize the object. You can even rotate an object by tapping and dragging on one of the sides. Figure 13.11 shows the chair in the office drawing after being grouped, rotated, and moved to fit the layout a little differently.

Recording Mode

The final input mode supported in Pocket Word is Recording mode, which is used to create and modify voice recordings. When you switch to Recording mode, the Pocket Word toolbar changes to become the Voice Bar that you learned about in

Chapter 6, "Staying Organized with Tasks and Notes." The Voice Bar serves as an alternative to the hardware Record button, and allows you to stop and play voice recordings, as well as change the volume of the device. To make a voice recording using the Voice Bar, just tap the Record button (red circle) on the Voice Bar, wait for the beep, and begin speaking. When you're finished, tap the Stop button (black square) next to the Record button. To listen to the recording, tap the Play button (black triangle) next to the Stop button.

→ **See Also** Chapter 6, "Editing Notes," **p. 107**.

After making a voice recording, a small icon appears in the top-left corner of the Pocket Word document. Tapping this icon plays the recording. You can think of a voice recording in a Word document as a form of annotation that is used to provide additional information about a document. Figure 13.12 shows how a voice recording icon appears in the context of a document.

Shortcut
A shortcut to making voice recordings is to use the hardware Record button. Using this approach, you hold down the button to make the recording, as opposed to using the Voice Bar.

Figure 13.12
Voice recordings are represented by icons in Pocket Word documents.

Working with Documents in Pocket Word

The main view in Pocket Word is a document list that displays Pocket Word documents available for viewing and editing. Pocket Word includes a variety of features for managing documents; most of these features can be found in the Tools menu. The first of these features has to do with how Pocket Word documents are saved. When you create a new Pocket Word document, the name of the document is automatically set to the first characters appearing in the document. One option to change the name of a document is the Save Document As command, which is located in the Tools menu. This command allows you to save a copy of a document under a different name.

Of course, you could also just rename the document instead of making a copy of it. This is accomplished by using the Rename/Move command in the Edit menu. This command also allows you to move a document to a different folder or even to a CF storage card. A document can be deleted by using the Delete Document command in the Tools menu. Keep in mind that these document management features in Pocket Word can also be accomplished with File Explorer; they are provided in Pocket Word primarily for convenience. As with most standard Pocket PC applications, you can select multiple documents in Pocket Word by tapping and dragging the stylus over the documents.

The Pocket PC hardware buttons play a small role in Pocket Word when it comes to document management. Actually, the Action button is the only button that really does anything specific to documents. Scrolling the Action button moves up and down the document list, while pressing the Action Button will open the currently selected document. Speaking of hardware buttons, the Record button is also used in Pocket Word to record voice recordings as part of Record input mode.

Customizing Pocket Word

Pocket Word can be customized slightly via the Tools menu. To customize Pocket Word, tap Options in the Tools menu. This displays the Pocket Word Options window, which is shown in Figure 13.13.

Figure 13.13
The Pocket Word Options window allows you to customize Pocket Word.

The Default template setting determines the type of template used to create Pocket Word documents by default. In addition to creating blank documents, Pocket Word includes standard templates to help in creating commonly used documents. The default template can be set to one of these templates:

- Meeting Notes

- Memo

- Phone Memo

- To Do

You might recognize these templates from Chapter 6, when you learned about a similar set of templates for the Notes application.

The Save To option allows you to change the location to which documents are saved. You can choose between main system memory and a CF storage card. If you choose the main system memory option, which is the default option, then all documents will be stored in the My Documents folder.

The last option, Display in List View, is used to determine what types of documents are included in Pocket Word's document list. The default setting is Known types, which displays the widest range of document types. More specifically, known document types consist of Pocket Word documents, text documents, and HTML documents. Other settings allow you to limit the document list to Pocket Word and text documents, or just Pocket Word documents.

Synchronizing Documents with Pocket Word

One of the benefits to using a Pocket PC is its capability of synchronizing with a desktop PC. Synchronization allows you to share documents between machines, effectively having one copy of a given file that floats back and forth as it is edited on each machine. Pocket Word documents can be synchronized with your desktop PC via ActiveSync. If you recall, ActiveSync is the desktop software that manages the connection between a Pocket PC device and a desktop PC. ActiveSync supports synchronization of Pocket Word documents by allowing you to specify documents that you want synchronized between your device and desktop PC.

To synchronize Pocket Word files in ActiveSync, open ActiveSync and click the Options button on the ActiveSync toolbar. This opens the Options dialog box shown in Figure 13.14.

Figure 13.14
The ActiveSync Options window allows you to set up synchroniza-tion for Pocket Word files.

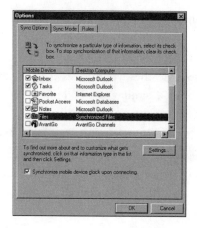

In the list of information types that can be synchronized, click Files. When you click files in the list, a message box is immedi-ately displayed that explains about a synchronization folder that is created on your desktop PC; just click OK to continue.

The synchronization folder on your desktop PC is created beneath your existing My Documents folder, and is named according to the name of your Pocket PC device. More specif-ically, the synchronization folder is named with the device name prepended to "My Documents." As an example, my device is named "Michael_PPC," so the synchronization folder is named "Michael_PPC My Documents." If you want to share Word documents with Pocket Word, just copy files into this folder and they will automatically be synchronized. Another option is to click the Settings buttons with Files selected in the ActiveSync list. This takes you to the File Synchronization Settings window, which allows you to identify specific files for synchronization (see Figure 13.15).

Figure 13.15
The File Synchronization Settings window allows you to identify specific files for synchronization.

When you add a file to the Synchronized File list in the File Synchronization Settings window, you effectively copy the file into the file synchronization folder; the original file is kept intact while any changes are made to the synchronized file. Upon selecting a file or files for synchronization for the first time, the Combine or Replace dialog box is displayed to clarify how you would like the synchronization to proceed for Pocket Word files (see Figure 13.16).

Figure 13.16
The Combine or Replace dialog box allows you to specify how synchronization should proceed for Pocket Word files.

The default setting is to combine files on the Pocket PC with files on the desktop PC, which is probably your best option. Another option is to replace files on the Pocket PC with files on the desktop computer, which is primarily useful if you are using Pocket Word only to view Word documents. After clicking OK in this dialog box, synchronization will begin and Word documents in the synchronization folder will be converted and copied onto your device in the My Documents folder. Figure 13.17 shows a menu that I created in Word as it appears in Pocket Word after being synchronized on the device.

Essential Information

- Even though Pocket Word supports a subset of the functionality in Word, it does fully understand the Word document format.

- Word documents are capable of losing some document information when converted to Pocket Word, due to features in Word that aren't supported in Pocket Word.

- Pocket Word offers several different input modes for entering different types of information.

- Pocket Word includes basic support for manipulating document files, which keeps you from having to use File Explorer.

- You can keep documents in sync between your desktop PC and Pocket PC by using ActiveSync's synchronization support for Pocket Word files.

GET THE SCOOP ON...
The Relationship Between Pocket Excel and Excel ▪
Limitations of Pocket Excel ▪ Using Formulas and
Functions in Pocket Excel ▪ Managing Pocket Excel
Workbooks and Worksheets ▪ Customizing Pocket Excel ▪
Synchronizing Workbooks Between Pocket Excel and Excel

Using Pocket Excel

Chapter 14

THERE WILL PROBABLY COME A TIME when it will be hard to imagine what life was like back when you couldn't do serious number crunching on the go in the palm of your hand. The Pocket PC is the first device to offer such power in the form of Pocket Excel. Pocket Excel is the Pocket PC counterpart to Microsoft Excel, the desktop spreadsheet application of choice for many professionals. Like Pocket Word, it is a trimmed-down version, but even with its compact size, Pocket Excel includes a surprising number of features found in Excel.

This chapter takes a look at Pocket Excel and explores its feature set. You learn about its relationship with Excel, including the specific features that are supported, and more importantly, the ones that aren't supported. By the end of this chapter, you'll have a solid grasp on mobile number crunching and what Pocket Excel is capable of handling.

Pocket Excel Versus Excel

Similar to Pocket Word, Pocket Excel is a compact version of the popular desktop spreadsheet application, Microsoft Excel. Pocket Excel supports a limited feature set of Excel, but is still quite useful and performs a wide range of interesting functions. Not surprisingly, the biggest benefit of Pocket Excel is its support for the Excel workbook format (.xls files). This allows you to carry Excel workbooks around on your Pocket PC to view and modify on the go.

Excel workbooks undergo a conversion process when they are transferred to a Pocket PC for use in Pocket Excel. The converted files are stored in a special Pocket Excel format with a .pxl file extension, as compared to Excel's .xls file extension. Excel templates are converted from their .xlt file type to Pocket Excel templates with a .pxt file extension. Excel workbooks are converted to Pocket Excel when any of the following situations occur:

Undocumented
Pocket Excel documents are automatically converted back to Excel documents when they are transferred back to a desktop computer. The conversion of Excel documents is actually handled by ActiveSync, which is why no conversion takes place if you transfer Pocket Excel documents between two Pocket PC devices.

- An Excel workbook is synchronized with Pocket Excel.

- An Excel workbook is manually copied from a desktop PC to a Pocket PC device.

- An Excel workbook is opened as an email attachment using Pocket Outlook.

When an Excel workbook is converted to Pocket Excel, it retains most of its data content but is capable of losing some important information, such as functions that aren't supported in Pocket Excel. You need to understand what workbook attributes are lost in the conversion so that you can avoid losing information when working with an Excel workbook in Pocket Excel. To help assure that information isn't lost when working with Excel workbooks in Pocket Excel, I recommend using Pocket Excel as a workbook viewer, which involves not saving a workbook after opening it. This obviously doesn't work for workbooks that you would like to edit in Pocket Excel. To edit workbooks in Pocket Excel without the fear of data loss, you need to become acquainted with the limitations of Pocket Excel.

Following is a list of the Excel workbook attributes that are fully supported in Pocket Excel:

- Built-in number formats
- Custom number formats
- Wrapping text
- Worksheet names (within the same workbook)

In addition to these fully supported workbook attributes, a few things are retained in the conversion to Pocket Excel, but might be slightly altered:

- **Formulas with arrays**—Changed to a value.

- **Formulas with unsupported functions**—Changed to a value.

- **Pivot table data**—Changed to a value.

- **Borders**—Changed to a single line.

- **Vertical text**—Changed to horizontal text.

- **Hidden names**—Displayed.

For the purposes of successfully managing Excel workbooks in Pocket Excel, the most important Excel workbook attributes are those that aren't supported at all, in which case they are actually lost when converting workbooks. These attributes follow:

- AutoFilter

- Data validation

- Cell notes

- Cell patterns

- Add-ins

- Protection

- Scenarios

- Object charts

- Vertical alignment

- Text boxes

- Embedded OLE objects

- Hyperlinks

- Picture controls

- Drawing objects

Shortcut
A good way to avoid the risk of losing workbook attributes when working with an Excel workbook in Pocket Excel is to make a copy of the workbook file on your desktop PC before copying/synchronizing with your Pocket PC. You can then compare the modified file when it is converted back to Excel and correct or reject any unwanted modifications.

If you aren't an avid Excel user, you might not even recognize all these features. If that's the case, you probably won't have to worry too much about them. Otherwise, you should be very careful when converting and editing files in Pocket Excel that use any of these features, as they will be lost during conversion.

Pocket Excel Essentials

As a compact version of Microsoft Excel, Pocket Excel is an application that is straightforward to use. To get started with Pocket Excel, tap Programs from the Start menu and then tap the Pocket Excel icon. Upon being launched, Pocket Excel first appears with a list of Pocket Excel workbooks that can be opened for viewing and editing. If you're using Pocket Excel for the first time, you probably won't have any workbooks in the list. In this case, you'll probably want to create a new one. To create a new workbook, just tap New in the lower-left corner of the screen.

Upon creating a new workbook or opening an existing workbook, the menu at the bottom of the screen changes to reflect commands and options available for Pocket Excel. The Edit menu contains commands used to alter the content and appearance of workbook data. The View menu allows you to enable or disable the various Pocket Excel user interface bars, as well as set the currently active worksheet and the manner in which the current worksheet is viewed. The Format menu allows you to manipulate and format cells, as well as work with rows and columns of data. The Tools menu includes a variety of commands for manipulating workbooks, such as sorting, filtering, inserting functions and symbols, and sending the workbook via infrared or email, to name a few commands. The Save Document As command on the tools menu allows you to save a Pocket Excel workbook in a variety of different formats including Pocket Excel 1.0, Excel 97/2000, and Excel 5.0/95. The Pocket Excel and Excel 97/2000 formats support saving as either a document or a template.

Figure 14.1 shows the Pocket Excel application upon creating a new workbook, which looks surprisingly similar to the desktop Excel application (minus a bit of real estate).

Figure 14.1
The Pocket Excel
application looks
a lot like the
desktop Excel
application.

Just above the Pocket Excel menu you'll notice a status bar that contains information about the status of Pocket Excel, as well as a couple of other interesting things. The word "Ready" in this status bar indicates that Pocket Excel isn't busy crunching numbers and is ready for you to work with the currently selected worksheet. As you might know from using Excel, a workbook can contain multiple worksheets. You can view and edit only a single worksheet at a time in Pocket Excel. You select a worksheet by tapping the Worksheet button next to the status text on the status bar; this button has the name of the worksheet and a down arrow on it (see Figure 14.2).

Next to the Worksheet button is the AutoCalculate button, which is used to perform a quick calculation on a selected range of cells in the worksheet. Tap the AutoCalculate button to select one of the following calculations (see Figure 14.3):

- **Average**—Determines the average of the cells selected.

- **Count**—Determines the number of cells selected.

- **Count Nums**—Determines the number of numeric cells selected.

- **Max**—Determines the maximum value of the cells selected.

- **Min**—Determines the minimum value of the cells selected.

- **Sum**—Adds the selected cells together.

Watch Out!
For some reason, the standard Pocket PC applications (including Pocket Excel) recognize files up to only one folder level beneath the My Workbooks folder. For example, if you place a Pocket Excel file in the Personal subfolder beneath the My Workbooks folder, Pocket Excel will display it in the workbook list when you select All Folders. However, if you create a subfolder named More Personal beneath the Personal folder and place files in it, Pocket Excel will not be able to access the files. The rule of thumb here is to create only a single level of folders beneath My Workbooks to avoid confusion.

To select cells for use with the AutoCalculate button, just tap a cell and drag the stylus over the other cells you want to select. The AutoCalculate button automatically updates to show the appropriate calculation for the cells selected. Figure 14.4 shows how the AutoCalculate button automatically calculates the sum of the currently selected cells.

In addition to the status bar, Pocket Excel also supports a tool-bar that contains various buttons for manipulating worksheets. To display the Pocket Excel toolbar, just tap Toolbar in the Views menu. Alternatively, next to the Tools menu you'll notice an icon with two arrows pointing up and down; tapping this icon also shows the toolbar. Figure 14.5 shows Pocket Excel with the toolbar displayed.

The first button on the toolbar is the Format button, which displays a window containing a variety of formatting options for use in formatting cells. You'll learn more about formatting cells a little later in the chapter.

Just to the right of the Format button are three buttons for setting the alignment of cells. The button next to the alignment buttons is the AutoSum button, which is used to automatically calculate the sum of a series of cells. Unlike the AutoCalculate button in the status bar, which can also calculate sums, the AutoSum button is used to create a sum and insert it into a cell in the worksheet.

Remember
If you don't see the status bar in Pocket Excel when it first starts, just tap Status Bar in the View menu to show the status bar.

Figure 14.5
The toolbar in Pocket Excel provides convenient access to worksheet manipulation options.

Sitting next to the AutoSum button, you'll find three style buttons that are used to apply common styles to selected cells. The following style buttons are included in the Pocket Excel toolbar:

Undocumented
Unfortunately, Pocket Excel only allows users to select a group of cells that are adjacent to each other. You cannot select multiple individual cells as you can in the desktop version of Excel.

- Currency—Displays numbers with two decimal places, a comma separator after every thousand (thousand, million, and so on), and a currency symbol (dollar sign) to the left of the number.

- Comma—Displays numbers with two decimal places and a comma separator after every thousand (thousand, million, and so on).

- Decimal—Displays numbers with two decimal places.

As you might have noticed, the three style buttons are progressively less detailed in the styles applied. For example, the Decimal button displays numbers with two decimal places, while the Comma button applies the Decimal style and also adds a comma separator after every thousand. Figure 14.6 shows how the Currency style button impacts the style of cells.

The last button on the Pocket Excel toolbar is the Zoom button, which allows you to alter the zoom level of the worksheet. Pocket Excel supports five standard zoom levels (50%, 75%, 100%, 125%, and 150%) that can be set via the Zoom button. You can also change the zoom level by tapping Zoom in the View menu. Figure 14.7 shows how a 125% zoom level makes the worksheet easier to read, with the obvious trade-off of being able to see less information.

That wraps up the Pocket Excel toolbar, but it doesn't tell the whole story in terms of viewing Pocket PC worksheets. Another very interesting feature in Pocket Excel is the Full Screen view, which is initiated by tapping Full Screen in the View menu (see Figure 14.8).

Figure 14.8
The Full Screen
command allows
you to view the
worksheet with
much more screen
space.

The full screen view mode is extremely helpful for getting a better perspective on a worksheet. However, it obviously results in you having to work within a more limited user interface. To change back to normal view mode, just tap the Restore button near the upper-right corner of the screen.

Formatting Cells

Pocket Excel includes several formatting options that can be used to format cells. To format cells, first select the cells you want to format, and then tap Cells in the Format menu. The Format button on the Pocket Excel toolbar can also be used to format selected cells. This results in the display of the Format Cells window, which is shown in Figure 14.9.

Figure 14.9
The Font tab of
the Format Cells
window is used to
select font options
for cells.

You'll notice in the figure that the Format Cells window contains several tabs, and the Font tab is selected by default. The Font tab allows you to alter the font, font color, font size, and font style of the current selection. Other tabs allow you to alter other aspects of cells, such as the cell size, number format, alignment, and borders.

The Size tab, which is shown in Figure 14.10, is used to set the size of cells in the worksheet.

Figure 14.10
The Size tab of the Format Cells window is used to alter the size of cells.

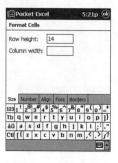

The Number tab in the Format Cells window is used to alter formatting that is specific to numerical data. This tab includes several different categories of number types, which each have their own formatting options. Figure 14.11 shows the formatting options for numeric currency data.

Figure 14.11
The Number tab of the Format Cells window is used to alter the formatting of numeric data, such as currency.

The Align tab is used to tweak the alignment of cells, as shown in Figure 14.12.

Figure 14.12
The Align tab of the Format Cells window is used to alter the alignment of cells.

The last tab in the Format Cells window is the Borders tab, which allows you to create visual borders around cells. Borders are very useful for dividing and calling out information in worksheets. Figure 14.13 shows the Borders tab, which in this case is being used to provide a visual cue for a header by adding a border along the bottom of the cell, as well as a fill color.

Figure 14.13
The Borders tab of the Format Cells window is used to create borders around cells.

Pocket Excel supports the manipulation of cells beyond the Format Cells window. For example, you can insert and delete cells using the Insert Cells and Delete Cells commands in the Format menu. You can also hide entire rows or columns of cells using the Hide command that is located in the Row and Column submenus of the Format menu. Hidden rows and columns are retained in a worksheet but are hidden from view. There is also an Unhide command that can be used to show hidden rows and columns. One final cell formatting option is the AutoFit feature, which is used to automatically size cells to fit their contents. You can enable this feature by tapping AutoFit in the Row or Column submenu of the Format menu.

Pocket Excel allows you to assign a name to a cell, which is very useful when creating formulas. To name a cell, select the cell and then tap Define Name in the Tools menu. This displays the Define Name window, which allows you to enter a name for the selected cell (Figure 14.14).

To name the cell, enter the name and tap the Add button. If there are any other names in the workbook, they will appear in the list of names shown in the Define Name window; you can

Inside Scoop
To select a hidden row or column, tap Go To from the Tools menu, and then enter a reference that is in the hidden row or column. The most likely reference is the row number (displayed to the left of the worksheet) or column letter (displayed above the worksheet).

assign any of the names to a cell. You can assign a list of names to a list of cells by tapping the Paste List button.

Using Panes

Pocket Excel supports panes, which are used to provide different views on the same worksheet. To split a worksheet into multiple panes, tap Split in the View menu. A splitter bar will appear between the two panes, which you can tap and drag with the stylus to alter the pane sizes. Figure 14.15 shows two panes divided by a splitter bar.

As you move around within a worksheet using the scrollbars, both of the panes change to reflect the selection point in the worksheet. If you want to keep one of the panes focused on a particular section of the worksheet, you can freeze it. To freeze a pane, tap Freeze Panes in the View menu. This results in the top pane freezing, while the bottom pane changes to show the remainder of the worksheet. This can be a little confusing at first because the splitter bar disappears, but when you scroll around, it becomes apparent that the bottom pane is the only pane moving.

To unfreeze the panes, tap Unfreeze Panes in the View menu. You can also remove the splitter bar, and therefore the extra pane, by tapping Remove Split in the View menu.

Working with Formulas and Functions

Formulas and functions are components of Pocket Excel workbooks that really allow you to get work done. Formulas are used to perform calculations on cells, whereas functions are standard mathematical operations used within formulas. Pocket Excel includes a Formula box near the upper-right corner of the screen that is used to enter formulas. To create a formula, you must first select a cell with which the formula is associated; this is the cell where the formula result will appear. After selecting a cell, create a formula by entering an equal sign (=) followed by the formula in the Formula box. Besides entering them by hand, you can specify cells in a formula by tapping them; to specify a range of cells in a formula, tap and drag over the cells. Figure 14.16 shows a formula that performs a simple calculation on a cell in the worksheet.

Inside Scoop
Pocket Excel allows a maximum of four separate panes divided by splitter bars. The panes are adjusted by tapping and dragging the splitter bar. In most cases, it is helpful to have only two panes visible at almost at any given time given the limited screen space on a Pocket PC.

Figure 14.16
The Formula box allows you to enter formulas that perform calculations on other cells.

This formula calculates the average sales in the first quarter of the worksheet, which involves adding the values for the three months and dividing by three. Notice that the named cell, JanSales, appears as a name instead of as a cell reference (A2).

Although it's fine to create your own formulas, use functions whenever possible to avoid reinventing the wheel. The standard AVERAGE() function is particularly useful in this example. To select a function while editing a formula, tap the fx button to the left of the Formula box. This displays the Insert

Function window, which provides a list of functions organized by category that can be used in formulas (see Figure 14.17). If you spend some time in this window, you'll see that Pocket Excel supports a surprising number of functions.

Figure 14.17
The Insert
Function window
provides a list of
categorized func-
tions available for
use in formulas.

Figure 14.18 shows how the earlier formula is modified to use the AVERAGE() function, as selected in the Insert Function window. Pay close attention to the Formula box, which shows how the AVERAGE() function is now being used instead of averaging the cells manually.

Figure 14.18
Functions can
eliminate the
need to create
custom formulas.

Managing Workbooks and Worksheets in Pocket Excel

Similar to Pocket Word, Pocket Excel's main view consists of a workbook list that displays Pocket Excel workbooks available for viewing and editing. Pocket Excel's Tools menu includes a variety of features for managing workbooks. Because the features found in the Tools menu act on the current workbook, you'll need to create a new workbook or open an existing one for the commands to appear in the menu. The first of these features has to do with how Pocket Excel workbooks are saved. When you create a new Pocket Excel workbook, the name of the workbook is automatically set to the word Book followed by a number, such as Book1. One option to changing the name of a workbook is the Save Workbook As command, which is located in the Tools menu. This command allows you to save a copy of a workbook under a different name.

A simpler option is to just rename the workbook instead of making a copy of it. This is accomplished by using the Rename/Move command in the Edit menu. This command also allows you to move a workbook to a different folder or to a CF storage card. A workbook can be deleted by using the Delete Workbook command in the Tools menu. Understand that these workbook management features in Pocket Excel can also be accomplished with File Explorer; they are provided in Pocket Excel as a convenience. As with most standard Pocket PC applications, you can select multiple workbooks in the Pocket Excel workbook list by tapping and dragging the stylus over the workbooks.

The Pocket PC hardware buttons play a small role in Pocket Excel when it comes to workbook management. The Action button is the only button that really does anything specific to workbooks. Scrolling the Action button moves up and down the workbook list; pressing the Action Button opens the currently selected workbook. Within a workbook, you also can scroll the Action button to move up and down cells; pressing the button closes the workbook.

Pocket Excel workbooks typically consist of multiple worksheets. You learned earlier in the chapter how to switch worksheets via the status bar. You can also switch worksheets by tapping Sheet in the View menu, followed by the worksheet you want to view. To add or remove worksheets, tap Modify Sheets in the Format menu. Doing so displays the Modify Sheets window shown in Figure 14.19.

Shortcut
You can perform most of the workbook management features of Pocket Excel by tapping and holding on a workbook in Pocket Excel's workbook list. This can often be faster than navigating to a menu command.

This window is pretty straightforward in that it provides buttons to rename, insert, delete, and change the order of worksheets.

Customizing Pocket Excel

You can customize some of the functionality of Pocket Excel via the Tools menu. To customize Pocket Excel, tap Options in the Tools menu. This displays the Pocket Excel Options window, which is shown in Figure 14.20.

The Template for New Workbook setting determines the type of template used to create Pocket Excel workbooks by default. In addition to creating blank workbooks, Pocket Excel supports standard templates to help in creating commonly used workbooks. The only standard template included in Pocket Excel is the Vehicle Mileage Log template, which helps in keeping track of mileage on a vehicle while traveling. You can also create your own templates in Excel and use them in Pocket Excel by copying them to the My Documents folder on your device.

The Save New Workbooks To option allows you to change the location to which workbooks are saved. You can choose between main system memory and a CF storage card. If you choose the main system memory option, which is the default option, all workbooks will be stored in the My Documents folder.

The last option, Files to Display in List View, is used to determine what types of workbooks are included in Pocket Excel's workbook list. The default setting is Known Types, which displays the widest range of workbook types. The other setting allows you to limit the workbook list to just Pocket Excel workbooks.

Synchronizing Workbooks with Pocket Excel

Pocket Excel workbooks can be synchronized with your desktop PC by using the ActiveSync synchronization software. ActiveSync supports synchronization of Pocket Excel workbooks by allowing you to specify workbooks that you want synchronized between your device and desktop PC. To synchronize Pocket Excel files in ActiveSync, open ActiveSync and click the Options button on the ActiveSync toolbar. This results in the Options dialog box being displayed, which you saw in the previous chapter while synchronizing Word documents.

In the list of information types that can be synchronized, click Files. If you recall from the previous chapter, this is the same setting used to synchronize Pocket Word files. When you begin synchronizing Excel files with Pocket Excel, you'll place them in a special synchronization folder on your desktop PC that is located beneath your existing My Documents folder. The synchronization folder is named with the device name prepended to "My Documents," such as "Michael_PPC My Documents."

Another synchronization option is to click the Settings buttons with Files selected in the ActiveSync list. This takes you to the File Synchronization Settings window, which allows you to identify specific files for synchronization. When you add a file to the Synchronized File list in the File Synchronization

Settings window, you effectively copy the file into the file synchronization folder; the original file is kept intact while any changes are made to the synchronized file. Upon selecting a file or files for synchronization for the first time, the Combine or Replace dialog box is displayed so you can clarify how you want the synchronization to proceed for Pocket Excel files.

The default setting is to combine files on the Pocket PC with files on the desktop PC, which is probably your best option. Another option is to replace files on the Pocket PC with files on the desktop computer, which is primarily useful if you are only using Pocket Excel to view Excel workbooks. After clicking OK in this dialog box, synchronization begins and Excel workbooks in the synchronization folder are converted and copied onto your device in the My Documents folder. Figure 14.21 shows a spreadsheet that I created in Excel as it appears in Pocket Excel after being synchronized on the device.

Figure 14.21
Most synchronized Excel workbooks retain their look in Pocket Excel, given the obvious screen-size limitations.

Essential Information

- Pocket Excel supports only a subset of the functionality in Excel, but it fully understands the Excel workbook format.

- Because Pocket Excel doesn't support all the features in Excel, it is possible for Excel workbooks to lose some information when converted to Pocket Excel.

- Pocket Excel supports panes, which are used to divide a worksheet into separate views.

- The Pocket Excel Formula box is a convenient place to enter formulas, which can use functions to perform calculations on cells.

- Pocket Excel includes basic support for manipulating workbook files, which keeps you from having to use File Explorer.

- You can keep workbooks synchronized between your desktop PC and Pocket PC by using ActiveSync's synchronization support for Pocket Excel files.

GET THE SCOOP ON...
The Relationship Between Money for Pocket PC and Money
2000 ▪ Install MS Money for Pocket PC ▪ Synchronization of MS
Money for Pocket PC with Money 2000 ▪ Managing Accounts in
Money for Pocket PC ▪ Entering Transactions in Money for
Pocket PC ▪ Tracking Investments with Money for Pocket PC

Using Pocket Money

Chapter 15

B EING SOMEWHAT OF A DETAIL person, I really like to keep
a close tab on finances. I regularly use Microsoft Money
2000—the desktop personal finance software—to track
bank accounts, investments, and other assets. The weak link in
my financial bookkeeping, and I suspect the weak link for just
about everyone, is keeping up with checks, debits, and credit
card purchases. It's hard to keep track of all those receipts, and
then come home and carefully enter and categorize them.
Wouldn't it be nice if you could record financial transactions
electronically at the time they are made, instead of later when
you get back to your desktop PC? Pocket PC includes an application called Microsoft Money for Pocket PC that makes it possible to do this and more.

This chapter tackles the issue of mobile financial management
and how it can be improved dramatically with your Pocket PC.
You learn about the capabilities of Money for Pocket PC, as
well as how to synchronize it with Money 2000, its desktop con-
fidant. You might find that Money for Pocket PC is one of
those applications that you can't live without after using it for
a few days.

Money for Pocket PC Versus Money 2000

In the past two chapters, you've already heard the song and
dance about pint-sized versions of popular Microsoft desktop
applications such as Word and Excel. Money for Pocket PC is a

little different from Pocket Word and Pocket Excel in that it isn't really intended for use as a standalone Pocket PC application. Even though Pocket Word and Pocket Excel can be synchronized with Word and Excel, they still function more or less as independent applications in which you can view and edit files from your Pocket PC. Money for Pocket PC can also be used as such an application, but that's not where you will realize its true benefits. Money for Pocket PC is designed to provide a quick view on your most important financial accounts, as well as a convenient place to enter transactions while on the go.

Money for Pocket PC is not the ideal application to use as the sole means of managing personal finances; desktop applications such as Money 2000 and Quicken offer significantly more features and are relatively inexpensive. What Money for Pocket PC offers is the capability to view and enter financial data from anywhere, because you can carry it around in your pocket. If you already use personal finance software on your desktop PC, you probably realize the significance of being able to enter transactions and manage accounts while away from your desktop computer.

The point is that Money for Pocket PC is really more of a companion for Money 2000. Yes, Money for Pocket PC technically can be used as your primary personal finance software, but you are much better served using it in conjunction with Money 2000. Money 2000 excels at financial analysis, of which Money for Pocket PC is virtually devoid. This is not to criticize Money for Pocket PC—it merely demonstrates its supporting role. Following are the three main tasks for which Money for Pocket PC proves most useful:

- Entering financial transactions

- Reviewing account balances

- Tracking investments

Unlike Pocket Word and Pocket Excel, which you might or might not decide to synchronize with their desktop counterparts, synchronizing Money for Pocket PC with Money 2000 is

Watch Out!
Money for Pocket PC is compatible only with Microsoft Money 2000, so you'll need to upgrade to Money 2000 if you plan on synchronizing with Money for Pocket PC.

Inside Scoop
Money for Pocket PC is not directly compatible with Quicken. However, you can import a Quicken file into Money 2000 and then synchronize with Money for Pocket PC.

a must if you use Money 2000. In fact, you should synchronize Money for Pocket PC with Money 2000 before you ever even run Money for Pocket PC, because it is tricky trying to preserve information that you've entered in Money for Pocket PC prior to synchronization. Another potentially tricky issue with Money for Pocket PC is that you must install it from the ActiveSync CD-ROM regardless of whether it is already in your Pocket PC's ROM. This installation is necessary because there are special files required by ActiveSync that are included in the installation.

Installing Money for Pocket PC

Some Pocket PCs ship with Money for Pocket PC in ROM, which means you don't have to install anything to begin creating accounts and entering transactions. However, if you ever plan on synchronizing with Money 2000, you should perform the ActiveSync installation for Money for Pocket PC that is located on the ActiveSync CD-ROM. This installation needs to be performed before you enter any information in Money for Pocket PC. Before performing this installation, you need to make sure Money 2000 is installed on your desktop PC.

To understand the importance of installing Money for Pocket PC from the ActiveSync CD-ROM, try running Money for Pocket PC before performing the installation. To do so, just tap Programs in the Start menu, and then tap the Microsoft Money icon. Money for Pocket PC will start up and display a warning about performing the installation from the ActiveSync CD-ROM (see Figure 15.1).

Remember
If you don't plan on ever synchronizing Money for Pocket PC with Money 2000, there is no need to install Money for Pocket PC from the ActiveSync CD-ROM. However, it is difficult to preserve financial data from Money for Pocket PC if you ever change your mind and decide to synchronize later without having performed the installation.

Figure 15.1
When you first run Money for Pocket PC, it displays a warning about installing and synchronizing it with Money 2000.

Assuming that ActiveSync is already installed and working, connect your Pocket PC to your desktop computer. To begin installing Money for Pocket PC, open the \Extras\MSMoney\ pocketpc folder on the ActiveSync CD-ROM and run setup.exe. You'll be presented with a few standard installation windows, which you can click the Next button on to navigate through. I recommend accepting the default installation location on your desktop PC. This installation location is used to store the Pocket PC install files, which are installed to the Pocket PC in the next part of the installation. Click the Next button to continue on with the Pocket PC portion of the installation.

After analyzing your device for a few moments, the setup program will prompt you to confirm the default installation directory on your Pocket PC (see Figure 15.2). To accept the default installation folder, click the Yes button. To change the installation folder, click No and enter the new folder.

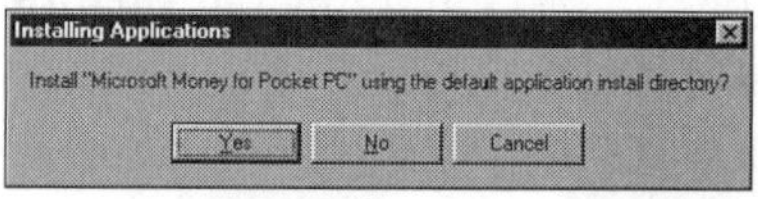

Figure 15.2
The Money for Pocket PC setup program prompts you to confirm the default installation directory on your Pocket PC.

You'll then see a progress bar that displays the progress of the installation. After the setup program finishes installing files, you'll see a message box notifying you that additional steps might be necessary on your device. This is a standard Pocket PC installation message box, and doesn't apply to Money for Pocket PC. Click the OK button to continue to the last step of the installation. The last window displayed by the setup program announces that the setup is complete; click the Finish button to wrap up the installation of Money for Pocket PC.

At this point, Money for Pocket PC is installed, but you still need to set it up for synchronization with Money 2000 before getting started using it.

Synchronizing Money for Pocket PC

ActiveSync is the software responsible for synchronizing Money for Pocket PC with Money 2000. Before performing the synchronization for the first time, you need to set up synchronization settings for Money for Pocket PC. There is an ActiveSync synchronization limitation for Money that you need to be aware of before starting to use it: You can synchronize Money between only one desktop PC and one Pocket PC. If you have two Pocket PC devices, you cannot synchronize between the two of them from a single desktop. Likewise, you can't synchronize from two desktop PCs with a Pocket PC device. This synchronization restriction applies only to Money for Pocket PC and Money 2000; other types of data synchronized via ActiveSync aren't affected.

To begin synchronizing Money in ActiveSync, open ActiveSync on your desktop computer and click the Options button in the toolbar. The Options window is displayed, which is shown in Figure 15.3.

Figure 15.3
The ActiveSync Options window allows you to select synchronized information types.

The list of information types in the Options window includes an entry for Microsoft Money, which you must check to enable the synchronization of Microsoft Money data. Before clicking the OK button to begin synchronizing Money data, click the Settings button to fine-tune the specifics regarding the Money data that is synchronized. This displays the Money Synchronization Settings window, which is shown in Figure 15.4.

Figure 15.4
The Money
Synchronization
Settings window
allows you to
specify the exact
Money data that
is synchronized.

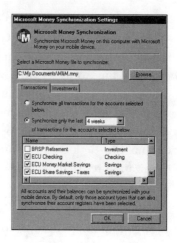

Inside Scoop
Although you can
synchronize all the
data in Money
2000 if you
choose, it is impor-
tant to assess
how much informa-
tion you're syn-
chronizing so as
not to waste
Pocket PC
resources. The
main usage of
Money for Pocket
PC is in entering
and maintaining
current transac-
tions, which proba-
bly means that you
can get by without
synchronizing your
entire financial his-
tory. Because
large data files will
inevitably slow
down Money for
Pocket PC, I
encourage you to
carefully select
the Money data
that you
synchronize.

The first option in the Money synchronization settings allows you to select a different Money 2000 file for synchronizing with Money for Pocket PC. Money 2000 stores all of your financial information in a special file with an .mny file exten-sion. If several people in your household use Money 2000, then you might have multiple Money files and need to be sure to look for the one that applies to you. Below the file setting is a tabbed view that displays the Transactions tab initially. This tab allows you to specify the accounts that are synchronized, as well as the transactions for the accounts. You have the option of synchronizing all transactions for the accounts, or specify-ing a number of weeks of data to synchronize. The default set-ting of 4 weeks is a good place to start from, but you can adjust this to suit your needs (between 1 and 52 weeks). The list near the bottom of the window takes its information from Money 2000 and allows you to choose the accounts you want to syn-chronize.

By default, ActiveSync enables only accounts that support an account register in Money for Pocket PC. This includes the fol-lowing account types:

- Cash

- Checking

- Savings

- Credit Card

- Line of Credit

Other account types can be synchronized with Money for Pocket PC, but you won't be able to add or view transactions with the account; the account balance is all that is retained. This is totally acceptable for some accounts, such as Investment accounts, because you probably care only about the balance anyway.

The other tab in the Money Synchronization Settings window is the Investments tab, which allows you to select the individual investments that are set up in Money 2000 (see Figure 15.5). You can choose whether to synchronize all investments or just the ones selected in the list.

Figure 15.5
The Investments tab in the Money Synchronization Settings window allows you to select investments for synchronization.

Watch Out!
Be careful not to turn off your Pocket PC or otherwise interrupt the synchronization of Money data. Doing so can cause the Money for Pocket PC database to get corrupted, which requires you to delete the Pocket PC partnership and set up Money for Pocket PC again to fix it.

Click the OK button to accept the settings and return to the ActiveSync Options window, and then click OK in the Options window to allow ActiveSync to get to work synchronizing Money data. Depending on how much data you've selected for synchronization, ActiveSync will churn for a few moments synchronizing Money data on your Pocket PC (see Figure 15.6).

→ **See Also** "Avoiding and Solving Problems with Money for Pocket PC," **p. 254**.

Synchronizing Existing Data

Earlier in the chapter, I mentioned that you shouldn't enter data into Money for Pocket PC prior to synchronization if you plan on synchronizing later. The reason for this warning is because there is no straightforward way to synchronize Money for Pocket PC data that was entered prior to setting up Money synchronization. However, it is possible. In fact, the following steps outline exactly how it's done:

1. Create a new Money 2000 file, and set it as the Money synchronization file in ActiveSync.

2. Synchronize Money for Pocket PC with the new Money 2000 file, which will enter your Money for Pocket PC data into Money 2000.

3. Export the Money 2000 data to a QIF (Quicken Interchange Format) file.

4. Open your original Money 2000 file, and import the data from the QIF file.

5. Set the original Money 2000 file as the Money synchronization file in ActiveSync.

This series of steps is required because during the initial Money synchronization, ActiveSync expects one of the Money files (Money 2000 or Money for Pocket PC) to be empty of any data. Because you've entered data in Money for Pocket PC, neither of the files is empty, which presents a problem. Creating a temporary Money 2000 file that is empty circumvents the problem. Keep in mind that this is only an issue when initially synchronizing Money data.

Using Money for Pocket PC

With Money for Pocket PC full of Money 2000 data, you're almost ready to start using it to enter transactions and monitor accounts and investments. Before doing so, you might want to consider setting a password for the application that keeps your financial data from prying eyes should they get their hands on your Pocket PC. To set a password for Money for Pocket PC, tap Password in the Tools menu. You'll be prompted to enter a password, after which you'll have to enter it each time you run Money for Pocket PC.

With a little financial security in place, you can get started working with accounts and managing your finances. To launch Money for Pocket PC, tap Programs on the Start menu, and then tap the Microsoft Money icon. Money for Pocket PC begins by displaying the Account Manager screen, which contains a list of the accounts that are set up for use in Money for Pocket PC (see Figure 15.7).

Remember
Just in case you're curious about the Money data used throughout this chapter, the account names, transactions, and amounts are entirely fictitious. Hackers will have to look for their fun elsewhere!

Microsoft Money	11:07p
Account Manager ▾	
ECU Checking	965.48
ECU Money Market S...	19,055.60
ECU Share Savings - ...	3,669.68
ECU VISA	(971.12)
Masheed's Roth IRA	3,450.30
MECU West Share Sa...	69.91
MECU West VISA	(308.77)
Michael's Roth IRA	2,862.86
Michael's SEP IRA	3,648.36
Balances:	32,442.30
New ▲ Tools	🖮 ▲

Figure 15.7
The Account Manager screen displays a list of accounts set up in Money for Pocket PC.

The Account Manager screen provides a quick view of each account balance. To create a new account, tap New near the lower-left corner of the screen. To find out more about an account, just tap the account in the account list. Figure 15.8 shows the Account Register screen, which is displayed when you tap an account that supports an account register in Money for Pocket PC, such as a checking account.

Figure 15.8
The Account
Register screen
displays a list of
transaction
entries in an
account.

Figure 15.8
The Account
Register screen
displays a list of
transaction
entries in an
account.

The Account Register screen resembles a register used to enter transactions in your checkbook, and is a simplified version of the Money 2000 account register. To edit an individual transaction, just tap it in the list. To enter a new transaction, tap New in the lower-left corner of the screen. Figure 15.9 shows a transaction being edited.

Figure 15.9
When editing a
transaction, you
can modify infor-
mation such as
the type, account,
payee, date, and
amount of the
transaction.

Shortcut
Most of the fields
used to enter and
edit transaction
information
use the
AutoComplete+
feature, which
automatically
enters data based
upon previously
entered informa-
tion. This helps to
significantly
speed up the
entry of common
transactions.

You'll notice in the transaction that the Required tab is initially selected; this tab reflects information that is required for the transaction to be considered complete. The Optional tab is used to enter additional information that isn't as critical to the transaction. Figure 15.10 shows the Optional tab information for the transaction.

The Optional tab includes optional fields such as the check number. I like to categorize transactions in Money, so I use the Category and Subcategory fields whenever possible. The Status field is used to signify if a transaction has been cleared, reconciled, or voided. Finally, the Memo field is used to provide additional information about the transaction. Tapping OK in the upper-right corner of the screen commits the changes to the transaction and returns you to the Account Register screen.

Figure 15.10
The Optional tab is used to enter optional information while editing a transaction.

Back in the Account Register screen (refer to Figure 15.8), you'll notice two drop-down lists near the top of the screen. In the upper-right area of the screen is a drop-down list that allows you to select an account; all the accounts that are set up in Money for Pocket PC are shown in the list. The list on the upper left allows you to choose from the following screens to manipulate Money data:

Shortcut
If you should need to perform a quick calculation while entering a transaction, just tap Calculator in the Tools menu to launch the Pocket PC Calculator.

- Account Manager

- Account Register

- Investments

- Categories

- Payees

You've already learned about the Account Manager and Account Register screens, so let's move on to the others. To switch to the Investments screen, tap the upper-left drop-down list and then tap Investments. Figure 15.11 shows the Investments screen, which contains a list of the investments being tracked in Money for Pocket PC.

The total market value for all the investments is displayed at the bottom of the screen. To add a new investment, tap New near the lower-left corner of the screen. To edit an investment, just tap the investment in the list of investments. Figure 15.12 shows an investment being edited.

Figure 15.11
The Investments screen contains a list of the investments being tracked in Money for Pocket PC.

Figure 15.12
When editing an investment, you can modify information such as the name, ticker symbol, last price, and number of shares held.

Remember
There is a difference between an investment and an investment account. Although you can edit investments, you can't add or remove transactions for an investment account.

Editing investments is pretty straightforward in that you enter information such as the name, ticker symbol, last price, and number of shares held for the investment. Notice that there is no reference to how much was paid for an investment or any commissions paid. This keeps you from being able to determine the performance of an investment, which is not the role of Money for Pocket PC; you should use Money 2000 for analytical purposes. Getting back to editing an investment, tapping OK in the upper-right corner of the screen commits the changes to the investment.

Back in the Investments screen, you might have noticed a button to the right of the Tools menu. This is the Update Quotes button, which is used to update the quotes for the investments shown in the investment list. The Update Quotes button is handy for keeping tabs on your investments while traveling with your Pocket PC. You do need an Internet connection to retrieve the quotes, but a CF modem or Ethernet card makes this an easy task. Please refer to Chapter 8, "Getting Online," for more information on how to get online with a CF modem or Ethernet card.

In addition to the Investments screen, Money for Pocket PC also includes Categories and Payees screens, which allow you to customize the categories and payees used throughout Money. To access the Categories screen, tap the upper-left drop-down list and then tap Categories. Figure 15.13 shows the Categories screen, which contains a list of all the categories used in Money for Pocket PC.

Figure 15.13
The Categories screen contains a list of all the categories.

To create a new category, tap New near the lower-left corner of the Categories screen. To edit a category, just tap it in the category list. Figure 15.14 shows a category being edited.

Figure 15.14
When editing a category, you can modify information such as the name and type of the category.

Inside Scoop
If you don't have access to an Internet connection, you can manually update investment prices by editing the investment and entering a share price directly in the Last Price field.

To accept the changes to the category, tap OK in the upper-right corner of the screen.

Similar to being able to add and edit categories in the Categories screen, you can also add and edit payees in the Payees screen, which is shown in Figure 15.15.

Figure 15.15
The Payees
screen contains a
list of all the pay-
ees used in
Money for
Pocket PC.

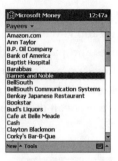

Figure 15.15
The Payees
screen contains a
list of all the pay-
ees used in
Money for
Pocket PC.

To create a new payee, tap New near the lower-left corner of the Payees screen. To edit a payee, just tap it in the payee list. Figure 15.16 shows a payee being edited.

Figure 15.16
When editing a
payee, you can
modify information
such as the name,
address, phone
number, and
account number
of the payee.

Although you might sometimes find it useful to edit payees via the Payees screen, I typically enter new payees by just entering them when I enter a transaction for them. Money for Pocket PC will automatically add the new payee to the payee list, in which case you can edit the details using the Payees screen.

Customizing Money for Pocket PC

Money for Pocket PC includes a few options that can be customized to alter the way the application works. You customize Money for Pocket PC by tapping Options in the Tools menu. This displays the Microsoft Money Options window, which is shown in Figure 15.17.

The first check box in this window enables the AutoComplete+ feature, which automatically fills in Money information when entering transactions and payees. This is a very useful feature and I've never encountered a scenario where it would be beneficial to disable it. The second check box is used to enable large fonts, which makes text in the various screens through-out Money a little easier to read. The large font setting is the default, and is used in the figures you've seen throughout this chapter. I have found that the smaller fonts, however, look much cleaner on the screen.

Figure 15.17
The Microsoft Money Options window allows you to customize Money for Pocket PC.

You might have noticed in Figure 15.17 that there is another tab in the Microsoft Money Options window named Proxy Server, which is shown in Figure 15.18. This setting is useful if you are on a network that requires a proxy server for accessing the Internet. If you do require a proxy server, this information is necessary so that Money can update investment quotes from the Internet.

Figure 15.18
The Proxy Server tab in the Microsoft Money Options window allows you to set a proxy server for accessing the Internet to retrieve investment quotes.

If you require a proxy server, you'll definitely want to enter the relevant information in this window to update investment quotes in Money for Pocket PC. You should be able to obtain this information from your network administrator.

Avoiding and Solving Problems with Money for Pocket PC

It's only fitting to close this chapter with a few words of caution regarding Money for Pocket PC. It is apparent that the application is relatively sensitive when it comes to encountering problems during synchronization. More specifically, it is surprisingly easy to accidentally corrupt the Money database and render Money for Pocket PC worthless.

In a moment I'll explain how to fix a corrupted Money database, but it's more important for you to understand how to avoid corrupting it to begin with. Following are some suggestions for keeping Money for Pocket PC running smoothly:

- Do not disconnect your device during synchronization; doing so will almost guarantee a corrupt database.

- Do not use Money for Pocket PC while your device is connected to your desktop PC (use Ctrl+Q to shut it down if you've already been running it); it's a good idea to physically disconnect the device before running Money for Pocket PC.

- Do not use Money 2000 on your desktop PC while your device is synchronizing.

- Do not use the Continuously synchronization option in ActiveSync; instead use the On Connection option or Manual option (these options are accessible from the Sync Mode tab in the ActiveSync Options dialog box).

- If ActiveSync reports that Money items need to be resolved during synchronization, do not click Resolve to resolve the problem; instead, disconnect the device, perform a soft reset, and reconnect the device.

I realize that this is a strict set of suggestions; however, you will have problems with Money for Pocket PC if you don't adhere to these guidelines. Unfortunately, synchronization is not very robust in the current release of Money for Pocket PC, so you must be careful to use it safely. Just stick to the previous suggestions and you shouldn't have any problems at all.

However, if something does happen that results in the Money database getting corrupted, you'll need to know how to solve the corruption problem. Fortunately, there is a reasonably straightforward fix. If you should get a database corruption error upon running Money for Pocket PC, follow these steps to recover from it:

1. Disconnect your device from the desktop PC, and perform a soft reset.

2. Click the Options button in the ActiveSync toolbar to display the ActiveSync Options window.

3. Click Microsoft Money in the list, and then click the Settings button to display the Money Synchronization Settings window.

4. Change the Money synchronization file to a dummy Money file; you can use the Sample.mny file in the Money directory or create a temporary Money file.

5. Click the OK button to accept the synchronization settings, and then click OK again to get out of the Options window.

6. Reconnect your device to the desktop PC and synchronize.

7. When the synchronization finishes, disconnect your device from the desktop PC again.

8. In ActiveSync, change the Money synchronization file back to the original file.

9. Reconnect your device to the desktop PC and synchronize once more.

These steps basically outline a trick that involves synchronizing Money for Pocket PC with a dummy Money file to fix the database problem, and then synchronizing with the original Money file that contains your data. Although the fix might sound strange, it does work quite well and will save you a lot of headaches should you ever end up with a corrupted Money database.

Essential Information

- Unlike some of the other standard applications included with the Pocket PC, Money for Pocket PC is truly designed as more of a companion to Money 2000, as opposed to serving as a standalone financial tool.

- It is important to synchronize Money for Pocket PC with Money 2000 before entering data in Money for Pocket PC if you intend to eventually synchronize it with Money 2000.

- Although it might be tempting to synchronize all the data in Money 2000 with Money for Pocket PC, keep in mind that a large Money database will impact the performance of Money for Pocket PC.

- Money for Pocket PC supports an account register for cash, checking, savings, credit card, and line-of-credit accounts, whereas other types of accounts display only the current balance.

- The Investments screen includes a button on the toolbar to update investment quotes from the Internet.

- Money for Pocket PC is a sensitive application, so you should exercise caution when synchronizing with Money 2000, and follow a few simple guidelines to preserve data integrity.

GET THE SCOOP ON...

The Usefulness of Pocket Streets ▪ The Different Versions of
Pocket Streets Currently Available ▪ How to Properly Install
Pocket Streets ▪ Creating Custom Maps for Use in Pocket
Streets ▪ Using Pocket Streets As a Mobile Map ▪ The Potential
for Using Pocket Streets As a Global Positioning Tool

Using Pocket Streets

Chapter 16

I T'S COMMON KNOWLEDGE THAT most men hate to ask for directions when they aren't sure where they are going. Call it rugged individualism or hardheaded stubbornness, but there is something almost degrading about having to admit that you have managed to get lost in a world as well mapped as the one we live in. Fortunately, help has arrived. Included on the ActiveSync CD-ROM that ships with all Pocket PCs is a nifty little application called Pocket Streets that will allow you to navigate yourself out of just about any situation.

Pocket Streets is an application that allows you to navigate maps at surprisingly high levels of detail. It is compatible with several of Microsoft's popular desktop mapping applications, which means you can create maps in a desktop application and view them in Pocket Streets while traveling. This chapter shows you how to get the most out of Pocket Streets, and will leave you with no excuse for getting lost again.

Pocket PC: The Ultimate Road Atlas

With the advent of Pocket Streets, the days of thumbing through an old worn-out road atlas are over. In fact, a Pocket PC running Pocket Streets is the ultimate road atlas. Not too many printed road atlases allow you to zoom in and out, and there definitely aren't any that allow you to enable and disable specific points of interest. Are you interested in seeing only bowling alleys and movie theatres? That's not a problem

Inside Scoop
Maps compatible with Pocket Streets are currently available for the United States and Great Britain.

Remember
Because Microsoft Streets & Trips 2000 is the most commonly used mapping application for the PC, I use it later in the chapter to demonstrate how to create maps for Pocket Streets. The technique is similar for the other mapping applications.

because Pocket Streets allows you to enable or disable points of interest at will.

Because maps can get fairly large due to the large amount of information contained within them, you might find it useful to create specific maps using a desktop mapping application. Pocket Streets is compatible with the following desktop mapping applications:

- Microsoft Streets & Trips 2000

- Microsoft MapPoint 2000

- Microsoft AutoRoute Express Great Britain 2000

If you don't have access to one of these applications, I encourage you to consider buying one of them if you plan to use Pocket Streets. Later in the chapter, I'll show you how to download maps so you can use Pocket Streets without a desktop mapping application, but the capability of creating custom maps in such a desktop application is very significant.

Pocket Streets and Pocket Streets 2001

Before moving on to the installation of Pocket Streets, it's important to understand some of the compatibility issues with Pocket Streets and its larger siblings. The version of Pocket Streets (version 3.02) that ships on the ActiveSync CD-ROM with Pocket PCs is compatible with the desktop mapping applications mentioned earlier. There is also a newer version of Pocket Streets available, Pocket Streets 2001, which is compatible with the very latest desktop mapping applications. Pocket Streets 2001 is available for free download from Microsoft's Pocket PC Web site at `http://www.microsoft.com/pocketpc/downloads/streets.asp`. Following are the desktop mapping applications that are compatible with Pocket Streets 2001:

- Microsoft Streets & Trips 2001

- Microsoft MapPoint 2001

- Microsoft AutoRoute 2001

As you can see, these are the 2001 versions of the same mapping applications listed earlier. The determination in using Pocket Streets or Pocket Streets 2001 is largely dependent on the version of the desktop mapping application you are using, because they aren't compatible between versions. In other words, you can't use Pocket Streets 3.02 with Microsoft Streets & Trips 2001. Likewise, Pocket Streets 2001 is incompatible with Microsoft Streets & Trips 2000. If you haven't yet purchased desktop mapping software and you intend to do so, you might as well get the newer one.

The good news about all this is that there is very little difference between Pocket Streets and Pocket Streets 2001 in terms of using the applications. For this reason, I focus on the use of Pocket Streets throughout this chapter. Besides it being the version on the ActiveSync CD-ROM, right now, more users are likely to have access to one of the 2000 desktop mapping applications.

Installing Pocket Streets

Although Pocket Streets is a very powerful and useful application, it is not included in the ROM of your Pocket PC like other standard applications such as Word and Excel. Instead, you must install Pocket Streets from a desktop PC. Pocket Streets is included on the ActiveSync CD-ROM, and Pocket Streets 2001 is available for download from Microsoft's Web site. I'm going to focus on the installation of Pocket Streets from the ActiveSync CD-ROM, but Pocket Streets 2001 installs in much the same way.

To begin installing Pocket Streets from the ActiveSync CD-ROM, you first need to connect your device to the desktop PC via a cradle or some other (serial/USB) cable connection. You'll also need to establish a connection via the ActiveSync software because ActiveSync is responsible for handling communication between the desktop PC and the device. With an ActiveSync connection established, you must navigate to the Extras\Pstreets\PocketPC folder on the ActiveSync CD-ROM using Windows Explorer on the desktop PC. You'll see a file named Setup.exe, which is the setup program for Pocket

Watch Out!
There is another compelling reason to use the newer version of Pocket Streets: The older version won't run on the Intel StrongARM processor, which is used in the Compaq iPAQ H3600 series of Pocket PCs. So, if you are an iPAQ H3600 user, you will have to use Pocket Streets 2001, and therefore one of the 2001 desktop mapping applications if you want to be able to create custom maps.

Remember
For the sake of brevity, when I refer to "Pocket Streets" without a version number throughout the remainder of the chapter, I'm referring to Pocket Streets 3.02, which ships on the ActiveSync CD-ROM.

Watch Out!
The Pocket
Streets applica-
tion must be
installed in your
device's RAM; it
cannot be
installed on a CF
storage card.
However, maps for
Pocket Streets
can be placed on
a storage card,
provided they are
located in the My
Documents folder
or a folder imme-
diately under My
Documents.

Streets. Double-click this file to launch the Pocket Streets setup program.

The first window you see after running the Pocket Streets setup program is the Welcome window, which gives the usual program installation warnings and advice. To get the setup process going, click the Next button, which will display the software license agreement for Pocket Streets. Click the Yes button to agree to this and continue on with the setup of Pocket Streets.

The User Information window comes up next. After entering your name and company name, click the Next button and then click the Yes button to confirm the registration information. From there you can alter the install directory from the Choose Destination Location window. The default destination is just fine, unless you have a specific place you want to see Pocket Streets installed. Clicking the Next button accepts the destination location and quickly installs the appropriate files on the desktop PC.

After the setup program installs Pocket Streets files to your desktop PC, the Pocket PC side of the installation takes place. This is evident by a small window that prompts to see whether you want Pocket Streets installed to the default application directory on your Pocket PC (see Figure 16.1).

Figure 16.1
The Installing
Applications win-
dow in the Pocket
Streets setup pro-
gram prompts you
to confirm the
Pocket PC appli-
cation install
directory.

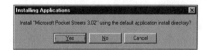

Clicking the Yes button accepts the default application install directory, which I recommend you use. At this point, the setup program begins installing files to your Pocket PC. This part of the setup process might take a couple of minutes, depending on the speed of your device's connection.

After the setup program finishes copying files, it will prompt you to make sure that additional steps aren't required on your Pocket PC; just click the OK button to go to the final step of the installation process. The last step of the process displays the Setup Complete window, which includes a check box that allows you to view the Read Me file for Pocket Streets upon completing the installation. I encourage you to accept this setting and read the file, because it might contain late-breaking information regarding Pocket Streets. Click the Finish button to complete the setup of Pocket Streets and view the Read Me file. Pocket Streets is now installed and ready to use on your Pocket PC.

Obtaining Maps for Pocket Streets

With Pocket Streets installed to your device, you're probably ready to get started viewing and working with maps. Unfortunately, the Pocket Streets setup program doesn't install any maps by default, so Pocket Streets has nothing to view. Because maps can take up a lot of space, it's important for you to be very selective about the maps you store on your device for use with Pocket Streets.

Obtaining maps for Pocket Streets is very straightforward, and can be done in three ways:

- Copy them from the ActiveSync CD-ROM

- Download them from the Web

- Create them using a desktop mapping application

The next few sections explain how to use each of these approaches to obtain maps for Pocket Streets.

Copying Maps from the ActiveSync CD-ROM

The quickest way to get started with maps in Pocket Streets is to just copy them off the ActiveSync CD-ROM. The CD-ROM includes maps for several, but not all, U.S. cities. Following are the cities for which maps are included on the ActiveSync CD-ROM:

- Atlanta

- Boston

- Chicago

- Houston

- Las Vegas

- Los Angeles

- Miami

- New York

- Philadelphia

- Phoenix

- San Francisco

- Seattle

- Washington D.C.

Watch Out!
Pocket Streets maps with the .mps file extension are usable only within Pocket Streets, and therefore aren't capable of being viewed in a desktop mapping application such as Microsoft Streets & Trips. However, several popular desktop mapping applications, including Microsoft Streets & Trips, are capable of generating .mps maps for use in Pocket Streets.

If you are interested in viewing a map for one of these cities, open the Extras\PStreets\Maps folder on the ActiveSync CD-ROM. You'll see several files with the .mps file extension, which indicates the file contains maps for use with Pocket Streets. The filenames should be obvious in identifying the city whose map they contain. Use ActiveSync to copy the map files you want to use to your device, making sure to place the files in the My Documents folder.

After you've copied maps to your device, you can start viewing them with Pocket Streets. We'll get into the specifics of that a little later in the chapter in the section titled "Using Pocket Streets." For now, let's move on to learning how to download maps from the Web.

Downloading Maps from the Web

The maps included on the ActiveSync CD-ROM only work with the version of Pocket Streets included on the CD-ROM. If you are using Pocket Streets 2001, then you can't use those maps. Another option for you is to download maps from Microsoft's Pocket Streets Web site at `http://www.microsoft.com/pocketpc/downloads/streets.asp` (shown in Figure 16.2). To download a map from Microsoft's Pocket Streets Web site, just click the link to the appropriate city on the page.

After clicking the link, follow your Web browser's directions for saving the map file to your hard disk. After the map file finishes downloading, use ActiveSync to copy the file from your desktop hard disk to the My Documents folder of your Pocket PC. The map is now ready to be viewed in Pocket Streets 2001.

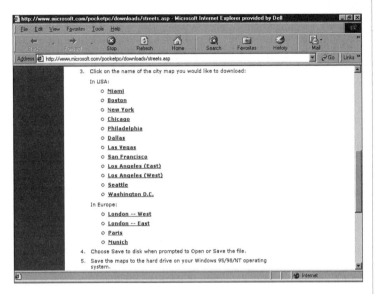

Figure 16.2
Microsoft's Pocket Streets Web site allows you to download individual city maps for Pocket Streets 2001.

Shortcut
You can also copy maps to your Pocket PC by placing them in the synchronized files folder of your desktop PC (assuming that you've set one up), in which case, ActiveSync will automatically copy them to your device.

You can download and view as many maps as you want in this manner, just be careful not to overdo it in terms of using up precious memory. You can always keep maps on your desktop PC and copy them to your Pocket PC on an "as needed" basis.

Creating Maps Using a Desktop Mapping Application

I encourage you to use ready-made maps whenever possible, but in reality you are likely to want a map for a locale that isn't readily available on the ActiveSync CD-ROM or for download on the Web. In this situation, you must use a desktop mapping application to create custom maps for use in Pocket Streets. You learned earlier in the chapter that the application you use determines the version of Pocket Streets with which the resulting maps will be compatible. To recap, if you are using Pocket Streets 3.02 off the ActiveSync CD-ROM, you must use the 2000 edition of Streets & Trips, MapPoint, or Autoroute. If you are using Pocket Streets 2001, use the 2001 editions of these same applications.

Watch Out!
Map files must be placed in the My Documents folder of your device, or in a folder one level beneath the My Documents folder. Otherwise, Pocket Streets won't be able to find the map.

Watch Out!
The city maps available for download from the Microsoft Pocket Streets Web site are compatible only with Pocket Streets 2001.

The remainder of this section focuses on using Microsoft Streets & Trips 2000 to create maps for Pocket Streets. If you are using one of the other desktop mapping applications, the process should be very similar. Keep in mind that the focus of this chapter is on using Pocket Streets, so my intention is to cover just enough of Microsoft Streets & Trips to create maps for use with Pocket Streets. I encourage you to experiment and learn more about your desktop mapping application of choice if you so desire, but for the purposes of this chapter I'm covering only the bare essentials.

To get started, launch Streets & Trips by clicking its icon in the Start menu's Programs folder. Make sure you have the Microsoft Streets & Trips 2000 CD-ROM in the drive because it contains all the map data that is required to run the application. Streets and Trips displays a Start Screen that gives you quick access to its most useful features. Unless you have a specific street address for a place you want to map, the best way to start in Microsoft Streets & Trips 2000 is to click the binoculars button, which finds a place in the United States. Clicking this button opens the Find window.

As an example of how to find a place, let's plan a trip to visit the scenic red rocks of Sedona, Arizona. On this trip, you're staying at the Enchantment Resort, and you need to know where it's located in Sedona. Entering "Enchantment Resort" in the Find window and clicking the Find button results in a list of matches for the place. In this case, the first match is exactly what you're looking for (see Figure 16.3). Notice the small icon to the left of the item in the list of matching places. This icon indicates that the Enchantment Resort is a hotel; there are many icons used throughout Microsoft Streets & Trips 2000 to represent different kinds of places.

Clicking the OK button in the Find window results in Microsoft Streets & Trips 2000 changing the map to view the selected place. Figure 16.4 shows the Enchantment Resort selected in the center of a map of Sedona, Arizona.

Figure 16.3
The Find window comes up with a match for the place for which you are looking.

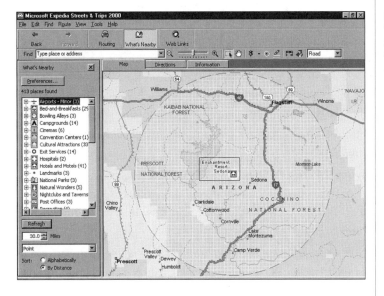

Figure 16.4
The map is zoomed and centered on the selected place.

At this point, you're ready to create a map for Pocket Streets, but it's important to select only the part of the map that you absolutely need to limit the size of the map. To do so, click the mouse and drag to create a box around the portion of the map you want to use.

After you've selected the portion of the map that you're interested in, you can right-click inside the box and select Create Map for Pocket Streets from the pop-up menu. Alternatively, you can select Create Map for Pocket Streets from the Tools menu. When you initiate the Pocket Streets map creation by issuing this command, a window is displayed that indicates the size of the resulting map (see Figure 16.5).

Figure 16.5
A window is displayed that notifies you of the size of the Pocket Streets map.

Inside Scoop
Map files exported for use with Pocket Streets have the file extension .mps. It is possible to have pushpins defined within a map, in which case an additional file is created with a file extension .psp. Pushpins are used to mark locations on a map and are covered later in this chapter.

You are given the option to confirm or reject the map at this point, because a large map would likely prove cumbersome on a Pocket PC. In this case, the map is 303KB, which is very reasonable. Clicking the OK button in this window results in your being prompted to enter a filename and location for the map on your desktop PC. This filename and location is entirely up to you. After providing a filename for the map, Microsoft Streets & Trips 2000 starts exporting the map for Pocket Streets. This can take a few minutes, depending on the size of the map.

When Microsoft Streets & Trips 2000 finishes exporting the map file, it brings up a window that clarifies the location of the map file on your desktop PC and how to use it with Pocket Streets.

Now that the map file is created, all that is left to do is copy it to your Pocket PC using ActiveSync. Keep in mind that it must be placed in the My Documents folder or a folder one level beneath My Documents for Pocket Streets to have access to it.

Using Pocket Streets

With a map or two stored away on your Pocket PC, you're ready to take Pocket Streets for a spin. To launch Pocket Streets, tap Programs in the Start menu, and then tap the Pocket Streets icon. Depending on how many maps you have on your device, Pocket Streets will start by showing a map or an Open window. In this case, Pocket Streets opens the Sedona map created in the previous section (see Figure 16.6).

Figure 16.6
The most recently displayed or down-loaded map is shown by default when you run Pocket Streets.

As you can see in the figure, the map has lost a lot of detail in the conversion from Microsoft Streets & Trips 2000 to Pocket Streets. Even so, a lot of information is still present, as you'll soon see.

Along the bottom of the screen in Pocket Streets is the menu, which is used to navigate and manipulate maps. The Tools menu contains various features for finding addresses and places, as well as managing pushpins and controlling the map view. Next to the Tools menu are two Zoom buttons, which allow you to zoom in and out of a map. If the road or location you want to see isn't fully in the window, you can use the scroll buttons (up, down, left, and right) to bring it into view.

The last icon on the menu is the pushpin icon, which allows you to create a pushpin that is used to remember a location on the map. Although you can tap anywhere on the map and create a pushpin, I usually find it better to find a place and then create a pushpin for it. To do this, tap Tools near the lower-left corner of the screen, and then tap Find Places. A screen appears that allows you to enter the name of a place to find. After entering the name of the place to find, tap OK in the upper-right corner of the screen to find matching places. Figure 16.7 shows the only match returned when trying to find the Enchantment Resort in Sedona.

After finding the place you want, tap OK in the upper-right corner for the place to be displayed on the map. Figure 16.8 shows the Enchantment Resort displayed on the map.

Remember
If you have Transcriber installed, you can use it to write the name of the place to find in Pocket Streets.

Figure 16.7
To find a place in Pocket Streets, you must first enter its name.

Figure 16.8
After you find a place, the map is automatically zoomed and scrolled to show the place.

It's a good idea to mark a place with a pushpin so you can easily find it again. Pocket Streets maintains a list of pushpins that you can use to find places after you've marked them. To convert the Enchantment Resort place into a pushpin, for example, tap the pushpin button in the menu at the bottom of the screen, and then tap the caption on the map that says "Enchantment Resort – Sedona." Figure 16.9 shows the window that appears, which allows you to customize the specifics of the pushpin.

Figure 16.9
Creating a pushpin involves entering the name of the pushpin, along with optionally providing a note and selecting a different visual symbol.

When you create a pushpin from an existing place, as in this example, the name of the pushpin will already be filled out. You have the option of accepting it or changing it to something else. You can also enter a note to go along with the pushpin. Every pushpin is represented on the map by a visual symbol, which you can change by tapping the Choose Symbol button. The default symbol for a pushpin is a yellow pushpin image, which is suitable in most cases. Ultimately, the visual appearance of a pushpin is a personal preference.

After entering information regarding the new pushpin, tap OK to create it. The pushpin symbol is then displayed along with the caption on the map where the place is located.

After a pushpin has been created, you can always use it to find a location on the map. This can be handy for finding the location of a place with respect to a zoomed-out map. For example, the Zoom Full command on the Tools menu zooms out the map as far as possible, which gives you a large view of the map. Figure 16.10 shows the Enchantment Resort pushpin as viewed with the map zoomed out.

Figure 16.10
Pushpins help you see places within the big scheme of things when a map is zoomed out.

The Tools menu contains some other interesting commands that you might find useful. One of the more interesting features of Pocket Streets is the ability to view points of interest on the map such as restaurants, hospitals, and ATMs. You can selectively enable and disable certain kinds of points of interest by tapping Points of Interest on the Tools menu. Figure 16.11 shows how the different points of interest are enabled and disabled.

Figure 16.11
Pocket Streets
allows you to
selectively view
certain types of
points of interest.

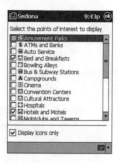

To see how powerful points of interest can be, I navigated to a different area of Sedona that is a little more commercial than the area surrounding the Enchantment Resort. Figure 16.12 shows the area surrounding the Tlaquepaque shopping village, which includes several restaurants and a hotel. Notice in the figure that the hotel (Inn On Oak Creek) is denoted by a hotel symbol, while the restaurant northwest of it is denoted by a restaurant symbol. You can view the name of a point of interest by tapping its symbol.

Figure 16.12
Points of interest
are identified on
the map with spe-
cial icons.

Inside Scoop
When several
points of interest
are too close
together for
Pocket Streets to
display their dis-
tinct symbols, a
special symbol is
displayed that
looks like three
overlapping
boxes. If you
zoom in further,
you will be able to
see the individual
symbols.

If a map is getting cluttered by pushpins and points of interest, you can disable them by tapping Display Pushpins or Display Points of Interest in the Tools menu.

If you have several maps stored on your Pocket PC, you'll need to use the Maps submenu of the Tools menu to access them. There are also some other commands for working with maps in this menu. The Open Map command is used to open a map stored on your Pocket PC; this command displays a window from which you can browse for a particular map file. The Copy Map command copies the current map view so that it can be pasted into other Pocket PC applications such as Notes or Pocket Word.

The last command on the Map submenu is the Map Styles command, which allows you to alter the background color of the map (light or dark), as well as the street detail (less detail or full detail). The default settings are Light Background and Less Street Detail, which are acceptable. If you don't mind the map updating a little slower, the Full Street Detail setting is nice because it shows much more detail when zoomed out on a map. Figure 16.13 shows how the Full Street Detail setting adds more interest to the zoomed-out Sedona map.

Figure 16.13
The Full Street Detail setting adds much more interest to maps when zoomed out, although it does result in them updating a little slower.

Global Positioning and Pocket Streets

A relatively new topic related to Pocket Streets is the capability of using it with a GPS (Global Positioning System) receiver to pinpoint your location on a map. Imagine a pushpin that tracks your position on a map as you travel and you can easily understand the power of coupling Pocket Streets with a GPS receiver. A GPS receiver communicates with satellites in orbit and provides positional data. Using the data provided by these satellites, a GPS receiver can determine its exact location, direction, and speed.

Several hardware manufacturers have CF GPS cards in the works, which will plug into your Pocket PC's CF port. Casio has a very compact GPS card that is due for imminent release as of this writing. I fully expect GPS cards to change the way Pocket PCs are perceived by many users, because it will open up the usage of Pocket PCs to many new and interesting applications.

Essential Information

- There are several applications that can be used to create custom maps for Pocket Streets.

- The version of Pocket Streets on the ActiveSync CD-ROM (version 3.02) won't run on the Intel StrongARM processor, which is used in the Compaq iPAQ H3600 series of Pocket PCs; if you are an iPAQ H3600 user, you must use Pocket Streets 2001.

- Several maps are included on the ActiveSync CD-ROM, while others can be obtained by downloading them from Microsoft's Pocket Streets Web site.

- Custom maps are selected for export in Microsoft Streets & Trips 2000 by clicking and dragging the mouse over the desired area of the map.

- Pocket Streets allows you to mark locations on a map with pushpins for easy reference.

- Special symbols are used on Pocket Streets maps to identify points of interest such as restaurants, hotels, and hospitals.

- Global positioning is a technology likely to create unique, real-world applications for Pocket PCs when used in conjunction with Pocket Streets.

Pocket PC: The Multimedia Entertainer

PART V

GET THE SCOOP ON...

Using the Pocket PC As a Portable Music Player ▪ Working with Digital Audio Files ▪ Using Windows Media Player to Organize and Play Digital Music ▪ Customizing the Look of Windows Media Player with Skins ▪ Controlling Windows Media Player with Custom Mapped Hardware Buttons

Fun with the Windows Media Player

Chapter 17

I N ADDITION TO BEING VERY CAPABLE productivity tools, Pocket PCs are also surprisingly effective as entertainment devices. One of the most exciting features of Pocket PCs that arouses interest in even the most die-hard PDA purists is its support for playing digital music. With music available in digital form, you can move it around just like any other file on your computer, and then listen to it on your Pocket PC using the Windows Media Player. Windows Media Player, with its support of several digital music formats, effectively turns a Pocket PC into a high-tech Walkman, which adds significantly to its allure as a mobile computing device. As practical as it is to edit Word documents, check your email, and enter financial transactions, kicking back and listening to music is a luxury many of us appreciate while traveling.

Before getting into the specifics of the Windows Media Player and how it works, it's worth mentioning that we are in the midst of a radical shift in terms of how music is purchased and managed. Now that music can be downloaded and copied just as any other binary file, there is a huge debate over copyright issues and how digital music should be distributed. Throughout the chapter, I try hard to just present the facts and steer clear of my own personal opinions on the subject; just keep in mind that digital music is still a new technology whose distribution model is still evolving.

Pocket PC: The Ultimate Walkman

The Pocket PC operating system includes the Windows Media Player, which is specifically designed for playing digital music. The Media Player allows you to use your Pocket PC as a digital Walkman that is capable of playing music stored in digital form. Windows Media Player supports similar functions to a traditional compact disc player such as Play, Stop, Pause, Next Track, Previous Track, Shuffle, and Repeat, not to mention volume control. You interact with these controls via the Windows Media Player software user interface, which resembles the front panel on a high-end stereo system. You can also customize the look and placement of the controls to suit your own tastes.

Inside Scoop
The speaker on most Pocket PCs isn't quite adequate for playing high-quality audio, so you might want to use a pair of headphones if you're serious about your music.

To use Windows Media Player as a digital Walkman, you must first download digital music files into your Pocket PC. You can also store digital music on CF storage cards, in which case you can insert a card to have the music available to Windows Media Player. You then have the option of playing the music through the standard Pocket PC speaker, or plugging headphones into the headphone jack. Windows Media Player makes it easy to listen to digital music using your Pocket PC. Except for the rugged construction of some traditional portable audio players, you're quite likely to find yourself using Windows Media Player and your Pocket PC as the primary means of listening to music on the go.

Unlike a traditional Walkman, Windows Media Player is designed to support the playback of audio in several different digital audio formats. I use the word "audio" instead of "music" because you can also use Windows Media Player to listen to sampled audio and voice recordings. Following are the types of digital audio formats supported by Windows Media Player:

- **MP3**—MPEG Audio Layer 3.

- **WAV**—Waveform.

- **WMA**—Windows Media Audio.

- **ASF**—Advanced Streaming Format.

You are probably familiar with the first two types of digital audio. MP3 files have been greatly popularized as the standard format for digital music, and form the basis of popular music-sharing applications such as Napster. MP3 is also the format used in Walkman-style digital audio (MP3) players such as the Creative Labs Nomad players and Diamond Multimedia's RIO players. The popularity of MP3 is largely based upon the fact that it compresses audio into more manageable file sizes than prior digital audio formats such as WAV. When referring to the Pocket PC's capability to play digital music, you will often hear people refer to it as an "MP3 player," because MP3 is the digital music format with which most people are familiar.

The WAV format is a digital audio format that has been around for a while, and is known more for sampling sounds than for storing music. WAV is the standard audio format used in the Windows operating system. For example, all the Windows system sounds you hear while working within Windows are actually WAV sounds. The WAV format doesn't employ any type of compression to optimize file size, and therefore is not very efficient at storing audio. Nevertheless, it is still used a lot and is a convenient format for sharing sampled audio such as voice recordings.

WMA is a relatively new audio format created by Microsoft that is intended to provide a more efficient alternative to MP3. WMA uses a different compression scheme to further whittle down the size of digital audio files. Although MP3 is currently the industry standard for storing digital music, WMA will likely grow in popularity as users realize the benefits of its improved compression.

ASF is a multimedia format that is designed to support streaming multimedia, which typically involves a media object being transmitted over a network connection such as the Internet. The ASF format is particularly useful for listening to music or watching videos over an Internet connection, in which case the

Inside Scoop
Napster is an extremely popular and controversial desktop application that allows people to share MP3 music files with each other over the Internet. As of this writing, Napster is involved in a messy lawsuit with the Recording Industry Association of America (RIAA) regarding the legality of enabling people to share copyrighted music over the Internet. The outcome of this lawsuit will likely have significant ramifications in terms of deciding the future of digital music distribution.

Watch Out!
Unlike the MP3 audio format, the WMA format supports the Secure Digital Music Initiative (SDMI) and Digital Rights Management (DRM), both of which require you to have an electronic license to listen to an audio file. DRM is designed to prevent the piracy of copyrighted audio. If you obtain audio in the WMA format and are having trouble getting it to play, you might not have obtained a proper license for it. You learn how to play licensed audio in the next section of this chapter, "Managing Digital Audio."

streaming benefits are very apparent. The streaming support in ASF allows music or video to begin playing before the entire file is transferred. This is a very important feature for audio and video that is played over the Internet, as it typically takes a little while for the relatively large files to transfer. In terms of the Windows Media Player, the ASF format is similar to MP3 and WMA in that it compresses audio to help optimize file size. The streaming benefits of ASF don't really come into play with the Windows Media Player, and you are less likely to encounter audio in ASF format unless you are playing it directly from a Web site.

By supporting several different audio formats, the Windows Media Player is kind of like a Walkman that can play 8-track tapes, cassettes, CDs, and mini-discs. Because no such Walkman exists in the real world, you can see why I've referred to the Pocket PC with Windows Media Player as the "ultimate Walkman." Before getting into the details of how to use it, however, it's worth taking a moment to learn how to manage digital audio.

Managing Digital Audio

When it comes to managing digital audio for use with Windows Media Player, it is very important to distinguish between audio that is licensed and audio that isn't licensed. Currently, the MP3 audio format does not support licensed audio, which means that you can play any MP3 file after you've successfully obtained it. Of course, I'm speaking in technical terms not legal terms. Legally, you are required to obtain a license for copyrighted audio, which includes virtually all commercial music. When you purchase a music CD, you automatically obtain a license to listen to it, and can make copies for your own personal use. So, it's okay for you to create MP3 files from your own CDs. However, you start to enter murky waters legally when you download MP3 files through an application such as Napster, which allows people to freely share MP3 files with each other. The legal implications of sharing copyrighted music are being hashed out in court as I write this, so it's up to you to decide how to make use of MP3 files in terms of the legality of copying them.

The WMA audio format supports licensed music, which requires you to obtain an electronic license before being able to listen to the music. Not surprisingly, unlocking the electronic license takes a few extra steps toward making licensed music available to Windows Media Player. The concept of licensed digital music is fairly new, and hasn't exactly caught on as a viable alternative to MP3. However, as the legal battles surrounding MP3 begin to shake out, it's quite likely we'll see licensed music gain momentum. You learn how to purchase and install licensed music later in the chapter in the section titled "Working with Licensed Music." Fortunately, the steps required to unlock a licensed piece of music are very straightforward.

$\rightarrow$ **See Also** "Working with Licensed Music," **p. 284**.

Regardless of whether you are dealing with unlicensed or licensed music, there is a desktop application that can help you manage digital music and the task of sharing it with your Pocket PC. I'm referring to Windows Media Manager, which is included on the ActiveSync CD-ROM that came with your Pocket PC. Windows Media Manager is primarily designed to help you move audio files back and forth between your desktop PC and Pocket PC. One of the significant features of Windows Media Manager is its support for packaged content, which is a term used to describe licensed audio files. Packaged content is encrypted so that it can't be played without first obtaining a license.

Windows Media Manager is located on the ActiveSync CD-ROM that ships with all Pocket PCs. To install Windows Media Manager, navigate to the Extras\Media folder and execute the setup program named wmmsetup.exe. After running the setup program, the first window you'll see is the usual installation Welcome window. To get started with the setup process, click the Next button, which displays the Installation Directory window that allows you to choose where on your hard disk to install the Windows Media Manager. The default installation directory is suitable unless you have a specific place you want Windows Media Manager to be installed. Clicking the Finish button accepts the installation directory and allows the setup program to begin copying files. Before the actual file copying takes place, however, you must confirm the creation of the installation directory in which the application is placed. After clicking the OK button, the setup program begins copying files.

When finished, the setup Complete window appears, allowing you to click OK once more to return to the desktop. You should read the Read Me file that is displayed after installing Windows Media Manager, as it contains late-breaking information about the application that might impact how you use it.

Working with Unlicensed Music

The simplest way to use Windows Media Manager is to share MP3 music files with your Pocket PC. Because the MP3 audio format doesn't support any type of licensing, placing an MP3 file on your Pocket PC is as simple as copying it to a folder on your Pocket PC using Windows Media Manager. The process is a little more involved with licensed WMA files (packaged content), as you learn a little later in the chapter.

Undocumented
If a CF storage card is present in your device, Windows Media Manager automatically navigates to the My Documents on it. If there is no My Documents folder on the CF card, Windows Media Manager creates one. If you have no CF storage card installed, Windows Media Manager navigates to the My Documents folder in main system RAM.

Before running Windows Media Manager, you must connect your device to the desktop PC via a cradle or some other (serial/USB) cable connection. To begin launching Windows Media Manager, click Start, Programs, Windows Media and then Windows Media Manager. Figure 17.1 shows Windows Media Manager upon being launched.

As you can see in the figure, Windows Media Manager includes two views: a desktop PC folder and a Pocket PC folder. You are capable of copying audio files from the desktop PC folder to the Pocket PC folder, as well as deleting files from the Pocket PC folder. Windows Media Manager automatically navigates to the My Documents folder on your Pocket PC; if you have a CF storage card installed, Windows Media Manager navigates to its My Documents folder. You can click the combo box to change the folder in which you want files placed on your Pocket PC.

However, keep in mind that Windows Media Player recognizes only audio files stored in or one level beneath the My Documents folder.

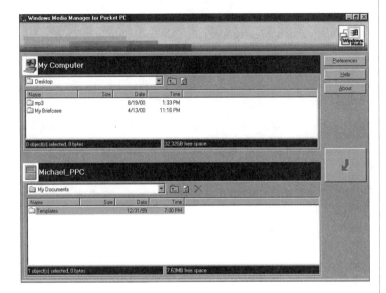

Figure 17.1
Upon first being launched, Windows Media Manager shows the Desktop folder on your desktop PC and the My Documents older on your Pocket PC.

To transfer music files from your desktop PC to your Pocket PC, you must navigate to the folder on your desktop PC where you keep your media files. Figure 17.2 shows Window Media Manager with the desktop PC folder changed to one of the subfolders where I keep music on my computer. Also notice in the figure that the Pocket PC folder has been changed to the My Documents folder in main system RAM, as opposed to the My Documents folder on the CF storage card. This was necessary because my CF storage card, in this case, didn't have enough room for music; free space on both your computer and Pocket PC is shown below the file list for each section.

After you've located and selected the audio file or files that you want to transfer to your Pocket PC, just click the large button on the right side of the Windows Media Manager screen to transfer the file. You can also drag and drop the file from the desktop PC folder to the Pocket PC folder in Windows Media Manager. Windows Media Manager begins copying the file, and displays a progress bar to indicate the status of the transfer.

Figure 17.2
The desktop PC folder is changed to a folder that contains MP3 music files, whereas the Pocket PC folder is changed to the My Documents folder in main system RAM.

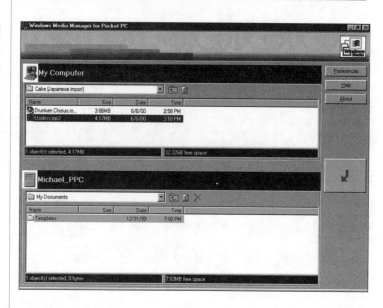

In the case of a non-WMA file format such as MP3, the Windows Media Manager actually converts these files to WMA before copying. Because Pocket PCs are capable of playing files such as MP3, you might be wondering why this conversion takes place. The reason Windows Media Manager uses the WMA audio format is because it generally increases file efficiency, not to mention support for licensed audio files. So, when an MP3 file is transferred to a Pocket PC using Windows Media Manager, the file is automatically converted to the WMA format while being copied. The benefit for you is a significant reduction in file size in many cases, as evident in Figure 17.3.

This size of the file in this example went from 4.17MB as an MP3 to 2.12MB in WMA. The degree to which Windows Media Manager reduces the file size is determined by the quality of the resulting WMA file. You can modify the quality of WMA files by clicking the Preferences button in Windows Media Manager, which displays the Preferences window shown in Figure 17.4.

The default WMA encoding format is "64kps, 44kHz, Stereo," which is a good trade-off between quality and storage space. Windows Media Manager recommends this setting for converting 128Kbps MP3 files, which is the format of most MP3 files. You can reduce the WMA quality to "32kps, 22kHz, Stereo" to save on space, but I wouldn't recommend doing so for music files. You can also increase the WMA quality to "128kps, 44kHz, Stereo" for better quality, but don't expect to see any file size savings versus MP3.

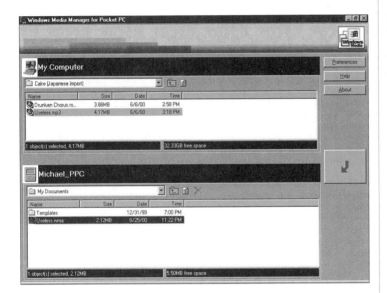

Figure 17.3
The conversion of MP3 files to the WMA audio format can result in a significant reduction of file size.

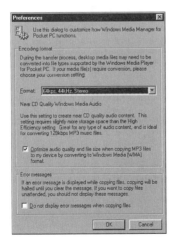

Figure 17.4
The Windows Media Manager Preferences window is used to change the quality of WMA files, among other things.

Working with Licensed Music

Licensed music is copyrighted music that is distributed in a locked form, and requires an electronic license to be unlocked and played. Prior to being unlocked, licensed music is encrypted so you can't listen to it. When you purchase licensed music, you are actually purchasing a license to listen to the music. The licensing aspect of licensed music is involved only when you first purchase the music. You must use the license to unlock the music file, after which you can listen to the music as much as you want without ever having to hassle with the license again. After you've gone through the licensing process, working with licensed music is no different from working with unlicensed music.

To demonstrate how to download and unlock a licensed music file using an electronic license, I purchased a song from MusicMaker.com, a Web site that allows you to buy individual songs for creating custom CDs or just for download. In this case, I used the download feature of MusicMaker.com. The song I purchased is "Bird of Paradise" by Charlie Parker and Miles Davis.

The cost of the song in this case was $1.00, which is very reasonable for an individual song given the cost of most complete CDs. Songs are priced differently, but most of them currently fall within the $1.00 to $2.00 range. Payment is handled in a manner that is very similar to other online shopping sites. After paying for the music, MusicMaker.com displays a link from which you can download the songs you selected. The songs are then transferred to your hard disk, but they are still locked because you haven't applied an electronic license.

Watch Out!
If your desktop audio player doesn't support electronic rights management, then you won't be able to play licensed music with it.

If your desktop audio player supports electronic rights management (SDMI or DRM), then you will be prompted to unlock the file before being allowed to play it. When using the desktop Windows Media Player application to attempt to play a locked song, it will transfer you to the site holding the license. In the case of my newly purchased file, the Windows Media Player sent me to the MusicMaker.com Web site.

Because MusicMaker.com uses email addresses as IDs for storing electronic licenses, you are required to enter your email address and click a button. At this point, the electronic license is automatically accessed, verified, and used to unlock the music file. The resulting Web page informs you that your file is now unlocked.

At this point, you have an unlocked WMA music file that is ready to be played. From here on, the file can be treated as if it were an unlicensed music file, at least in terms of playing it and transferring it to your Pocket PC. In other words, the music file is unlocked and ready for use on your desktop PC and your Pocket PC by virtue of the license. However, you can't email the file to a friend and have them be able to listen to it because it hasn't been unlocked on their machine; they don't have the license for it. You can use Windows Media Manager to transfer the file to your Pocket PC just as you learned how to do with unlicensed audio files.

Using Windows Media Player

Windows Media Player is a standard Pocket PC application that is built into system ROM. It has a user interface that should be familiar to anyone who has used a CD player. To run Windows Media Player, tap Windows Media in the Start menu. If you've placed any audio files in the My Documents folder, one of them will appear as the currently selected track in Windows Media Player upon it being launched. Figure 17.5 shows the song, "Bird of Paradise" as the selected track in Windows Media Player.

Figure 17.5
The Windows Media Player user interface has a feel very reminiscent of a CD player.

The user interface in Windows Media Player consists of the name of the currently selected track near the top of the screen. Below that is the name of the current playlist, followed by a timeline of the current track as it is being played. You can tap and hold the circular control on this timeline and drag it to move around within a track. The buttons in the center of the screen perform familiar media control functions such as Play, Pause, Stop, Next Track, Previous Track, Shuffle, and Repeat. Below these buttons is a sliding volume control, as well as a speaker icon that allows you to mute the audio output entirely.

The Tools menu includes a Track Info command that allows you to view additional information about the currently selected track. This results in the display of the Track Information window, which is shown in Figure 17.6. The Options command on the Tools menu allows you to assign hardware buttons to Windows Media Player, which is covered in "Customizing the Hardware Buttons" later in this chapter.

Figure 17.6
The Track Information window displays additional information about the currently selected audio track.

The Playlist command that appears next to the Tools menu displays the Windows Media Player Playlist, which is a listing of the tracks that are currently queued for play (see Figure 17.7). You can create multiple playlists that include different songs arranged in a specific order. The default playlist is "All My Music," which includes all the songs stored on your device, regardless of in which folders they are located.

You add a new playlist by tapping the name of the current playlist and then tapping New Playlist from the menu that appears. You also use this menu to choose between playlists when you have more than one. There is a toolbar along the bottom of the Playlist screen that allows you to manipulate tracks in the list. The Add Tracks button (plus sign) is used to add tracks to the currently selected playlist, while the Remove Tracks button (red X) is used to remove tracks from the list. The Move buttons, which are represented by up- and down arrows, are used to move tracks up and down to change the order of the playlist. Finally, the Play button is used to play the currently selected track.

Figure 17.7
The Playlist screen in Windows Media Player displays the currently active playlist, which is "All My Music" by default.

A playlist is really nothing more than a list of songs, but they are not actually the song file. Although a song must be on your device in order to reside in a playlist, there is no intrinsic connection between a playlist and the songs that are stored on your device. If you want to play all the songs on your device, just select "All My Music" as the playlist.

Personalizing Windows Media Player

Like most Pocket PC applications, Windows Media Player can be customized to some degree. One customization technique allows you to alter the look and feel of the user interface. This is accomplished through special graphical looks called skins. Windows Media Player skins are roughly similar to the schemes that are used to alter the look of the Windows desktop. However, skins go a bit further by actually altering the number and positions of buttons in the Windows Media Player user interface.

Another customization technique for Windows Media Player involves assigning functions to your device's hardware buttons. For example, you might assign the Play and Pause functions to

Inside Scoop
The Playlist automatically updates whenever you add new music to your device. This includes plugging in a CF storage card that has music stored on it—the music on the CF card is combined with the music already stored on the device.

Watch Out!
If you delete a song from your device while it is part of a playlist, the playlist will become inaccessible. The only way to fix the playlist is to copy the song back to the device. The easy way around this problem is to always remove songs from any playlists before deleting them from the device.

Inside Scoop
As of this writing, Microsoft is offering a free Pocket PC Fun Pack, which is a 4MB CF memory card loaded with goodies. The Skin Chooser application is included in the Fun Pack, along with several skins. This saves you the trouble of having to download the Skin Chooser. If you don't have the Fun Pack, I highly recommend ordering it from http://orders.one.microsoft.com/pocketpc.

the up and down motion of the Action button. These button mappings apply as long as Windows Media Player is active in memory.

The next couple of sections explore Windows Media Player customization using both skins and hardware button mapping.

Beauty Is Skin Deep

Skins are special graphical "looks" that can be applied to Windows Media Player to give it a different look and feel. Skins are a great way to personalize your Pocket PC, and are freely available for download from Microsoft's Windows Media Web site. Before downloading a skin, however, you must download and install the Pocket PC Skin Chooser, which is an application that allows you to choose between the skins that you've installed on your device. To download the appropriate Skin Chooser application for your device, visit the Install Skins page at the Windows Media Web site, which is located at http://www.microsoft.com/windows/windowsmedia/en/software/players/Install.asp. This page includes versions of the Skin Chooser application that are designed for use with each of the major Pocket PC processors.

After downloading the Skin Chooser application to your desktop PC, you must copy it to your device to use it. The best place to store the application is in the Start menu, which makes it readily accessible. To store the application in the Start menu, use the Explore feature in ActiveSync to navigate to the Windows\Start Menu folder on your device, and then copy the Skin Chooser executable file (skin chooser.exe) to it. With the Skin Chooser application in place, you can start downloading skins.

A skin consists of a group of bitmap files and a text file with an .skn file extension that includes organizational information about the skin. Because skins consist of multiple files that are named similarly, you should place each skin in its own folder to keep them separated. You can download skins from Microsoft's Download Skins Web page at http://www.microsoft.com/windows/windowsmedia/en/software/players/Skins.asp. Each skin is packaged in a self-extracting Zip file. When you extract a skin, allow it to unzip to the folder it suggests because you will copy this entire folder directly to your Pocket PC. The folder will be placed in one of two places: your desktop PC's Windows folder or a new folder on your desktop PC called skins. It is an unfortunate inconsistency that there isn't one standard folder to which all skins are unzipped, so remember to pay close attention to where the Zip self-extractor places the files.

To install a skin on your Pocket PC, copy the skin folder from your desktop PC to the Windows Media Player folder on your device; this folder is named Program Files\Windows Media Player. To copy the skin folder, you can use the Explore feature in ActiveSync to navigate to the Windows Media Player folder, and then copy the skin folder over from your desktop PC. After the skin folder is copied, you can begin using the Skin Chooser to select a new skin. Figure 17.8 shows the Skin Chooser in action.

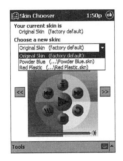

Figure 17.8
The Skin Chooser application allows you to choose a skin from the skins that you've installed.

After selecting a new skin, the look of Windows Media Player immediately changes to reflect the newly selected skin. Figure 17.9 shows how the Powder Blue skin impacts the look of Windows Media Player.

As you can see, skins not only change the graphical look of Windows Media Player, but also the size and location of the buttons and track information. Some skins have an overly simplified look and feel, which might not seem appealing at first. Figure 17.10 shows the Red Plastic skin, which is a good example of a skin with a very simple look.

Figure 17.9
The Powder Blue
skin dramatically
changes the look
of Windows Media
Player.

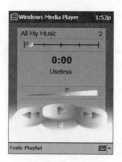

Figure 17.10
The Red Plastic
skin is very clean
and simple, but
the buttons are
big enough that
you can use your
fingers instead of
the stylus.

Although the Red Plastic skin is certainly very simple, one advantage it has is that the buttons are so large you can push them with your fingers and forgo using the stylus. This might not seem like a big deal, but keep in mind that Windows Media Player is attempting to make Pocket PCs as intuitive and easy to use as traditional Walkmans. Alleviating the need for a stylus is one way of accomplishing this goal.

There is one caveat worth mentioning in regard to skins and Windows Media Player that involves storing skins on CF storage cards. It is possible to store a skin on a CF storage card and have it work with Windows Media Player. However, if you ever remove the card, Windows Media Player will mysteriously stop working with no warning. This is somewhat of a bug in Windows Media Player because it should either complain about the missing skin or automatically revert to the default skin. Unfortunately, it does neither of these things. Instead, it will flash on the screen briefly and disappear, which is very annoying.

The way to avoid this problem with Windows Media Player is to not install skins on a CF storage card. It's worth noting that this is mainly a problem with Microsoft's Pocket PC Fun Pack CF storage card, because it gives you the option of installing skins in main RAM or leaving them on the card. I strongly recommend you always install skins to main system RAM so that you don't forget and remove the card, only to find that Windows Media Player has stopped working. If you do get into trouble, you can easily fix the problem (with or without inserting the CF storage card) by selecting the default skin using the Skin Chooser application.

Customizing Hardware Buttons

Another neat Windows Media Player customization is mapping hardware buttons to Windows Media Player functions. You perform this mapping by tapping Options in the Tools menu of Windows Media Player. This displays the Options window, which is shown in Figure 17.11.

Figure 17.11
The Options window allows you to map Windows Media Player functions to Pocket PC hardware buttons.

The figure shows the different hardware buttons and combinations to which you can associate Windows Media Player functions. Following are the functions available for the associations:

- Play

- Pause

- Stop

- Next Track

- Previous Track

- Mute

- Volume Up

- Volume Down

- Screen Toggle

Inside Scoop
Devicewide button mappings are handled by tapping Settings in the Start menu, and then tapping the Buttons icon. Button mappings made on this screen apply to the entire system, not just a specific application. However, button mappings created within a specific application, such as Windows Media Player, will override the systemwide mappings as long as the application is in memory. After the application closes, the mappings return to their normal functions.

To map a function to a button, select the function in the drop-down list and then press the desired button on the device. The Button Mapping list in the Options window will reflect the mapping. To unmap a button, tap and hold over the button in the list and then tap Unmap this button.

Button mappings are very personal and will likely vary a great deal among different people. A few mappings I suggest are to map the Volume Up and Volume Down functions to the Up and Down buttons, which correspond to rotating the Action button up and down. One other useful mapping is to map the Screen Toggle function with the Action button. The Screen Toggle function turns off your device's screen, which helps conserve battery life. After all, you don't necessarily need the screen on while you're listening to music.

Essential Information

- Windows Media Player gives Pocket PCs the functionality of a traditional compact disc player by supporting familiar functions such as Play, Stop, Pause, Next Track, Previous Track, Shuffle, and Repeat.

- Windows Media Player supports the popular MP3 digital music format, which has been popularized by controversial music-sharing applications such as Napster.

- The WMA audio format provides better compression than MP3, and also supports licensed music, which requires users to purchase an electronic license to play a downloaded song.

- Windows Media Manager is a desktop application that simplifies the task of transferring digital audio files from a desktop PC to a Pocket PC.

- Playlists are used in Windows Media Player to organize songs for playback.

- Skins are special graphical "looks" that are used to alter the look and feel of Windows Media Player.

- The hardware buttons on your device can be customized to control individual functions in Windows Media Player.

GET THE SCOOP ON...

■ Using Your Pocket PC As a Portable Library ■ Purchasing and Downloading eBooks ■ Reading eBooks Using the Microsoft Reader Application ■ Customizing the Microsoft Reader Application ■ Creating Your Own eBooks ■ Listing to Audible eBooks

Reading eBooks with Reader

Chapter 18

W HEN I FIRST HEARD THAT MICROSOFT was incorporating an eBook technology into Pocket PC, I thought it sounded like an interesting idea. It's a natural fit because a lot of people like to carry books around with them and read when they have spare time. Even though I thought it was a good idea, I never anticipated how dependent I would become on my Pocket PC as an electronic reader. Because most users like to keep their Pocket PC close when out and about, you might find that you actually end up doing a lot more reading because it's so easy to keep plenty of reading material on the device ready to go. Obviously, you can't replace the feel of a physical book, but I have to admit that being able to carry around several books and other articles on a Pocket PC helps offset the comfortable familiarity of flipping real pages.

This chapter introduces you to the Microsoft Reader application, and the underlying ClearType technology that makes text on the screen look more like printed text. ClearType represents a huge step forward in making it possible to use computers and mobile devices as replacements for printed material. Microsoft Reader for the Pocket PC uses ClearType, and provides yet another killer Pocket PC application that, once familiar with, you will likely use on a regular basis to read books, magazine articles, and other text-based content.

Pocket PC: The Ultimate Library Card

It's been a while since I used a library card, but when you think about it, a library card is pretty powerful. On a small card that you can fit in your wallet or purse, you have access to hundreds of thousands of books. Everyone is amazed by the capacity of CD-ROMs and DVDs, but we've always had access to tons of information via our library cards. Admittedly, it takes more effort to go check out a book than to search a CD-ROM, but the point is that often a lot of useful information gets overlooked because the methods for getting it are becoming antiquated.

Watch Out!
Before I get too carried away with the library card analogy, let me clarify that no libraries are supporting Reader as of this writing. In other words, you can't yet carry your Pocket PC into a library and download eBooks. Currently, you must download or purchase eBooks from online retailers to use them with Reader. The potential, however, is there for eBook resources to become much more established and eventually rival the convenience and availability of printed books.

Now imagine a library card that not only allows you easy access to an information source as vast as a library, but also stores the books themselves and provides an interface for reading them. Although the medium is still in its infancy, the Microsoft Reader application for Pocket PC provides this functionality in that it allows you to store and read books on your Pocket PC. Admittedly, even the smallest Pocket PC is somewhat larger than a library card, but then it's also much smaller than most books.

The idea of reading books on computers is nothing new. However, as anyone who uses computers regularly can attest, for some reason it takes longer to read text on the screen than it does to read printed text. My profession dictates that I read a lot of technical documentation that is typically in electronic form, so I have a real appreciation of the difference between reading screen text versus printed text. Even so, the benefits of electronic publishing are huge: No more printing means information can be made available much faster, and less printing overhead means a savings for consumers. Both publishers and readers benefit from the move to electronic publishing; the significant blocks have been the difficulty in matching screen typography with that of the printed page and the more practical issue of making eBooks as rugged and convenient as printed books.

Microsoft researchers have been trying to figure out the exact reasons why the typography in books is ideal for reading. We often take them for granted, but the physical structure of books along with the typography used for the text has evolved over several centuries. Microsoft engineers developed a technology called ClearType that draws upon the superior typography of books to provide an immersive reading experience for computers. This technology is used by Microsoft Reader, and results in a book-style interface that is simple yet elegantly useful. Although, ultimately, Reader's success is measured by how little you notice that it is a software application imitating a book, there are clearly still many hurdles to leap before people start clearing out their bookshelves.

Even if you're sold on the technical merits of Microsoft Reader, the availability of eBooks is another factor to consider before proclaiming success or failure. It is true that we are witnessing an industry shift, and we are very much at the beginning of this shift. It might still be a while before you can go searching for any book you want on Amazon.com and download an eBook version of it. However, many new books are being released in both print and eBook form. Also, the push by some prominent authors such as Stephen King to explore new electronic distribution methods will certainly spur on the shift toward electronic book publishing. Stephen King's *The Plant* is a story being offered directly from his Web site in separate parts that cost $1 to $2 each. The Plant is very much an example of experimental book distribution that is testing the waters to see whether authors can go directly to their readers.

For a slightly more traditional approach to acquiring eBooks, take a stroll through the eBooks section of the Barnes and Noble Web site at `http://ebooks.barnesandnoble.com`. A large selection of eBooks is already available, with more on the way. There are also some special offers for Pocket PC users on the Barnes and Noble site that allow you to download several eBooks for free. The next section clues you in on how to take advantage of these offers.

Obtaining and Managing eBooks

The availability of eBooks is obviously critical to the success of Microsoft Reader and the Pocket PC's usage as an electronic reading device. You might not have realized this when purchasing your Pocket PC, but every device comes with enough eBooks to keep you busy for quite some time. More specifically, two fairy tales (*The Emperor's New Clothes* and *The Little Match Girl*) are preinstalled on every Pocket PC. If fairy tales aren't your thing, check out the eBooks that are included on the ActiveSync CD-ROM that accompanies every Pocket PC. Following are these eBooks:

- *Little Women* - Louisa May Alcott
- *Peter Pan* - J. M. Barrie
- *Wonderful Wizard of OZ* - L. Frank Baum
- *Kai Lung's Golden Hours* - Ernest Bramah
- *Wuthering Heights* - Emily Bronte
- *Secret Garden* - Francis Hodgson Burnett
- *Tarzan of the Apes* - Edgar Rice Burroughs
- *Alice's Adventures in Wonderland* - Lewis Carroll
- *Innocence of Father Brown* - G. K. Chesterton
- *Great Expectations* - Charles Dickens
- *My Bondage and My Freedom* - Frederick Douglass
- *Study in Scarlet* - Arthur Conan Doyle
- *Wind in the Willows* - Kenneth Graham
- *Riders of the Purple Sage* - Zane Grey
- *Legend of Sleepy Hollow* - Washington Irving
- *Three Men in a Boat* - Jerome K. Jerome
- *Call of the Wild* - Jack London
- *Light Princess* - George MacDonald
- *The Prince* - Machiavelli

- *Extraordinary Popular Delusions and the Madness of Crowds* - Charles McKay

- *Fall of the House of Usher* - Edgar Allan Poe

- *Captain Blood* - Raphael Sabatini

- *Unbearable Bassington* - Saki (H. H. Munro)

- *Treasure Island* - Robert Louis Stevenson

- *Dracula* - Bram Stoker

- *Tom Sawyer* - Mark Twain

- *Time Machine* - H. G. Wells

- *Importance of Being Earnest* - Oscar Wilde

- *Encarta® Pocket Dictionary* - Bloomsbury Publishing

That is quite an impressive list of books, some of which are sure to be worthy of transferring to your Pocket PC and trying out in Reader. All these books are located in the Extras\MSReader\Books folder of the ActiveSync CD-ROM. If that's not enough, following are some places online that you can go to download and purchase additional eBooks:

- Microsoft Reader Web Site - `http://www.microsoft.com/reader/read`

- Barnes and Noble Pocket PC Web Site - `http://pocketpc.barnesandnoble.com/pocketpc`

- Peanut Press Web Site - `http://www.peanutpress.com`

- Slate's eBook Web Site - `http://slate.msn.com/eBook`

The Microsoft Reader Web site includes several eBooks that you can download, along with links to other eBook sites. The Barnes and Noble Pocket PC Web site is a section of the Barnes and Noble eBooks site that includes special offers for Pocket PC owners. Slate is an online magazine edited by Michael Kinsley that tackles all kinds of topics, usually social or political in nature. Slate is the first periodical to be offered in eBook format. This means that you can download articles from Slate;

Inside Scoop

Digital eBooks are stored in a special format that supports encryption to make sure that only licensed users can read the books. Unfortunately, there are several levels of encryption and the version of Reader that ships with most Pocket PCs doesn't support all of them. There are still many eBooks currently available that are compatible with Pocket Reader's DRM support, but a lot of eBooks use a more advanced level of DRM encryption and therefore won't work with the current version of Pocket Reader. As of this writing, Microsoft is working on an updated version of Reader that will be made freely available for download from its Reader Web site at http://www.microsoft.com/reader.

more specifically, you can download an entire week of Slate articles as a single eBook. With Slate getting on board with eBook support, your Pocket PC is not only capable of allowing you to read books, but you can stay up on current events with a virtual magazine subscription, too. It will be very interesting to see whether and when other periodicals become available in eBook form.

Now that you know about several sources for acquiring eBooks, I want to focus on how you get an eBook from your desktop PC to your Pocket PC. It's also important to understand how to manage eBooks on your Pocket PC after you've transferred them. Transferring an eBook from your desktop PC to your Pocket PC is really no different from transferring any other file, as long as you make certain to place the file in the My Documents folder.

The file format used to store eBooks uses a file extension of .lit. When you purchase or download an eBook, you receive a file with an .lit extension—this is the file you must copy to the My Documents folder on your Pocket PC. As an example, I downloaded Michael Crichton's novel, *Timeline*, from the Barnes and Noble Web site, and I received an eBook file named Timeline.lit. To copy an eBook file to your Pocket PC, follow these steps:

1. Connect your device to your desktop computer.

2. Launch ActiveSync on your desktop computer and click the Explore button.

3. Navigate to the device's My Documents folder in the ActiveSync Explore window.

4. Use Windows Explorer on your desktop PC to drag the eBook file (.lit file extension) to the ActiveSync Explorer window.

After an eBook is copied to the My Documents directory on your Pocket PC, it is ready for viewing in the Reader application. To launch the Reader application, tap Programs on the Start menu, and then tap the Microsoft Reader icon.

Following a brief title screen, the main screen displayed in the Reader application is the Library, which is a list of all the eBooks installed for use with Reader (see Figure 18.1).

Figure 18.1
The Library displays all the eBooks installed for use with Reader.

You'll notice just above the listing of books are two drop-down lists that are used to sort and filter the list of books. The drop-down list on the left allows you to sort the list of books by any one of the following criteria: title, author, last opened, book size, date acquired. The drop-down list on the right is used to filter books from the list. By default, all books are displayed in the list, but you can elect to enter a word or phrase that is used to filter the books so that only books containing the word or phrase in their title or author are displayed. This feature really comes into play only when you have a lot of books installed and you're having trouble managing them.

The Library allows you to delete books when you are finished with them, which is a good idea because books take up valuable device memory. Fortunately, individual books aren't too bad in terms of hogging memory, but there's still no reason to leave a book around that you aren't planning on reading any time soon; you can always store it on your desktop computer and copy it back to your Pocket PC later. As an example, Michael Crichton's *Timeline* takes up about 550KB of memory. To delete a book from your device, tap and hold on the book in the Library, and then tap Delete in the pop-up menu that appears.

Inside Scoop
If you have more books installed than will fit on the Library screen, Reader automatically divides the book list into pages. You can then flip through the pages of the Library much as you flip through a book.

Watch Out!
Books that were preinstalled on your device are installed in ROM and cannot be removed from the Library. On most devices, this includes the Microsoft Reader Guidebook and Two Fairy Tales eBooks.

If you were previously reading a book in Reader and then try to delete it, it's possible for Reader to refuse the deletion. This is because Reader still has the book open, and therefore doesn't want you to delete the file. If this happens, try opening a different book and then deleting the original book. Another option is to close the Reader application, launch it again, and then delete the book in the Library.

→ **See Also** in Chapter 2, the section "Closing Applications," **p. 33**.

Reading eBooks

To read an eBook in the Reader application, you just tap the name of the book in the Library. Along the bottom of the screen are several buttons that are used to navigate throughout Reader. The first button, Library, takes you to the Library. The second button, Guidebook, takes you to the Microsoft Reader Guidebook, which is a built-in book that provides help on how to use Reader. The Return button takes you to the last screen displayed. These three buttons appear on the cover page of all books, and serve as a means of getting back to the Library and accessing the Guidebook whenever you have a book open.

The Microsoft Reader Guidebook is a default book that is installed in the ROM of all Pocket PCs, and is always available because it cannot be deleted. The Guidebook is a great reference and general resource for learning how to get the most out of the Reader application (see Figure 18.2). You can open the Guidebook by tapping it in the book list or by tapping the Guidebook navigational button along the bottom of the Reader screen.

You'll notice several text links displayed on the Guidebook cover page; you can tap these links to go to specific areas of the guidebook. Several of these links are standard and appear in all eBooks. Following are the standard links that you can expect to find in all eBooks:

- **Annotations Index**—A list of all the annotations (highlights, bookmarks, notes, and drawings) for the book.

- **Table of Contents**—The table of contents for the book.

- **First page**—The first page of the book.

- **Most recent**—The most recently read page of the book.

- **Furthest read**—The furthest read page of the book.

Figure 18.2
The Microsoft Reader Guidebook is a great reference and general resource for getting the most out of the Reader application.

These standard links are very handy navigational aids when it comes to moving around in a book and managing any annotations that you've entered. You learn how to annotate a book a little later in the chapter in the section titled "Working with Annotations." The Furthest read link is especially useful for returning to the furthest page you've read in a book. Even though you can set bookmarks wherever you want in a book, the Furthest read link functions somewhat like an automatic bookmark.

Tapping the Two Fairy Tales book in the book list brings up the title's cover page. Many of the standard links for the Guidebook are also included on this cover page to help in navigating and reading the book.

From the cover page of a book, you start reading the book by either tapping the First page link or by tapping the Table of Contents link and then tapping a specific section within the table of contents. Figure 18.3 shows the Table of Contents screen for the Two Fairy Tales book.

To begin reading a section from the Table of Contents screen, you just tap it. Figure 18.4 shows the first page of *The Emperor's New Clothes* fairy tale, which is representative of the user interface used to read books in Reader.

Time Saver
Tapping a book in the book list takes you to the cover page of the book if you haven't previously opened the book and begun reading it. However, if you have read some of the book, opening it in Reader takes you to the last page read.

Figure 18.3
The Table of
Contents page of
a book allows you
to select a sec-
tion to begin
reading.

Figure 18.4
The first page of
*The Emperor's New
Clothes* fairy tale
shows the user
interface used to
read books in
Reader.

Inside Scoop
I've found the
page navigation
buttons in Reader
to be annoying
because they are
so small that it
often requires sev-
eral taps to turn
the page. A more
efficient way to
turn the page is
to use the Action
button or
Gamepad button;
you can rotate the
Action button up
and down to turn
pages backward
and forward, or
tap different sides
of the Gamepad
button to achieve
a similar result.

Perhaps the most interesting aspect of the figure is the simplicity of the user interface. Keep in mind that Microsoft's goal
with Reader was to closely simulate the simplicity of the
printed page. This involved eliminating as much clutter as possible, reducing the page of a book to text and a few small user
interface elements. The drop-down list in the upper-left corner of the screen is easily identifiable because it shows the
name of the book. Tapping the name results in the display of
a drop-down list of familiar options such as Cover Page,
Annotations Index, Microsoft Reader Guidebook, Library, and
so on. Tapping this list and then tapping Library is how you
return to the Library from within a book.

The other important user interface element on each page of a
book consists of navigation buttons for turning the page. Near
the upper-right corner of the screen appear the page number
and arrows for turning forward or back a page. In addition to
tapping the right arrow to move forward a page, you can also
tap the page number itself to move forward. For even more
control over page navigation, tap and hold on the page number. This displays a pop-up menu that allows you to navigate to
a specific page number or jump to the last page of the book.

While reading a book in Reader, it is possible to search for text that appears in the content of the book. To search for additional occurrences of a given word, tap the word on the screen and a pop-up menu appears. Tapping Find in the menu opens a small Find window that allows you to change the word you are trying to find, along with specifying whether you want to find the first occurrence in the book or the next occurrence (see Figure 18.5). You can also search for phrases by tapping and dragging over the phrase, in which case the same pop-up menu appears.

Text that is found using the Find feature is highlighted on the page in which it is found. To close the Find window, tap outside of it. If the Find feature has moved you to another location in the book and you want to return to the page where you first started the search, tap the drop-down list in the upper-left corner of the page and then tap Return.

In addition to finding text, you can also copy text to the Clipboard by tapping it and then tapping Copy Text on the pop-up menu. After you copy text in this manner, it is on the Clipboard and available for pasting into other Pocket PC applications.

Inside Scoop
Unlike printed books, pages in Reader books aren't fixed in terms of the content they contain. This is apparent when you alter the font size used to display books in Reader, which results in books having more pages because less text can be fit on each page. You learn how to change the font size a little later in the section titled "Customizing Reader."

Figure 18.5
The Find window allows you to search for words and phrases in an eBook.

Undocumented
Reader allows you only to copy text that appears on a single page, so you can't copy text that spans more than that.

Inside Scoop
By default, the Find feature in Reader attempts to find an exact match for the word or phrase for which you are searching. It is also possible to search for an approximate match of the word or phrase. You do this by tapping Find exact in the Find window, and then tapping Find approximate in the pop-up menu that appears.

Remember
Studies have shown that when babies and toddlers share the same caregiver, toddlers tend to get the short end of the stick. Make sure that your child's caregiver is able to provide him with the time and attention he deserves.

When you're finished reading a book, the best thing to do is to return to the Library. This usually results in Reader releasing the book, which allows you to delete the book if you want. If you leave a book open in Reader, you won't be allowed to delete it from memory. Keep in mind that you return to the Library by tapping the title of the book in the drop-down list near the upper-left corner of the page, and then tap Library.

Working with Annotations

The Reader application supports several different approaches to providing additional information about a book while reading it. Information that you add to a book for your own use is generally referred to as annotations, and includes the following types of information:

- Bookmarks

- Highlighting

- Notes

- Drawings

Bookmarks are extremely useful if you want to mark a specific page so you can return to it later. To create a bookmark, highlight a word or phrase on a page and then tap it with the stylus. Even though a bookmark identifies an entire page, it is important to associate specific text with a bookmark because Reader uses it to identify the bookmark in the Annotations Index. For example, you might want to select the beginning of a sentence when creating a bookmark so that the bookmark is easily recognizable if you view it in the Annotations Index. You learn more about the Annotations Index later in this section.

To add a bookmark, tap and drag to select a word or phrase, and then tap Add Bookmark in the pop-up menu that appears. Figure 18.6 shows how this is carried out.

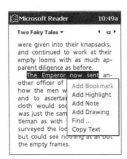

Figure 18.6
A bookmark is created by selecting a word or phrase and then tapping Add Bookmark in the pop-up menu that appears.

After you create a bookmark, a small colored icon appears in the right margin of the page. You can delete the bookmark by tapping the icon, and then tapping Delete in the pop-up menu that appears. When you are viewing any page other than the page identified by the bookmark, the bookmark appears as a small colored box in the right margin; tapping the box takes you to the bookmarked page. Each bookmark that you create automatically takes on a different color to distinguish them from one another.

Whereas bookmarks are useful for marking important pages, highlighting is used to mark important text. Highlighting in Reader works very much like a highlighter pen in a traditional printed book. To highlight a word or phrase, tap and drag to select the text, and then tap Add Highlight in the pop-up menu. Highlights can only be deleted from the Annotations Index, which you learn about in a moment.

In some cases, a highlight just doesn't provide enough information about a word or phrase in a book. Have you ever caught yourself taking notes by writing in the margin of a book? If so, then you'll find notes in Reader to be the perfect tool for attaching information to a word or phrase. To attach a note to a word or phrase, tap and select the text, and then tap Add Note. A note entry window appears, which you can use to enter a text note that is associated with the selected text in the book (see Figure 18.7).

Undocumented
Reader allows you only to copy text that appears on a single page, so you can't copy text that spans more than that.

Undocumented
Reader is capable of displaying up to only twelve bookmarks in the right margin of any given page, although you may create as many bookmarks as you desire. If you create more bookmarks than can be displayed in the margin, Reader will display the twelve most recent bookmarks.

Figure 18.7
Notes are associ-
ated with words
or phrases in a
book by entering
text in a special
note entry
window.

After entering a note, a special icon appears in the left margin of the page next to the text to which the note is attached. Unlike the icons for bookmarks, which appear on all pages, note icons appear only on the page in which they are associated. You can access all notes for a book from the Annotations Index. You can delete notes from the Annotations Index by tapping and holding the note icon on a page, and then tapping Delete in the pop-up menu that appears.

The last type of annotation supported in the Reader application is drawings, which are drawn by hand and associated with text in a book. To add a drawing to a book, tap and select a word or phrase, and then tap Add Drawing in the pop-up menu that appears. A small toolbar then appears along the bottom edge of the screen that includes three buttons for editing a drawing:

- **Change Color**—Change the color of the drawing stroke.

- **Undo**—Undo the previous drawing stroke.

- **Done**—Finish the drawing.

Creating a drawing is as simple as drawing on the screen with the stylus. Keep in mind that the drawing will appear on top of the page of text, although you can toggle the display of the drawing if it gets in the way of the text. You can make as many drawing strokes as you want, and change the color of each stroke by tapping the Change Color button at the bottom of the screen. When finished with the drawing, tap the Done button. Figure 18.8 shows a drawing being edited in Reader.

Figure 18.8
Creating a drawing
in Reader is as
simple as drawing
on the screen with
the stylus.

After creating a drawing, you'll notice a small pencil-shaped icon in the lower-left corner of the page. Tapping this icon toggles the display of the drawing on the page. You can tap and hold the pencil icon to display a pop-up menu of options for working with drawings. The Drawing pop-up menu includes commands for deleting, editing, hiding, and viewing drawings.

The Reader application provides a central location to view and edit drawings and other annotations. I'm referring to the Annotations Index, which is accessible from the drop-down menu near the upper-left corner of the page that appears when you tap the title of the book. Figure 18.9 shows the Annotations Index, which includes a listing of all the annotations associated with the book.

Figure 18.9
The Annotations
Index groups all
the annotations for
a book into one
convenient list.

You can identify Annotations in the Annotations Index by the special icons displayed to the left of each, as well as the text that is associated with each annotation. You can see in the Annotations Index how the text associated with an annotation is important because it becomes the name of the annotation. You can change the name of an annotation by tapping and holding on the annotation, and then tapping Rename in the pop-up menu that appears. You can also delete an annotation by tapping Delete in the same menu. Tapping an annotation immediately takes you to the page containing the annotation.

The Annotations Index allows you to sort and filter annotations by using the drop-down menus that appear just above the list of annotations. To alter the sort order of the annotation list, tap the drop-down list on the left side of the screen, and then tap one of the sort criteria (by Type, by Page Number, by Date Created, or by Last Opened). To alter the annotations that are displayed, tap the drop-down list on the right side of the screen, and then tap the filter criteria (show All, show Highlights Only, show Bookmarks Only, show Drawings Only, or show Notes Only).

Using the Encarta Pocket Dictionary

Microsoft Reader supports a dictionary that allows you to look up definitions of words. The dictionary is itself an eBook titled Encarta Pocket Dictionary, but it is not installed by default on most Pocket PCs. You must install the Encarta Pocket Dictionary from the ActiveSync CD-ROM to use it to look up definitions. The dictionary file is named msebdict.lit, and is located in the Extras\MSReader\books folder on the ActiveSync CD-ROM. You must use the Explorer feature in ActiveSync to copy the dictionary file from the ActiveSync CD-ROM to the My Documents folder of your Pocket PC.

Watch Out!
The Encarta Pocket Dictionary file is relatively large, approximately 2.5MB, so make sure you have room on your device before copying the file.

After copying the dictionary to your Pocket PC, Microsoft Reader recognizes it and adds a new command to the pop-up menu that appears when you tap text in the page of a book. This new command is Lookup, and allows you to look up the definition of a selected word in the dictionary. Figure 18.10 shows the definition of a word being displayed in the Encarta Pocket Dictionary.

Figure 18.10
The Encarta
Pocket Dictionary
allows you to look
up the definitions
of words in other
books.

You'll notice in the figure that the real power of the Encarta Pocket Dictionary is the tight integration it has with Reader. More specifically, when you look up a word in the dictionary, the definition of the word displays in a small pop-up window within the book you are reading. In other words, you don't have to open the dictionary eBook to look up words. Of course, if you are curious about the definition of a word without it being in the context of another book, you can always open the dictionary directly and find the definition there.

Customizing Reader

The Reader application includes several settings that you can modify to alter the manner in which it reads eBooks. The Reader settings are available from within the Guidebook—to access them, tap Quick Settings on the Guidebook cover page. Doing so results in the display of the screen shown in Figure 18.11.

Figure 18.11
The Quick Settings
screen provides
access to several
settings for the
Reader applica-
tion.

The Quick Settings screen includes several options for customizing the Reader application. Because each of these are toggle settings, to change an option, tap it in the Quick Settings screen. Following are the different options:

- Show/Hide Visual Guides

- Show/Hide Bookmarks

- Show/Hide Notes

- Show/Hide Drawings

- Show/Hide Highlights

- Use Small/Large Fonts

One other setting that isn't directly related to Reader but that nonetheless impacts how it displays books is the contrast setting for your device's screen. You might want to increase or decrease the contrast to change the way text is displayed in Reader. As an example, sometimes I read at night in the dark, in which case the default contrast is too bright. Following are the steps required to adjust the contrast of your device's screen:

Time Saver
If your device includes a hardware cursor button (gamepad), a quicker way to adjust the contrast is to hold down the Action button and then press up or down on the cursor button to adjust the contrast.

1. Tap Settings on the Start menu, and then tap the System tab.

2. Tap the Contrast tab if it isn't already selected.

3. Move the slider bar left or right to adjust the contrast.

In general, text is clearest in Reader with a high contrast setting, but this is obviously a personal preference. You'll want to return to Reader to see the difference as you tweak the contrast to suit your tastes.

Creating eBooks

The most common usage of Microsoft Reader clearly is to read published works that you would otherwise read in printed form. However, there exists quite another usage of Reader that doesn't get as much attention—self-publishing! That's right, you can create your own eBooks for use with Reader. This could include creating eBooks of personal essays and poetry, or be something as practical as offering your résumé in eBook form. Technically, you could even sell your own eBooks from your own Web site and effectively become your own publisher. Clearly, eBooks open up a lot of opportunities for the aspiring writer who wants to self-publish.

The software required to create eBooks for Microsoft Reader is called ReaderWorks by OverDrive. The Standard edition of ReaderWorks is available for free download from the ReaderWorks Web site at `http://www.readerworks.com`. The more advanced ReaderWorks Publisher software package is available for purchase from the same Web site, along with several other high-powered e-publishing packages.

Downloading and installing the ReaderWorks application is no different from downloading any other file. Click the link, choose where to store the file, and open it up when the download is complete. So, let's jump straight into how to use the application to create eBooks that you can view in Reader.

When launched, ReaderWorks opens a Quick Start window. Accepting the default option of creating a Blank ReaderWorks Project is sufficient for creating most eBooks. Upon selecting this option, the ReaderWorks application opens with an empty project, as shown in Figure 18.12.

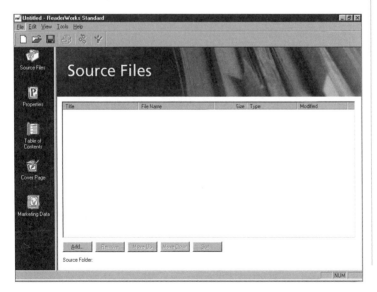

Figure 18.12
The ReaderWorks application initially opens and displays the source files in the current project.

Source files in ReaderWorks are the original documents and resources that go into a finished eBook. Examples of source files include text documents, HTML documents, and image files. For the purposes of this example, I can add a single source file to the project by clicking the Add button located at the bottom of the window. You are then given a chance to browse and locate the file on your hard drive. After locating the source file, it is added to the source file list.

In addition to specifying source files that drive the content of eBooks, ReaderWorks allows you to alter specific aspects of an eBook. For example, clicking the Properties icon along the left side of the application window switches to a Properties view that allows you to edit properties of the eBook. The list of properties you can edit is extensive, but some of the ones you can edit include Title, Author, and Subject.

Additional icons along the left side of the application window allow you to further detail an eBook by creating a Table of Contents, adding a cover page, and providing marketing data. Many of these detailed aspects of an eBook are editable only in the ReaderWorks Publisher edition, which is available for purchase from the ReaderWorks Web site.

To generate an eBook file (.lit file) in ReaderWorks, you click the Build eBook button (gear icon) in the application toolbar, or select Build eBook from the File menu. Initiating the build process results in the display of the Build eBook Wizard, shown in Figure 18.13.

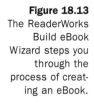

Figure 18.13
The ReaderWorks Build eBook Wizard steps you through the process of creating an eBook.

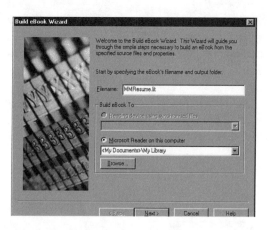

Although the Build eBook Wizard is implemented through a wizard user interface, the necessary information required to build the eBook is all gathered in the window shown in the figure. You must clarify the filename of the resulting eBook, along with the location the eBook is to be stored on your desktop computer. Clicking the Next button creates the eBook.

After creating an eBook, you must copy the .lit file from your desktop computer to your Pocket PC to view it in Reader. Figure 18.14 shows the cover page of my résumé eBook as viewed in Microsoft Reader on a Pocket PC.

Figure 18.14
The cover page of a custom eBook that was created by ReaderWorks.

Listening to eBooks

Although certainly not as popular as printed books, many books are available as audio books on tape or CD and are convenient for people who find it easier to listen than to read. Pocket PC supports a more advanced equivalent of audio books by allowing you to listen to eBooks using Microsoft Reader. Reader supports audio eBooks, also known as audible books, but you must use a special desktop application to manage audible books and transfer them to your Pocket PC. This application is called AudibleManager, and is freely available from Audible.com at `http://www.audible.com`. Audible.com is a Web site that offers audible books and articles for download and purchase.

Audible.com is somewhat of an online bookstore for audible books in electronic form. In addition to books, however, Audible.com also offers audible versions of periodicals such as The Wall Street Journal. There is even a weekly comedy series

Time Saver
If you don't like the idea of a lengthy download, you can have the AudibleManager software sent to you on a CD-ROM free of charge. The Audible.com Web site includes details on how this is done.

by Robin Williams available. Audible.com offers an interesting range of audio content that expands the media appeal of Pocket PCs considerably.

Before you can begin purchasing and downloading audible books from Audible.com, you need to download and install the AudibleManager software, which is freely available from the Audible.com Web site. The setup file for the AudibleManager application is around 8MB, so it takes a little while to download. After downloading the AudibleManager setup program, launch it to install it. The steps required to install are not much different from installing any other application onto your desktop.

With the AudibleManager software installed, you are ready to configure it for use with your Pocket PC. You must sign up for a free Audible.com account to purchase and download audio content. The first time you run the AudibleManager software, it presents you with the usual application Welcome window.

Clicking the Next button in the Welcome window takes you to the Device Selection window, in which you select the types of devices you plan on using to listen to audible books (see Figure 18.15).

Figure 18.15
Specify the devices you plan on using to listen to audible books.

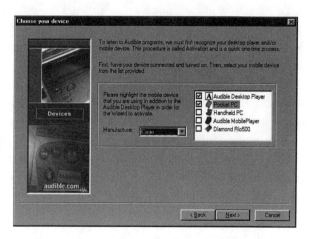

The Audible Desktop Player option will be selected by default, which is good to keep because you may want to listen to audible books on your desktop computer in addition to your

Pocket PC. You should check the Pocket PC check box and then select the manufacturer of your device in the combo box on the left. Clicking the Next button takes you to the Device Configuration window.

You must click the Upgrade button in the Device Configuration window to set up your device for playing audible books. Upon clicking the Upgrade button, the configuration program will copy files and configure your device for playing audible books. The next window displayed is the Audible User Information window, which is shown in Figure 18.16.

Figure 18.16
The Audible User Information window prompts you to create a new Audible account or log in with an existing account.

Click the Create New Account button to create a new account; if you already happen to have an Audible account, enter your username and password, and click the Next button. In the next window, you need to enter your name, email address, and an account name and password.

Clicking Next opens up the Activate Player(s) window, which is responsible for activating the Audible Player on your device. Clicking the Next button with the Activate radio button selected results in the Audible Player being activated.

At this point in the configuration process, you must have an Internet connection because the configuration program communicates with the Audible.com Web site to verify account information and enable the Audible Player on your Pocket PC.

As your device is being activated, an Activation window appears that monitors its progress.

After your device is activated, the Finish window is displayed, which confirms the successful configuration of the Audible software (see Figure 18.17); click the Finish button to complete the configuration.

Figure 18.17
The Finish window confirms that the Audible software has been successfully configured.

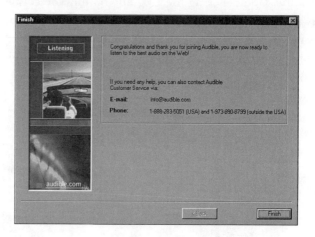

If you recall, AudibleManager is the software used on your desktop computer to manage and transfer audible books to your Pocket PC. To launch the AudibleManager application, click Start, Programs, Audible, and then the AudibleManager icon (see Figure 18.18).

Figure 18.18
The AudibleManager application is used to manage audible books and transfer them to your Pocket PC.

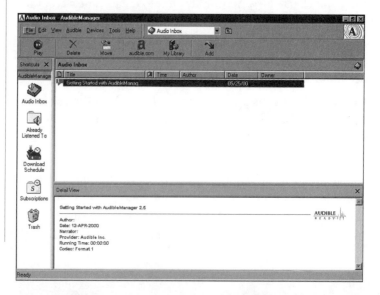

The AudibleManager application includes a lot of functionality for managing audible books. It's somewhat beyond the scope of this chapter to delve into the details of the AudibleManager application. Instead, I want to focus on how to access audible books and transfer them to your Pocket PC.

The Audio Inbox window is the main window in AudibleManager, and contains a list of the audible books stored on your desktop computer. The Audio Inbox window initially contains a sample audible book that welcomes you to AudibleManager. You can double-click the book to listen to it on your desktop computer. Because this book is just a sample book, I decided to purchase and download a real audible book (Dennis Miller's *I Rant, Therefore I Am*) from Audible.com to demonstrate how to use AudibleManager. A typical audible book actually costs much less than its print version. *I Rant, Therefore I Am* was on sale for $2.95, whereas the printed book retails for $18.00.

The purchasing and downloading of audible books is handled entirely on the Audible.com Web site. Purchasing the audible books is roughly akin to any e-commerce Web site in that you first add the books to a shopping cart and then check out to finalize the purchase. Instead of waiting for a package, however, you just download the file directly.

When you initiate an audible book download on the Audible.com Web site, the book begins downloading directly into the AudibleManager application. When the download finishes, the new book is shown in the Audio Inbox window. Figure 18.19 shows the Dennis Miller audible book. Notice that there is a windowpane beneath the Audio Inbox called the Detail View that includes details about the currently selected audible book.

To transfer an audible book to your Pocket PC, you must first add it to the AudibleManager playlist; this is accomplished by selecting the book in the Audio Inbox and then clicking the Add button on the main toolbar. After adding a book to the playlist, a Playlist Editor pane will open to the right of the Audio Inbox and show a vertical timeline of books in the playlist.

Watch Out!
Because computer audio files can get fairly large, it's important to consider space issues on your Pocket PC before purchasing audible books for it. The Dennis Miller book has over 2 hours and 20 minutes of audio, and even at the lowest-quality format supported by Audible.com, it weighs in at 5.5MB, which is quite a large file.

Inside Scoop
Audible.com supports different audio quality levels, numbered 1, 2, 3, and 4, in order of increasing quality. When you download a book, you must specify in which quality you want the book. Because of the file size issues with these books, the lowest standard you can handle listening to is usually the best.

Figure 18.19

The Dennis Miller audible book *I Rant, Therefore I Am* as it appears in the AudibleManager Audio Inbox window.

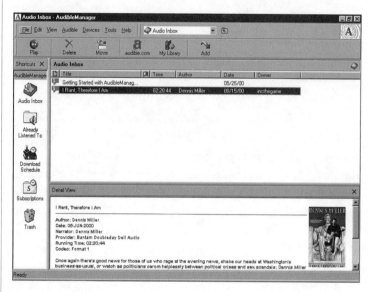

With the book added to the playlist, you are ready to transfer it to your Pocket PC. To transfer the book, click the Transfer button in the Playlist Editor window. A progress window will immediately appear that tracks the progress of the book being transferred to your device (see Figure 18.20). Keep in mind that the transfer can take some time because of the large size of most audible book files.

When the file finishes transferring, you are ready to launch Reader on your Pocket PC and listen to the audible book. Just like a normal eBook, Reader adds the audible book to its Library. To listen to the book, tap it in the list of books in the Library. Figure 18.21 shows the Dennis Miller audible book opened in Reader.

Figure 18.20
AudibleManager displays a progress window to indicate the progress of the transfer of audible books to your device.

Figure 18.21
The Dennis Miller audible book *I Rant, Therefore I Am* opened in Microsoft Reader for listening.

Instead of the normal eBook options, you'll notice that Reader includes a few different controls along the bottom of the screen that are used to control the playback of the audible book. You can use the buttons on the left side of the screen to move forward and backward in the audible book, as well as pause the book. On the right side of the screen is a small speaker icon that is used to alter the volume of Reader. To change the volume, tap and hold on the icon, and then tap Increase Volume or Decrease Volume in the pop-up menu that appears. Frankly, the user interface for audible books could use a little work—I would really like to see a sliding volume control and a mute option for the volume. Additionally, it

Inside Scoop
Audible.com offers a free audible book player for Pocket PC that you can use in lieu of Microsoft Reader to listen to audible books. Although the Audible Player eats up more memory real estate on your Pocket PC and doesn't integrate directly with Reader, it is a more full-featured player that addresses most of the user interface weaknesses of Reader. Audible Player is available for download from the Audible.com Web site at http://www. audible.com.

would be nice to be able to move forward and backward through entire segments of an audible book, but then I suppose that's what product updates are for.

Essential Information

- Microsoft's ClearType technology draws upon the superior typography of books to provide an immersive reading experience for computers.

- Several eBooks are included on the ActiveSync CD-ROM that accompanies all Pocket PCs.

- The Microsoft Reader Guidebook is a great reference and general resource for learning how to get the most out of the Reader application.

- Reader supports several types of annotations such as highlighting, which is very similar to highlighting words and phrases in a printed book with a highlighter pen.

- The ReaderWorks application allows you to create eBooks for use with Microsoft Reader.

- In addition to reading books, you can also listen to audible books using Reader.

GET THE SCOOP ON...
- The Role of Pocket PC As Portable Game Machine
- The Significant Hardware Muscle Pocket PCs Pack in Comparison to Dedicated Portable Game Systems
- The Games Included in the Pocket PC Fun Pack ▪ Jimmy Software and Their Pocket PC Games ▪ Using Your Pocket PC to Carefully Track Your Golf Game

Games in Your Pocket

A LTHOUGH FEW PEOPLE COULD JUSTIFY or admit that they would buy a Pocket PC device purely for its entertainment value, there is a lot to be said for the entertainment power that it packs in such a small package. Beyond playing music and reading books, however, you might not realize that Pocket PCs have plenty of hardware muscle to serve as portable game machines. Sure, the Pocket PC operating system includes Solitaire, which can certainly help kill time while waiting in a dentist's office, but there are incredibly slick action games available for Pocket PC that will force you to view it in a different way. As an example, there is a version of the hit 3D shoot'em-up game DOOM in the works for Pocket PC.

This chapter introduces you to gaming capabilities of Pocket PC, along the way highlighting many of the games that are current available. You learn about the games included in Microsoft's free Pocket PC Fun Pack, as well as some third-party games that are quite impressive.

Pocket PC: The Ultimate Game Boy

Nintendo's Game Boy is without a doubt the most popular and successful portable gaming machine to date. Knowing this, how can I possibly compare such a powerful game machine to a Pocket PC device that is geared more toward productivity? It's easy because the technical prowess of Pocket PC devices is

Chapter 19

literally more than a decade ahead of Game Boys. The Game Boy was introduced to America in 1991, and has undergone little change in the years since then. Granted, the screen is now color and there is more memory, but the system is essentially the same as it was back in 1991. To understand the device in terms of computing power, check out some of the technical details of the Game Boy Color, the latest Game Boy as of this writing:

- **Processor**—8-bit running at 8MHz.

- **RAM**—32KB.

- **Screen**—160×140 with 56 colors.

If you recall the technical specifics of Pocket PCs, you probably see where I'm headed with this. If not, take a look at a similar list of technical details for the Cassiopeia E-115 Pocket PC:

- **Processor**—32-bit running at 131MHz.

- **RAM**—32MB (that's megabytes, not kilobytes!).

- **Screen**—240×320 with 65,536 colors.

As you can see, comparing the technical capabilities of a Pocket PC with that of a Game Boy is way past the apples and oranges analogy. These are two very different machines that admittedly are designed for different purposes. Or, so we think. Why should a device with the technical capability to serve as a killer portable game machine not be exploited as such? The truth is Pocket PCs have more than enough horsepower to be a dominant portable game platform. However, there is little chance that games will be a major selling factor for Pocket PCs any time soon. In addition to being much more expensive than pure portable game machines such as the Game Boy, the Pocket PC still doesn't have enough support from game developers to build a large catalog of quality game titles. However, if you look at the game capabilities of Pocket PCs as yet another interesting facet of the devices, then you'll really appreciate what they have to offer.

Although nothing could match the Game Boy's extensive library of titles, game development for the Pocket PC is already well underway, with some impressive games already available. If, as I expect, Pocket PCs get the attention of larger game publishers, you'll probably start seeing some familiar titles appear for Pocket PC. At the very least, expect Microsoft's entertainment division to pump out some high-quality Pocket PC games to get the ball rolling. As is evident with its new Xbox game system, Microsoft is serious about becoming a force in the video game market. I expect to see Pocket PCs playing a role in establishing that force.

→ **See Also** "Outside of the Pocket," **p. 13**.

The Pocket PC Fun Pack

Because the out-of-the-box gaming options for the Pocket PC are slim, the best place to start is Microsoft's Pocket PC Fun Pack, which is available for order from Microsoft free at `http://orders.one.microsoft.com/pocketpc`. The Pocket PC Fun Pack consists of a CF card and a CD-ROM full of Pocket PC content, utilities, and games. Pac-Man is the only game included on the CF card; the remaining games are on the CD-ROM. Following are all the games included in the Pocket PC Fun Pack:

- Pac-Man
- Fire Drill from the upcoming Microsoft Mobile Games Pack
- Cubicle Chaos from the upcoming Microsoft Mobile Games Pack
- Hearts from the upcoming Microsoft Entertainment Pack
- Chess from the upcoming Microsoft Entertainment Pack
- PocketFriendly Backgammon by AnyWerx
- Bubblets by oopdreams (trial version)
- ZIOGolf by ZIO Interactive (trial version)

Each game is installed individually, which allows you to pick and choose which ones you think are worth keeping. Keep in mind that every application installed on your Pocket PC (including games) takes up valuable memory, so be careful to make sure you plan on using any applications you install. In regard to games, this means that you should make sure you really plan on playing a game before wasting memory on it. Of course, you can always install a game and remove it later if you don't like it or get tired of it.

Pac-Man

Ask just about anyone over 25 to name the single most popular arcade game of all time and the answer will likely be Pac-Man. Together with Asteroids and Space Invaders, Pac-Man is responsible for separating quite a few people from their hard-earned quarters. Microsoft obviously wanted to tip its hat to the golden age of video game arcades when it decided to make Pac-Man the headliner game in the Pocket PC Fun Pack. You can relive 1980 in the comfort of the 21st century by playing Pac-Man on your Pocket PC.

You can install Pac-Man from either the CF card or the CD-ROM that accompanies the Pocket PC Fun Pack. I'll step you through the installation from the CD-ROM, because that's how you'll have to install the other games in the Fun Pack. You can install Pac-Man from the Fun Pack CD-ROM by running the setup program, setup.exe, from the directory download\Games\PacMan. You can also initiate the setup program from the Fun Pack Welcome page that is automatically displayed when you first insert the CD-ROM into your CD-ROM drive. Upon executing the Pac-Man setup program, the Welcome window appears with some preliminary information. Click Next to proceed to the Software License Agreement window, to which you agree by clicking the Yes button.

You are then prompted to enter your name and company information, if relevant. After entering that information, clicking the Next button displays a window that allows you to select the destination directory on your desktop PC that is used to install Pac-Man. The default destination directory is fine, in which case you click the Next button to continue.

The setup program asks you to confirm the creation of the destination directory, which is done by clicking the Yes button. Finally, you get to the familiar Pocket PC installation window that prompts to confirm the default application directory for Pac-Man on your device.

If the default directory is acceptable, you can click the Yes button to begin copying files to your device. A progress bar, which you're no doubt accustomed to at this point, monitors the installer's progress as the Pac-Man files are copied to the device.

After the files finish copying, the Setup Complete window is displayed allowing you to click Finish to complete the installation. With Pac-Man successfully installed, you can try it out by tapping Programs in the Start menu, and then tapping Games to open the Games folder. Figure 19.1 shows the Games folder with all the Fun Pack games currently installed.

Remember
Although the Pocket PC device in Figure 19.1 has all the Fun Pack games installed, it is important to keep in mind that you do have to install each of these games individually. Installations for the other games in the pack are nearly the same as for Pac-Man.

Figure 19.1
All the games that you install from the Fun Pack are accessible from the Games folder on your device.

In the Games folder, you just tap the Pac-Man icon to launch the game. The Pac-Man title screen appears with options for adjusting the game's settings, resuming a saved game, and starting a new one.

To start a game, just tap Play Pac-Man on the title screen. You can also alter the game settings by tapping Game Settings. The Pac-Man game is identical to its historical arcade counterpart, as shown in Figure 19.2.

Figure 19.2
The Pac-Man game
in action.

You move Pac-Man around the maze by tapping or dragging the stylus just in front of him, which is an interesting way to play the game if you're accustomed to a traditional joystick in the arcade. If your Pocket PC has a multidirectional control button, then you can use it in lieu of the stylus for a more traditional control approach.

Fire Drill

Inside Scoop
Fire Drill is one of
the games that
will appear in
Microsoft's soon-
to-be-released
Mobile Games
Pack for the
Pocket PC.

Imagine an office engulfed in flames and only one person bold enough to grab a fire extinguisher and put out the fires to avoid disaster. This is the premise of Fire Drill, an action game by Rapture Technologies. Fire Drill employs a top-view scrolling approach to provide a view of a highly combustible office. As the fire retardant hero of Fire Drill, you must navigate cubicles and save your fellow employees by dousing fires with your trusty extinguisher. When you extinguish all the fires in one level, they spread to another and get more aggressive; your work is never done in Fire Drill.

Figure 19.3 shows the Fire Drill hero busy at work putting out fires with his fire extinguisher.

Figure 19.3
The Fire Drill game
in action.

You control the character in Fire Drill by tapping or dragging the stylus in the direction you want him to move. Tapping on a fire will move him toward the fire and cause him to shoot the fire extinguisher at it. Be careful not to walk into any fires if you'd like to avoid a trip to the burn ward.

Cubicle Chaos

Next to Pong, one of the original classic home video games that comes to mind for most people is Breakout. Breakout is a game that involves a row of bricks across the top of the screen and a small bar on the bottom of the screen. You control the bar and use it to keep a ball bouncing up and down around the screen. Each time the ball hits a brick the brick is destroyed; the object is to eventually clear all the bricks. You lose when you miss the ball with the bar and it falls off the bottom of the screen. The game gets more difficult with each new level as the bricks lower and the ball moves faster.

Cubicle Chaos is a contemporary remake of Breakout, also by Rapture Technologies, that uses an interesting office metaphor instead of bricks, bars, and balls. The premise of this game is that you fling balls at fellow co-workers in an attempt to collapse their cubicles. Having personally witnessed a co-worker getting beaned in the head with a Koosh ball at a previous job, I can certainly appreciate the premise of this game. In Cubicle Chaos, you sit at your desk along the bottom of the screen (the bar) and slide back and forth deflecting the bouncing ball. Your co-workers sit at their desks (the bricks) in different cubicle formations around the screen. The object of the game is to hit your co-workers and rid the office of them and their cubes.

Inside Scoop
Cubicle Chaos is one of the games that will appear in Microsoft's soon-to-be-released Mobile Games Pack for the Pocket PC.

Figure 19.4 shows the bouncing ball at work destroying fellow employees and their cubicles in Cubicle Chaos.

You control the desk-roving employee in Cubicle Chaos by tapping and dragging the stylus back and forth across the screen. Your only goal is to keep the bouncing ball alive by constantly deflecting it with the employee and his desk. Various items will fall on occasion when you destroy a fellow employee's desk;

some of these items give you extra powers whereas some of them cause strange things to take place that hinder you. All the effects brought on by falling items are temporary.

Figure 19.4
The Cubicle Chaos game in action.

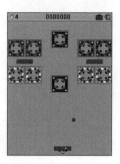

Hearts

If you've ever played the card game Hearts on a network against human opponents, then you understand the thrill of deviously setting up a run and pulling it off to perfection. Hearts is my favorite computer card game because it is so much fun trying to pull one over on the other players. The Pocket PC version of Hearts is just as much fun, and even supports two human players via an infrared connection between devices.

If you aren't familiar with Hearts, I highly recommend trying it out on your desktop computer and using it to learn how to play. Hearts is included with Windows 9x, ME, NT, and 2000. It is easy to learn; its online help includes a description of the game and how to play it.

When you first run Hearts on your Pocket PC, you are prompted for information (see Figure 19.5).

Figure 19.5
Hearts first requests that you enter your name and specify how you want to play the game.

If you don't plan on using an infrared connection to play with another human player, select Play against the computer and tap OK. Otherwise, you are playing with another player via infrared, and you must specify whether you are the dealer or not; one player must be the dealer and the other must be a player that connects to the dealer. There is no real significance to being the dealer other than you establishing the infrared connection; Hearts automatically does all the card dealing!

After you've established a game of Hearts, the cards are laid out and the action begins (see Figure 19.6).

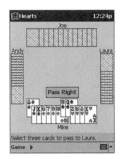

Figure 19.6
The Hearts game in action.

Hearts is played by simply tapping the card you'd like to play at any given time. There is no need to drag cards around since in Hearts you typically play one card at a time to the middle. The only exception to this is at the beginning of a turn, when you must pass three cards to another player. In this event, you tap to select the three cards, and then tap the button above your cards to pass them to the appropriate player.

Chess

Chess is a game than needs no introduction, except to say that this version is specially designed to run on Pocket PC. This version of Chess allows you to play against the computer or against another human player. However, unlike Hearts, you don't play against another player with two devices connected via infrared. Instead, you just share the same device and take turns making moves. Admittedly, this is more cumbersome than the infrared approach, but it does alleviate the need for two devices.

Figure 19.7 shows the Chess game in action as the computer player has me on the run.

To move pieces in Chess, tap and drag the piece to the location to which you'd like to move it. The rest of the game is intuitive if you have any familiarity with Chess.

PocketFriendly Backgammon

PocketFriendly Backgammon is a full-featured Backgammon game created by AnyWerx for the Pocket PC. PocketFriendly Backgammon is based upon the standard international rules of Backgammon, but also supports some variations on these rules. For those players, like me, lacking any knowledge of the game, one of the most significant features of PocketFriendly Backgammon is its help, which is quite extensive for a Pocket PC game.

PocketFriendly Backgammon supports skins that change the look of the board and pieces, somewhat like the skins for Windows Media Player. You can download additional skins from the AnyWerx Web site at http://www.anywerx.com.

The first screen that appears when you start PocketFriendly Backgammon prompts you to enter your name so the game can track your play.

Figure 19.8 shows the PocketFriendly Backgammon game in action using the default skin.

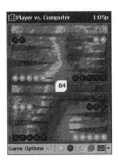

Figure 19.8
The PocketFriendly
Backgammon
game in action.

Bubblets

I was skeptical when I first read a review of Bubblets by oop-dreams Software that mentioned how addictive it could be. I installed it and starting tapping on the screen without reading any instructions. It took a couple of minutes to figure out what was going on, but the game is very intuitive to learn so I caught on pretty quickly. Half an hour later, I was still tapping away trying to beat my highest score. Tetris it is not, but this game can get a hold of you.

Bubblets is a game that consists of a grid full of bubbles of different colors. The object is to pop as many adjacent bubbles of the same color as possible; the more bubbles popped at once, the higher the points awarded. It might appear simple, but after you play the game a few times, you start realizing that there are subtle strategies involved in setting up groups of bubbles to be popped.

Unfortunately, the version of Bubblets included on the Fun Pack CD-ROM is a 15-day trial version. To order a full registered version of the Bubblets shareware game, visit the oopdreams Web site at http://www.oopdreams.com.

The Bubblets game is deceptively simple looking. Figure 19.9 shows a group of bubbles selected and ready to pop; the number in the small circle tells how many points will be awarded if you follow through with the pop.

To play Bubbles, just tap on a group of bubbles to see how many points they are worth if popped. To follow through with the pop, tap on the same group of bubbles again.

Figure 19.9
The Bubblets
game in action.

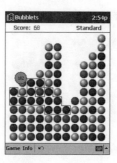

ZIOGolf

If you can't get enough golf in the real world and feel like playing a little extra golf on your Pocket PC, then look no further
than ZIOGolf, a very capable golf game by ZIOSoft. ZIOGolf is
similar to the popular desktop golf games that use a 3D view to
show the swing and flight trajectory of the ball along a ren-
dered golf course. The user interface is even similar to desktop
golf games in that it takes advantage of a round swing gauge
that requires you to carefully time taps with the stylus to swing
properly.

The version of ZIOGolf on the Fun Pack CD-ROM is a trial version that includes only two holes. To order the complete game,
along with additional courses, check out the ZIOSoft Web site
at http://www.ziosoft.com.

Figure 19.10 shows the title screen of ZIOGolf, which allows
you to set up the players for a round of golf. Up to four human
players can play, but keep in mind that you'll have to take
turns. You can also play with computer players for a little
added competition.

Figure 19.10
The ZIOGolf title
screen allows you
to set up players
for the game.

Figure 19.11 shows the ZIOGolf game in action. The game really does have excellent graphics, and is a good example of how much is capable in terms of Pocket PC gaming.

Figure 19.11
The ZIOGolf game in action.

Jimmy Software Games

Beyond the Fun Pack for Pocket PC, there are other games available for download and purchase that you should consider. After scouring the offerings for Pocket PC, I found myself constantly returning to Jimmy Software, which seems to have a significant leg up when it comes to Pocket PC game development. As the only game company focusing solely on Pocket PC gamed development, Jimmy Software has virtually defined the market for Pocket PC games. Their games are significantly ahead of much of their competition in term of both graphics and sound. I suspect we will see larger players enter the Pocket PC game arena soon, but for now Jimmy Software has center stage and their current work on porting the PC game classic, DOOM should allow them to keep that status for the immediate future.

Jimmy Software began as one guy (Jimmy) working with Windows CE back in 1997, and created several freeware utilities that were very popular. When he realized there was virtually no competition in the Windows CE game market, he switched his focus to games, and apparently hasn't looked back. His first game was JimmyARK, a Breakout-style game with impressive graphics and sound, and decent game play. Jimmy Software eventually grew to six programmers, six graphic designers, two musicians, and a game designer. This team can now take credit for the most innovative games to appear for Pocket PCs yet.

Following are some of the most popular Jimmy Software games available for Pocket PC:

- Turjah

- JimmyARK

- FireFrontier

- Boyan

- RallyCE

- PocketRunner

Watch Out!
As of this writing, not all the Jimmy Software games are available for all Pocket PC devices. In the upcoming coverage of each game, I clarify the devices for which it is available.

The next few sections introduce you to each of these games. To download a trial version of any of the games, visit the Jimmy Software Web site at http://www.jimmysoftware.com. To purchase any of the games, visit Handango, an online Pocket PC retailer, at http://www.handango.com.

Turjah

Turjah is a surprisingly fast-pace shoot'em-up game with excellent graphics, music, and sound effects. Jimmy Software has developed a powerful game engine that squeezes the most performance out of Pocket PC graphics. Turjah is a great example of the future of Pocket PC games, as it exhibits all the characteristics of a high-quality desktop game, minus big-name actors and screenwriters, of course. Turjah's game play is highly dependent on a multidirectional gamepad, which is why it is currently available only for the Cassiopeia E-115 Pocket PC. Granted, the Compaq iPAQ H3650 Pocket PC includes a suitable gamepad, but Turjah isn't available for it yet. I would expect an iPAQ version to be available very soon.

Figure 19.12 shows Turjah in action. As you can see, the game involves very high-quality graphics and a lot of action. The trial version allows you to play for only a few minutes, but it's enough to get fans of shoot'em-ups hooked.

Figure 19.12
The Turjah game in action.

JimmyARK

JimmyARK is Jimmy Software's take on Breakout, the bouncing ball game that also served as the basis for Cubicle Chaos. Although the graphics and sound in JimmyARK are excellent, I found the game play to be a little better in Cubicle Chaos. If you're into Breakout, I encourage you to try them both and see for yourself which one you prefer. Keep in mind, however, that you'll need to purchase JimmyARK to be able to play beyond the first level. JimmyARK is currently available for the Cassiopeia E-115 and Compaq iPAQ Pocket PCs.

Figure 19.13 shows a game of JimmyARK, which makes its similarity to Breakout (and Cubicle Chaos) quite apparent. In fairness to JimmyARK, this game was around for Windows CE long before Cubicle Chaos.

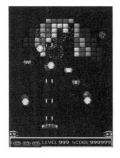

Figure 19.13
The JimmyARK game in action.

FireFrontier

Fire Frontier is a maze shoot-em-up that employs a top-view approach to presenting a maze full of tanks and other futuristic vehicles of war. You control a tank and basically drive around blasting everything that moves. There are a variety of different weapons at your disposal, which lends a certain amount of strategy to the game. The graphics and sound are excellent, and the game plays pretty well, too. However, as of this writing, Fire Frontier is available only for the Cassiopeia E-115 Pocket PC. FireFrontier is freely available in a trial version, which has a very short timeout period; you must purchase the game to play as long as you want.

Figure 19.14 shows FireFrontier in action, with a tank being assaulted from several directions.

Figure 19.14
The FireFrontier
game in action.

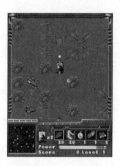

Boyan

Boyan is one of the few Jimmy Software games that is currently available for all Pocket PCs. The game itself is a horizontal shooting game in which you control a small spaceship and blast aliens as they drift from the bottom to the top of the screen hanging onto balloons. The idea is to keep the aliens from getting to the top of the screen, where they will join forces and create a great deal of havoc. Like all Jimmy Software games, Boyan is freely available in a trial version.

Figure 19.15 shows the Boyan game in action as the hero Boyan fires at an alien that is drifting toward the top of the screen.

Figure 19.15
The Boyan game in
action.

RallyCE

If you are a true child of the video game era, you will no doubt remember Rally-X, a great game that pitted you against a group of computer-controlled race cars in a large maze. In Rally-X, you control a race car of your own and attempt to pick up flags while avoiding the computer cars. Your secret weapon is a smokescreen that you can deploy when the computer cars get close behind you. Although Rally-X isn't as well known as Pac-Man or Asteroids, it is certainly a video game classic.

RallyCE is Jimmy Software's Pocket PC version of Rally-X. Of course, RallyCE goes several steps beyond Rally-X with improved music and sound effects, although it does retain a similar feel to Rally-X graphically. RallyCE is currently available for the Cassiopeia E-115, Compaq iPAQ, and HP Jornada Pocket PCs.

Figure 19.16 shows a shot of RallyCE as the player-controlled car leaves a smokescreen to block the computer car.

Figure 19.16
The RalleyCE game in action.

PocketRunner

PocketRunner is another game that is written closely in the tradition of a classic game. The classic game in this case is Lode Runner, which was a hit on the Commodore line of computers. Lode Runner has somewhat of a Donkey Kong feel to it, although the graphics are even more simplistic. PocketRunner is a faithful remake of Lode Runner that will be both nostalgic and enjoyable to anyone who liked Lode Runner. As of this writing, PocketRunner is available only for the Cassiopeia E-115 Pocket PC. You can download a free trial version from the Jimmy Software Web site (http://www.jimmysoftware.com).

Figure 19.17 shows PocketRunner in action, and gives you an obvious feel for the fact that this game is written in the spirit of an arcade classic. PocketRunner could have clearly been designed with higher-quality graphics, but then it wouldn't feel like the original Lode Runner game.

Figure 19.17
The PocketRunner game in action.

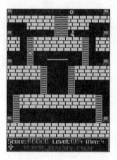

Tracking the Real Game of Golf

Throughout this chapter, I've introduced a variety of different video games that can be played on your Pocket PC. All these games qualify as virtual games because they are played entirely within the confines of your device. However, a Pocket PC can also be used as a tool to enhance your experience within a real game. One game in which Pocket PCs can come in quite useful is golf, which involves careful scorekeeping to establish a handicap and track your progress. Pocket PCs are ideal devices for this type of mobile bookkeeping because they allow you to quickly enter information on the go, store it in a reliable format, and then analyze it later.

Inside Scoop
Course maps for Pocket Golfwits are available for download from the Siscosoft Web site at http://www. siscosoft.com. If a course isn't available, you can request Siscosoft to create a map for it or create the map yourself using a special tool that is available from the Siscosoft Web site.

Siscosoft's Pocket Golfwits is a Pocket PC application that performs this very function. This application could change the way you think about your golf game. Pocket Golfwits is a powerful golf record-keeping application that allows you to tap to record each shot you take on a digital map of the course you are playing. You can specify how the shot was hit (slice, hook, and so on), as well as the club used to hit it. You can imagine how valuable this information can be in improving your game when you have each and every shot documented in detail.

Pocket Golfwits can be used as a standalone application, but it is particularly powerful when coupled with the desktop

Golfwits application. Pocket Golfwits includes many of the same features as its desktop counterpart, but the desktop application is easier to use when it comes to analyzing your play. Figure 19.18 shows the Golfwits desktop application with a hole displayed that has been played.

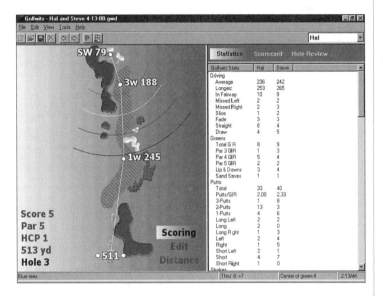

Figure 19.18
The Golfwits desktop application is a full-featured golf record-keeping and analysis tool.

Notice in the figure that the left side of the screen contains a graphical rendering of a golf hole. Lines and points are displayed to indicate the location of each shot that was made to complete the hole. The right side of the screen includes a wealth of very interesting statistics regarding the specifics of the shots made during the round. Figure 19.19 shows Pocket Golfwits, which displays only the left side of the desktop application's view due to the limited screen space.

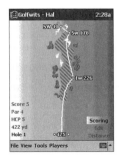

Figure 19.19
The Pocket Golfwits application is a great companion to the desktop application, and makes it very easy to keep a detailed record of your golf rounds.

The real power of Pocket Golfwits is that you can keep your golf score without ever entering numbers or doing any math. You enter everything visually by tapping on a map of the course, which is incredibly intuitive. Pocket Golfwits is then capable of determining a great deal of information about your game from the visual data you provide it. As an example, Figure 19.20 shows the Hole Review view in Pocket Golfwits, which provides a written summary of a hole based upon the data that was entered graphically.

Figure 19.20
The Hole Review view in Pocket Golfwits provides a great written record of a hole, even though you don't have to type anything.

There are clearly significant benefits to using Pocket Golfwits for the golfer who wants to keep up with his or her game. As Pocket PCs continue to catch on and spread in popularity, I wouldn't be surprised to see Pocket Golfwits start appearing fairly regularly on golf courses. It solves a need that is well suited to Pocket PCs, and does so in a manner that doesn't add any technical hassle. No one wants to fool with gadgets while trying to enjoy themselves outdoors. Keeping score in Pocket Golfwits is not much different from writing down numbers on a scorecard, and you end up with much more information at the end of the day.

Inside Scoop
You can make voice recordings and associate them with different holes in Pocket Golfwits. This is a great way to add any extra commentary about a particular hole.

One question you might have in regard to Golfwits and Pocket Golfwits is course availability. Obviously, the applications are useful only if you can obtain courses that you play. Siscosoft currently has several thousand courses available with many more in the works; new courses are being released on a regular basis. All the courses are freely available from the Siscosoft Web site. If you're antsy and can't wait for Siscosoft to get around to creating a map of your favorite course, you can map it yourself using the Mapwits software. Mapwits allows you to construct golf course maps for use in Golfwits. You can also send Siscosoft information about your course and have them map it for you, although this will take longer than doing it yourself.

For more information on Golfwits, visit the Siscosoft Web site at `http://www.siscosoft.com`. You can also purchase Golfwits online from Handango at `http://www.handango.com`.

Essential Information

- With a processor more than 16 times faster than a Game Boy Color, the average Pocket PC has plenty of processing power to serve as a portable game system.

- Microsoft's Pocket PC Fun Pack is loaded with fun games, and is freely available for order from Microsoft at `http://orders.one.microsoft.com/pocketpc`.

- Jimmy Software is the primary development company that has managed to create a market for Pocket PC games by developing games with high-quality graphics, sound, and game play.

- Siscosoft is perhaps showing us the future of golf scoring in its Pocket Golfwits golf scorekeeping application for Pocket PC, which allows you to enter every shot taken in a round of golf by tapping on a map of the course.

Watch Out!
Although Golfwits is available for all Pocket PCs, there are issues that make Golfwits better suited to the Compaq iPAQ H3650 Pocket PC. Along with its more compact size, the iPAQ alters its internal screen lighting to account for natural light. The screens on other Pocket PCs tend to wash out in sunlight and are difficult to read.

Remember
Pocket Golfwits has some competition in the IntelliGolf golf scorekeeping application for Pocket PC. If you want to learn more about IntelliGolf to do a comparison, visit the IntelliGolf Web site at `http://www.intelligolf.com`.

GET THE SCOOP ON...
How a Pocket PC Can Be Used As a Digital Camera ▪
Installing a Digital Camera Card ▪ Using a Digital
Camera Card to Take Pictures and Record Videos ▪
The Video Capabilities of Pocket PC ▪ Using Media
Players to Play Animations and Short Films

Photography, Video, and Your Pocket PC

A T THIS POINT IN THE BOOK, you certainly realize that a Pocket PC is capable of many things right out of the box, but you might be surprised to find out that with the right accessory it can also be a digital camera. It really isn't too much of a leap when you consider that a Pocket PC has a great viewfinder (screen) and a lot of storage options (memory), two requirements of any decent digital camera. All that's missing is the actual camera hardware, which can be placed conveniently on a CF card. It's pretty amazing, but you can get a digital camera CF card that plugs into your Pocket PC and allows you to take digital pictures and record short videos.

This chapter explores the role of Pocket PC as a digital photography tool. You learn how to use a popular digital camera card made by Casio, as well as a couple of software packages that make it possible to play videos on your Pocket PC in much the same way that Windows Media Player plays audio content.

Pocket PC: The Ultimate Digital Camera

Turning your Pocket PC into a digital camera is as simple as purchasing a special CF card that includes camera hardware. Casio makes a very compact digital camera CF card (JK-710DC) that includes a rotating lens for extremely flexible digital photo shoots. Because the Casio camera card is a CF card, it slides into the top of your Pocket PC using the CF slot. The camera lens rests on top of the device and can be rotated to shoot forward or backward. Unfortunately, the Casio camera card currently works only with Casio devices, which is a significant limitation. Hopefully, Casio (or some other manufacturer) will remedy this situation soon and release a camera card with wider support. Figure 20.1 shows the Casio camera card.

Figure 20.1
The Casio CF digital camera card (JK-710DC) is extremely compact and has a rotating lens.

Inside Scoop
The CMF file format is based upon the popular MPEG1 video format. You can view CMF videos on your desktop PC by using Casio's Mobile Video Player application. Casio offers utilities for converting from popular video formats into the CMF format, but there currently is no way to convert from CMF to another format.

Although it isn't fair to compare the Casio digital camera card to mega-pixel digital cameras that cost hundreds of dollars, it is a powerful Pocket PC accessory that turns your Pocket PC into a very capable digital camera. In terms of camera specifications, the Casio card uses a 350,000-pixel CCD with a focal range of 30.7 inches in Normal mode and 3.9 inches in Macro mode. The camera supports the JPEG file format for still images, and Casio's CMF file format for short videos. The camera card relies on the Pocket PC's main system battery for power, and puts a considerable drain on it. You should expect your battery life to drop sharply while using the camera.

As of this writing, Casio is alone in the CF digital camera market but I suspect they will have competition soon. It is totally logical to extend handheld computers and use them as digital cameras, so I believe this is an emerging market. The next few sections run through the installation and usage of the Casio card, which will demonstrate how natural it is to use a Pocket PC as a digital camera.

Installing a Digital Camera Card

Although it would be nice to plug in the digital camera card and immediately start taking pictures, you have to remember that Pocket PCs require drivers for new hardware, just like desktop PCs. Also, the Casio camera card comes with special software that is used to configure the card, take pictures, and record videos. This software is included on a CD-ROM that comes with the card. The CD-ROM includes a setup program that installs all the necessary software on your device.

The first two steps in the setup program for the Casio camera card, involve informing you that you need to have your device connected to your desktop computer and that you should NOT have the camera device attached to your Pocket PC when installing the software.

Clicking the Next button on the Remarks window displays the License Agreement window; you must agree to it to continue. After that, you can either accept the default destination folder for installing the software on your desktop or choose your own.

After clicking the OK button in the Destination Folder window, the setup program prompts you to confirm the creation of the new folder. After confirming the folder creation, a window appears that asks you to confirm the default installation directory for your Pocket PC. Clicking the Yes button accepts the default directory, which I recommend using. The final step in the installation process is copying the actual files to your Pocket PC, which takes a few moments.

After all the files are copied, the setup program finishes. At this point, you can turn your Pocket PC device off and insert the CF camera card. Turn the device back on and you're ready to start taking pictures!

Using Your Pocket PC As a Camera

The software installation for the Casio digital camera card results in the addition of an application to your Pocket PC called Mobile Camera. The Mobile Camera application is used to take pictures and record videos with the camera card. To launch the application, tap Programs in the Start menu, and then tap the Mobile Camera icon. Figure 20.2 shows the Mobile Camera application upon first being executed.

Figure 20.2
The Mobile
Camera applica-
tion initially con-
tains an empty
list of video
recordings.

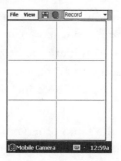

Shortcut
The two buttons
to the right of the
View menu allow
you to move
between different
views.

The initial view shown in the Mobile Camera application is a list of the video recordings that have been made, which is obviously empty to begin with. There are three views supported in Mobile Camera:

- **Record**—Take pictures and record videos.

- **Playback**—List of pictures you've taken or videos you've recorded.

- **Album**—Pictures and videos that you've organized for viewing.

The Playback view is a little misleading because you would think from its name that it would apply only to videos. However, the Playback view is used both to play back videos and to view still pictures. To switch to the Still screen in the Playback view, which is where you can see thumbnails of the digital pictures you've taken, tap View near the upper-left part of the screen, followed by Image Type, and then tap Still Screen. Of course, no pictures have been taken as of yet, so you might as well tap Record on the View menu to get started. Figure 20.3 shows the About Recording window, which is displayed each time you enter Record view.

The About Recording window provides information regarding the meaning of the buttons in the Record view. This window is displayed each time you enter Record mode or switch from still camera to video camera. For many, it will eventually get annoying, in which case you can uncheck the check box near the bottom of the window to disable it.

Figure 20.3
The About Recording window displays information about the buttons used to take pictures and record videos.

Record view supports two different approaches (modes) to using the digital camera card: still pictures and videos. By default, Mobile Camera always starts you off in Video mode. To switch to Picture mode, tap the button below the File menu that looks like a still camera. There is another button next to this one that looks like a video camera; these two buttons allow you to switch between modes. Regardless of what mode you're in, the Record view always shows a live image of what the camera is seeing in the middle of the screen.

To take pictures, you need to switch to Picture mode by tapping the Still Camera button just below the File menu. After you're in Picture mode, aim the camera at whatever you want to photograph and tap the Shutter button near the lower-right corner of the screen. After taking a few pictures, switch to the Still screen in the Playback view to see them. Figure 20.4 shows the Playback view with a few pictures stored away.

Figure 20.4
The Playback view allows you to view thumbnails of the pictures that have been taken.

Keep in mind that the Still screen in the Playback view is designed as a means of seeing what pictures you've taken and deciding which ones you want to keep. Although it initially

Remember
The Mobile Camera application has a fair amount of features built into it for fine-tuning the camera hardware to account for different lighting and focal points. Although it is important to understand these features to get the most out of your camera, keeping this chapter focused on the basics of using the Pocket PC as a photographic tool will hopefully allow users of non-Casio devices to apply this information to their own product (if/when other manufacturers put out camera devices of their own).

displays small thumbnails of the pictures, you can double-tap a picture to see it in a larger size. The pictures are stored in the JPEG image format, which is supported in just about all Web browsers and image-editing applications. You can keep pictures on your Pocket PC or move them over to your desktop PC using ActiveSync. By default, pictures taken with Mobile Camera are stored in the Record folder beneath the My Documents folder.

Recording a video using Mobile Camera is very similar to taking still pictures. The main difference is that you must use Movie mode in the Record window, which you switch to by tapping the video camera button below the View menu. To record a video, tap the Rec button near the lower-right corner of the screen to start recording. To stop the recording, tap the Stop button that is next to the Rec button. If you want to record a video without audio, there is a microphone button to the left of the Rec button that allows you to turn audio on or off for the video.

Like still pictures, videos are stored in the Record folder just beneath the My Documents folder. To view a video in the Mobile Camera application, just switch to the Playback view and select Movie Screen as the Image Type from the View menu. A thumbnail image of the first frame of the video is displayed for all movies in the directory.

To play a video that you've recorded, double-tap the thumbnail of the video in the Playback view. Figure 20.5 shows a video being played back in the Playback view. This video is a rare piece of footage of a Yeti that happened to walk through my office and pose for the camera.

Figure 20.5
The Playback view allows you to play back videos that have been recorded.

I mentioned a little earlier in the chapter that the Album view in the Mobile Camera application is used to organize pictures and videos. To create an album, tap Make Album in the File menu. An album consists of a folder that contains pictures and videos organized onto pages that you can flip through. An album gives you more control over the presentation of pictures and videos than the thumbnail list of files in the Playback view.

Pocket PC: The Not-So Ultimate Theatre

You've already learned that Pocket PCs are capable of recording and playing short videos using the Casio CF digital camera card. However, even without the camera card, it is possible to play videos using your Pocket PC. You might think that the Pocket PC Windows Media Player is capable of playing videos, but it isn't. Microsoft wanted to focus Windows Media Player on playing music, and not overburden it with video support. I agree with that strategy, but that doesn't mean there isn't a need for a Pocket PC video player. Instead, it means you'll have to go elsewhere for a video player.

Fortunately, a couple of different video players are available to use with Pocket PCs. Following are the two Pocket PC video players that are available as of this writing:

- PocketTV

- ActiveSky Media Player

The PocketTV video player supports the MPEG video standard, which is popular and in wide use. The ActiveSky Media Player currently only plays videos in the proprietary SKY format, but the company has plans to support the MPEG format at some point in the future. Even though the ActiveSky player supports only a proprietary video format, there are several content providers that offer interesting video content in the SKY format. One of these content providers is Atom Films (http://www.atomfilms.com), which is a Web-based film house that offers short films and animations for download. DEN (http://www.den.net) is another content provider whose focus is to provide an alternative to watching network and cable

Inside Scoop
You are limited to recording movies no longer than the available storage memory on your device. Of course, it would be nice to record straight to a CF card with lots of free memory, but that would be pretty difficult considering that Pocket PCs currently have only one CF slot at best, which the digital camera is using.

Remember
The desktop version of Windows Media Player includes extensive support for playing videos; the video limitation applies only to the Pocket PC version of Windows Media Player.

Inside Scoop
To be fair, Casio does offer a standalone video player, but it is based upon the same technology as the Mobile Camera application. Because you've already learned how to watch videos using Mobile Camera, and the Casio video player supports only Casio's own CMF video format, I thought it best to focus on the other two Pocket PC video players which can be used on Pocket PC devices other than Casio's.

television. Content is the name of the game when it comes to media players, so I recommend checking into the available content for each player when deciding which one to use.

Even though the two aforementioned media players are quality applications that do a good job of playing videos, you have to keep some perspective on the whole concept of using a Pocket PC to watch videos. Despite all their processing power (compared to competing devices), it's still pushing the envelope to expect Pocket PCs to perform well when managing the playback of video, a notoriously resource-intensive operation. In reality, they do a decent job of playing most videos but they're not going to replace VCRs or DVD players any time soon. Videos also hog a lot of storage space, so pay close attention to file sizes if you start cramming your device full of videos.

The PocketTV Video Player

Because video is very memory- and processor-hungry, it's not surprising that video players have demanding requirements. The PocketTV video player requires 500KB of storage space for the application, and an additional 2MB of free memory to run properly. So, be prepared to give up 2.5MB of space in your main system RAM to use PocketTV.

The PocketTV video player is freely available for download from the PocketTV Web site at `http://www.mpegtv.com/wince/pockettv`, or from Handango at `http://www.handango.com`. When you download the PocketTV player, a file named PocketTVSetup.exe will be placed on your desktop hard drive. To install the PocketTV player, just execute this file on your desktop PC.

When the Welcome window appears, clicking the Setup button takes you to the Destination Directory window, where you can specify the directory on your desktop PC in which PocketTV files are installed.

Clicking the OK button in the Destination Directory window takes you to the familiar Pocket PC installation window that prompts you to confirm the installation directory on your Pocket PC.

Clicking the Yes button to agree to the default installation directory will start the file copy portion of the installation, which takes a few moments.

When the PocketTV setup program finishes, the PocketTV video player is almost ready to run. Before you can start playing videos, however, you need to obtain a code and enter it in the PocketTV application to enable the application. Figure 20.6 shows the Register PocketTV screen, which is displayed when you first run the PocketTV application.

Figure 20.6
The Register PocketTV screen allows you to enter a code that enables the PocketTV application.

The key for this window is obtained from the PocketTV Web site. The site includes instructions for how to obtain the key, which involves filling out a brief registration form. The key is sent to you via email, after which you must enter it in the Register PocketTV screen. Upon entering the key and tapping OK in the upper-right corner of the screen, PocketTV displays a Thank You message and then takes you to the Open MPEG File window, which is shown in Figure 20.7.

Figure 20.7
The Open MPEG File window in PocketTV is where you open MPEG video files for playback.

As you can see, there is already a video listed in the Open MPEG File window, which I downloaded from the PocketTV Web site (http://www.mpegtv.com/wince/pockettv). The PocketTV Web site is a good place to start when it comes to acquiring MPEG-1 videos. As of this writing, there are a couple of movie trailers for download, as well as a five-minute South Park episode. To be fair, the South Park episode weighs in at 17MB, which can make it too large for Pocket PCs unless you're planning on storing the video on a CF storage card. Another place that has videos for download is the Palm Size Media Web site, which is located at http://www.palmsizemedia.com. This Web site includes several movie trailers and a few television commercials for download.

After you've located a video, download it to your desktop computer using a Web browser or FTP client. From your desktop computer, run ActiveSync and transfer the video file to the My Documents folder on your Pocket PC. After a video is stored in the My Documents folder, it is ready to be viewed in the PocketTV video player.

Getting back to the Open MPEG File window, all the videos on your Pocket PC are displayed in the file list. To play a video, tap it in the list and it will begin playing. Figure 20.8 shows a trailer for the Star Wars Special Edition movies being played in PocketTV.

Remember
Due to the relatively large size of most videos, it is a good idea to store them on a CF storage card if you have one. Just be sure to create a My Documents folder on the card if it doesn't already exist, and then place the video in it.

Figure 20.8
Tapping a video in the PocketTV video file list results in it being played.

You can control the playback of the video using the buttons located along the bottom of the screen in the PocketTV menu. There are buttons for Stop, Play/Pause, Fast Forward, and Step

Frame, as well as a Volume button. To the left of the buttons is a Tools menu that allows you to change parameters associated with the video such as how it is displayed. As an example, you can tap Options in the Tools menu, and then tap Size to set the manner in which a video is displayed. By default, PocketTV automatically determines the optimal size for a video, but you can also set the video to a nominal size to fit the screen while retaining the aspect ratio or to fill the screen. I find the automatic sizing feature to be adequate in most cases, but you can certainly change the video size according to your own preferences.

The ActiveSky Media Player

The ActiveSky Media Player is a video player similar to PocketTV but it is based on a different video format. The SKY video format used by the ActiveSky player is a proprietary format designed for use exclusively with the ActiveSky player. Although this might seem like a limitation, there is enough content available in the SKY format to make it a viable video format for Pocket PCs.

The ActiveSky Media Player is available for free download from the ActiveSky Web site at `http://www.activesky.com/download.html`. The actual downloadable file is hosted by Handango, which is automatically linked to by the ActiveSky Web page. To install the ActiveSky player, just execute the downloaded executable on your desktop PC after it finishes downloading.

Launching the install file brings up the Welcome window in which clicking Continue takes you to a second Welcome window with additional information about the setup process; just click the Next button to continue along with the installation. The Software License window is the next window displayed. To accept the ActiveSky software license and continue with the installation, click the Yes button. The Destination Location window is shown next, and is used to specify the directory on your desktop PC in which ActiveSky files are installed.

Clicking the Next button in the Destination Location window takes you to the Select Components window, in which you select the components to be installed. The components consist of the media player and user guide, both of which you should go ahead and install. Clicking the Next button begins the Pocket PC portion of the setup procedure, in which you are prompted to confirm the installation directory for ActiveSky on your device. You can modify this directory, or accept the default setting by clicking the Yes button. At this point, the setup program copies files from the desktop computer to the Pocket PC.

After copying files, the ActiveSky setup program displays the Setup Complete window, which states that the installation completed successfully. Clicking the Finish button closes the setup program.

Similar to the PocketTV player, the ActiveSky player requires a special registration code before it can be used to play videos. This code is obtained from the ActiveSky Web site; you are required to fill out a registration form to receive the code via email. The ActiveSky Web site will ask you for the device ID of your Pocket PC, which is displayed in the Registration screen that is first displayed when you run the ActiveSky player (see Figure 20.9). After you've obtained the registration code, enter it in the Registration screen to enable the application.

Figure 20.9
The Register screen allows you to enter a code that enables the ActiveSky application.

Tap OK in the upper-right corner of the screen, and the ActiveSky player opens and allows you to start playing videos. To open a video, you must tap the Open button near the lower-left corner of the screen; it resembles an open file folder. The Open window is then displayed, as shown in Figure 20.10.

Figure 20.10
The Open window
in the ActiveSky
player is where
you open SKY
video files for play-
back.

There is already a video listed in the Open window, which I downloaded from the Atom films Web site at http://www. atomfilms.com. The Atom Films Web site contains a lot of interesting animations and short films, and is a great place to start when it comes to acquiring SKY videos. The Content Page of the Active Sky Web site is also a great resource for hunting down SKY videos. This page is located at http://www.activesky. com/prod_content.html.

After locating a video, download it to your desktop computer using a Web browser or FTP client. You must then transfer it to your Pocket PC by using ActiveSync on your desktop computer. The video must be placed in the My Documents folder of your Pocket PC for ActiveSky to find it. You can also place a video on a CF storage card as long as it is in the My Documents folder on the card. After a video is stored in the My Documents folder, it is ready to be viewed in the ActiveSky video player.

To play a video, tap it in the list shown in the Open window and it will begin playing. Figure 20.11 shows a short animated movie titled "Planes, Trains, and Pocket PCs" that stars an Atom Films character known as the Suckup Guy. In this episode, the Suckup Guy bumps into Steve Ballmer of Microsoft and learns about Pocket PCs. This animation was shown at the initial rollout of Pocket PCs to demonstrate their power.

The video's playback is controlled via a series of buttons that line the bottom of the screen. There are buttons for Open, Play, Pause/Step Frame, Stop, Options, and Zoom; for some reason, there is no volume button. To the left of the buttons is a File menu that allows you to view the properties of a video and alter options for the player. Player options include the capability of changing the playback speed, continuous play, and zoom level, to name a few.

Figure 20.11
Tapping a video in
the ActiveSky
video file list
results in it being
played.

Essential Information

- You can turn your Pocket PC into a digital camera by installing a digital camera CF card (currently available only for Casio Pocket PCs).

- The Casio JK-710DC digital camera card allows you to take still pictures and record short movies with audio.

- Because Windows Media Player is designed solely around the playback of digital audio, it can't be used to play videos; you have to rely on third-party applications for video playback.

- The PocketTV video player supports the MPEG-1 video format, whereas the ActiveSky Media Player supports the proprietary SKY video format.

- Regardless of the video player you use or the format in which videos are stored, it's a good idea to store videos on a CF storage card to preserve main system RAM.

PART VI

Appendixes

A Guide to Pocket PC Accessories

POCKET PCS ARE INCREDIBLY POWERFUL devices straight out of the box. However, their power, flexibility, and usability can be greatly improved with the addition of a few choice accessories. Many of these accessories come in the form of CompactFlash (CF) cards that plug into standard Pocket PC CF slots. The current drawback with most Pocket PC devices is that they have only a single CF slot, which makes it impossible to have more than one CF card installed at any given time. As an example, this can be a problem when you use a CF card for additional memory as well as for modem communications. Right now, there is no good solution to this problem; you're basically left having to carefully decide what goes on a CF memory card so it can be removed without causing problems. Future Pocket PCs probably will come with multiple CF slots.

→ **See Also** "Memory," **p. 21**.

This appendix explores some of the more interesting Pocket PC accessories currently available. The accessories are broken down into the following categories:

- Storage
- Communication
- Multimedia and I/O

Remember
The reason most
Pocket PCs
include only one
CF slot is to
reduce the size of
the device. Two
CF slots would
most likely have
to be stacked one
on top of the
other, which
would increase
the thickness of a
device consider-
ably. Compaq
goes a step fur-
ther than most
manufacturers
with their iPAQ
series of Pocket
PCs, which add a
CF slot by sliding
the device into a
special CF sleeve.

- Carrying cases

- Pointing tools

Storage

Because memory is a limited resource in all Pocket PC devices, additional storage is likely the most useful accessory you'll purchase. The most popular accessory for expanding the memory of Pocket PCs is the CF memory card, which is a CF card containing RAM that is extremely valuable for storing data and installed applications. Because CF memory cards are an industry standard, they can be interchanged with some digital cameras.

The other type of storage accessory currently available for Pocket PCs is IBM's Microdrive CF cards. A Microdrive CF card is a tiny hard disk drive embedded in a CF card. The big advantage the Microdrive CF cards have over CF memory cards is price; as of this writing, Microdrive cards are roughly half the price of CF memory cards when you consider the price per megabyte (MB) of storage. Microdrive CF cards are also available in considerably larger sizes than CF memory cards. One drawback to Microdrive CF cards is that they (like any hard disk) are slower to access than RAM. Even so, the speed issue with Microdrive CF cards is not a deal breaker—they are speedy enough to use without too much of a wait problem.

Memory Cards

CF memory cards are currently available in sizes ranging from 8MB to 320MB, depending on the manufacturer. The primary manufacturers of CF memory cards are Kingston Technology, Pretec, and Sandisk. The cards themselves weigh approximately a half-ounce and are the size of a matchbook. CF memory cards are designed according to the CompactFlash Type I standard, which means they are usable on the widest range of Pocket PC devices; some Pocket PC devices support only CompactFlash Type I cards.

One compelling reason to use CF memory cards is because they are compatible with digital cameras such as the popular

Kodak DC280 camera. If you happen to own a digital camera that uses CF memory cards, you can take pictures, slide the card into your Pocket PC, and then view, edit, and email the pictures. In addition to storing photographic images, CF memory cards are great for storing other types of memory-hungry data such as MP3 or WMA music.

IBM Microdrive Cards

I've made the analogy earlier in the book that RAM in a Pocket PC plays the same storage role as a hard disk drive in a desktop or laptop computer. If you aren't a big fan of analogies, you can forgo a CF memory card and install a hard drive in your Pocket PC. As stated earlier, IBM Microdrive CF cards are tiny hard drives embedded within CF cards that can be used to expand the storage of Pocket PCs. Unlike CF memory cards, Microdrive CF cards are designed around the CompactFlash Type II standard, which means the cards are slightly thicker (5mm thick) than the Type I cards (3.3mm thick). This also means that you must have a Pocket PC that supports Type II cards.

The Microdrive CF cards are currently available in 170MB, 340MB, and 1GB. Even with the advantages of the Microdrive hard disk versus CF memory cards, there is one noticeable downside (other than the need for a CF Type II slot). Microdrive CF cards put a heavier drain on the main Pocket PC battery. The degree to which this drain affects your specific device varies according to the normal battery life, condition of the battery, and so on. Regardless of the specifics, you'll get a shorter runtime when using a Microdrive CF card. However, the dramatically increased storage just might be worth it! To learn more about IBM Microdrives, visit the Microdrive Web site at `http://www.storage.ibm.com/hardsoft/diskdrdl/micro`.

Watch Out!
Because the Microdrive CF card doesn't have a lip to grab to extract the card, you should make sure you can get the card out of your Pocket PC before inserting it. One approach is to stick an adhesive plastic tab to the card to use as a pull-tab for removing the card. Casio includes several of these tabs with the Cassiopeia E-115. Ideally, every Pocket PC device would have an eject switch that is used to push CF cards out when you want to remove them, but so far no devices have these switches.

Communication

Communication comes in a close second to storage as the most useful type of Pocket PC accessory. Communication accessories include 56Kbps modem cards, infrared modems, digital phone cards, wireless network cards, Ethernet cards, and serial cards.

As this list reveals, there are a lot of options when it comes to communicating with a Pocket PC.

56Kbps Modem Cards

56Kbps modem cards are CF cards that include tiny 56Kbps (kilobits per second) embedded modems. Not surprisingly, these modems function much like external modems for desktop or laptop PCs. From the Pocket PC's perspective, you establish a dial-up modem connection, which allows you to use the modem to connect to an ISP or some other dial-up network. CF modem cards are relatively power efficient, so you don't have to worry too much about them draining the battery of your Pocket PC.

Currently, the manufacturers of 56Kbps modem cards are Casio, Compaq, Kingston Technology, and Pretec. Because all the modem cards provide similar functionality, the primary difference between them is size. The Casio modem card is the same size as a CF memory card with an additional connector cable attached to it for plugging in a phone line. The Compaq, Kingston, and Pretec cards are considerably larger, and include the phone line connector on the modem itself. If you're looking for a modem that can be safely tucked away inside your Pocket PC, the Casio modem is a winner. However, it does require you to keep track of the connector cable, which could get lost. The Compaq, Kingston, and Pretec modems are larger and protrude from the CF card slot, but they are self-contained so there is nothing to worry about losing.

Psion Infrared Travel Modem

Perhaps one of the most interesting uses of the Pocket PC infrared port is the Psion infrared Travel Modem, which communicates with a Pocket PC at speeds up to 56Kbps using the infrared port. In other words, the modem sits next to your Pocket PC and doesn't involve any physical connection to the device. There are several advantages to the infrared modem approach taken by Psion:

- There are no wires connected to your Pocket PC.

- The CF slot is kept free for other accessories such as a memory card.

- There is minimal power drain on the Pocket PC battery.

The Travel Modem operates on two AA batteries or an optional power adapter, which explains why it doesn't eat into the Pocket PC battery. This is probably a benefit for most Pocket PC users, but it does mean that you have to concern yourself with buying new batteries when the modem goes dead, or possibly investing in rechargeable batteries. Expect a fresh set of AA batteries to be good for around four to six hours of continuous online use.

The obvious downside to the Travel Modem is that it has to be physically positioned next to a Pocket PC so their infrared ports line up. Additionally, the modem must be positioned reasonably close to the Pocket PC, typically within a few feet. Depending on how you are accustomed to using your Pocket PC, this might not be a big deal. At times, it would probably be beneficial to have the convenience of a CF modem card that is physically attached to the device, although at other times the Travel Modem would probably work just fine. It really comes down to an individual preference. One argument that cannot be refuted is the benefit of not having to give up your CF slot for the Travel Modem. To find out more about the Psion infrared Travel Modem, visit the Psion Travel Modem Web page at http://www.psionconnect.com/tm56kgsma.htm.

Socket Digital Phone Card

If you like the convenience of your digital mobile phone and would like to have the same convenience with Pocket PC connectivity, the Socket digital phone card is a product that might just meet your needs. The Socket card is a CF Type I card that slides into a Pocket PC and connects with a digital mobile phone using a special cable; the digital phone must be a CDMA or GSM phone. Currently Socket provides digital phone cards that are compatible with Qualcomm, Nokia, and

Ericsson phones. Aside from the obvious portable connectivity benefits, the Socket card is a very low-power accessory, which means it won't take too much of a bite out of the precious Pocket PC battery life. To learn more about the Socket digital phone card, visit the Socket Products Web page at `http://www.socketcom.com/prodinfo.htm`.

Sierra Wireless AirCard

For mobile Pocket PC users who want the utmost in connectivity flexibility, the Sierra Wireless AirCard 300 is a solid option. The AirCard is basically a wireless CF modem card designed to work on CDPD (Cellular Digital Packet Data) networks. The AirCard is a CF Type II card, and has a small antenna that it uses to reach the CDPD network. The glaring drawback to the AirCard is its slow maximum speed of 19.2Kbps. However, when you consider the flexibility of being able to surf the Web and check email from virtually any location, the speed is something you can probably learn to accept.

The AirCard is more expensive than its wired counterparts, and also requires CDPD service through a wireless ISP. The additional expense associated with the AirCard makes it impractical for some users, although it will be equally indispensable to others. Stop by the Sierra AirCard Web page at `http://www.sierrawireless.com/ProductsOrdering/pccards.html` for more information about the AirCard 300.

Socket Network Cards

Socket, the maker of the digital phone CF card, also offers traditional network cards for Ethernet and serial connections. Both cards are CF Type I cards, which means they can be used in any Pocket PC with a CF slot. The Ethernet card includes a removable RJ-45 cable that allows you to connect a Pocket PC to a 10BASE-T Ethernet network. There is also a rugged version of the Ethernet card that includes a fixed cable with a reinforced connector for use in industrial applications.

The Socket serial CF card effectively acts as a serial COM port for Pocket PCs. In other words, you can install the serial CF card and connect to serial devices such as modems, digital cameras, bar code scanners, and so on. If you're industrious enough to write your own driver, you might even be able to hook a mouse up to your Pocket PC! To find out more about the Socket network cards, visit the Socket Products Web page at http://www.socketcom.com/prodinfo.htm.

Multimedia and I/O

Multimedia accessories are in many ways the flashiest of Pocket PC add-ons because they provide sizzle with sounds and imagery. These accessories are composed of surprising pieces of hardware such as audio amplifiers, digital camera CF cards, portable scanners, portable printers, and Pocket PC keyboards.

Boostaroo Audio Amplifier

Even though Pocket PCs include the capability of playing music via MP3 or WMA music files, some of the devices are weak in terms of how much power they devote to audio playback. More specifically, it can be difficult to hear music on some Pocket PCs when there is ambient noise such as listening in a car, even with the volume cranked up high. For these devices, you might want to consider using an audio amplifier, which boosts the audio signal coming out of the headphone jack of the Pocket PC to give you a better (or at least louder) listening experience.

The Boostaroo is an audio amplifier designed to boost the signal of audio, and is perfectly suited for Pocket PC listeners. It is a small device powered by two AA batteries, and it plugs into the headphone jack of a Pocket PC. In addition to boosting the audio of a Pocket PC, the Boostaroo also provides two extra headphone jacks, which allows a total of three people to listen in at once. Now when you're traveling by plane, everyone on your aisle can listen in together as you spin MP3 tunes.

The Boostaroo doesn't have a volume control of its own; instead, it boosts the signal that it receives. So, you still control the volume of the Pocket PC using the standard volume control. The big difference is that you'll find half volume with the Boostaroo to be louder than full volume without it. For more

information on the Boostaroo, visit the Boostaroo Web site at
http://www.boostaroo.com.

Koss Audio Amplifier

Another option for boosting the audio signal on Pocket PCs is
the Koss EQ-30 audio amplifier. It performs a function similar
to the Boostaroo, but it doesn't provide the extra headphone
jacks. On the upside, the Koss amplifier includes a three-band
equalizer that allows you to fine-tune the audio signal to some
degree. This amplifier does include its own volume control,
which might be seen as a benefit or a drawback depending on
your own personal preference. The benefit would be that you
can clip the amplifier to your belt and have an easy to access
volume control; the drawback would be the complexity of having two volume controls with which to contend. For more
information on the Koss audio amplifier, visit the Koss Web site
at http://www.koss.com.

Casio Digital Camera Card

My favorite of all Pocket PC accessories is without a doubt the
Casio Digital Camera card. Being able to turn your Pocket PC
into a digital camera with the slip of a CF card is a gadgeteer's
dream. The Casio Digital Camera Card is a CF Type II card that
allows you to take digital photos and record short movies. The
length of the movies you can record is limited by the available
memory in your device. The card is extremely compact and
seamlessly integrates into the Casio E-115 Pocket PC. It will
technically work with any Pocket PC that supports a CF Type II
slot, but it is obviously designed to accompany Casio devices.

The camera extends above the CF slot where the lens is actually located, and has a small notch thoughtfully cut out of the
edge of it to allow access to the stylus. The camera is very
ergonomic, allowing you to swivel the lens around and take
pictures of yourself. Pictures taken with the camera are automatically stored as JPEG images, although movies are stored in
Casio's CMF (Casio Movie File) format. The camera includes
software for converting CMF movies into the more standard
AVI format.

The only significant drawback to the camera is its drain on a Pocket PC's battery. The camera drains an enormous amount of battery power, and therefore shortens Pocket PC battery life considerably. As long as you take this into consideration when you set out to take pictures, you can plan around the shortened battery life and keep your Pocket PC charged up accordingly. You also should take into consideration the fact that the camera doesn't have a flash, which means you'll need decent lighting in order to take pictures. Stop by the Digital Camera Card page on Casio's Web site at `http://www.casio.com/ products/index.cfm?act=0&PID=1644`.

Casio Freedio Palm-Sized Scanner

For those situations when you are in desperate need of a mobile scanner, Casio has just the accessory for you. The Casio Freedio FZ-700S palm-sized scanner is a miniature scanner designed for use with Pocket PCs. The scanner is designed for scanning small documents such as business cards, but can also be used to scan larger documents by hand scanning with multiple passes. The Freedio scanner uses the infrared port on a Pocket PC, and can also be connected to a desktop PC using a serial port. To make things even more interesting, you can connect the Freedio scanner directly to a parallel printer and print scanned images. In fact, Casio makes a companion handheld printer that is covered in the next section. To learn more about the Freedio palm-sized scanner, visit the Freedio scanner page on Casio's Web site at `http://www.casio.com/products/index. cfm?act=0&PID=1642`.

Casio Freedio Palm-Sized Printer

Pocket PCs aren't exactly known for their printing capabilities, but that doesn't mean printing isn't an option. In fact, Casio has a portable printer designed with Pocket PCs in mind. The Freedio FZ-500P palm-sized printer is designed for mobile printing from Pocket PC devices. Like the Freedio scanner, the Freedio printer uses the infrared port on a Pocket PC to receive data for printing. It also supports a parallel port interface for connecting it to a desktop PC or directly to the Freedio scanner. The printer prints 64 shades of gray at a resolution of 400dpi (dots per inch). To learn more about the Freedio palm-sized printer, visit the Freedio printer page on Casio's Web site at `http://www.casio.com/products/index.cfm?act=0&PID=1643`.

KeySync Keyboard

Text entry is a major limitation of any handheld device, including Pocket PCs. As efficient as you might get at using the stylus to write or peck keys on the soft keyboard, it's doubtful that you'll be able to match the speed and convenience of a traditional computer keyboard. That's why DS International offers a keyboard specifically designed for use with handheld devices such as Pocket PCs. The KeySync Keyboard is powered by three AAA batteries, and connects to Pocket PCs via a serial or USB port. For more information regarding the KeySync Keyboard, visit the DS International Web site at `http://www.notestation.com/dsintl`.

Carrying Cases

A relatively inexpensive accessory that you might consider picking up for your Pocket PC is a carrying case. Most Pocket PCs come with a carrying case of some sort, but it's possible to upgrade to a significantly nicer and more protective case if you so desire. If you carry your Pocket PC in situations in which it might be at risk of physical abuse, a rigid case might be a worthy investment. You might also consider a carrying case that folds open to provide space for other personal items such as credit cards.

RhinoSkin Cases

RhinoSkin makes several carrying cases that are designed specifically to hold Pocket PCs. From the sleek Executive Leather Case to the sporty RhinoPak 2000, there are cases to meet the needs of most Pocket PC users. The RhinoPak 2000 is a particularly interesting carrying case because it is designed for the rugged Pocket PC user. It resembles a mountain bike gear bag, and includes elastic straps inside to secure your Pocket PC in place. There are several pockets for storage of extra batteries and accessories. If you need extra space for other gadgets, you can move up to the RhinoPak 3000, which is similar to the RhinoPak 2000 but with extra room. At the other end of the spectrum is the RhinoPak 1100, which is a relatively slim-lined case with extra pockets for storing business cards, credit cards, and so on. To find out more about RhinoSkin cases, visit the Pocket PC page of the RhinoSkin Web site at `http://rhinoskin.com/palm_pc_page.htm`.

Incase Designs PDA Case

If you're looking for sleekness and style in a carrying case, you might want to check out Incase Designs' PDA Case for Pocket PCs. The oval shape of the case looks unique when compared to traditional rectangular cases. Even more unique is the graphite-colored neoprene material used for the exterior of the case. This case is so hip it was even featured in the January, 2000 *InStyle* magazine; of course, the Palm version of the case was featured because Pocket PCs had not even been released in January of 2000. To get the full scoop on the Incase Designs PDA Case, visit this Web site: `http://stores.yahoo.com/goincase`.

Otterbox

If you think your Pocket PC might run the risk of being trampled by an angry mob of loggers, run over by a dump truck, or tied to a concrete block and tossed in a lake, then the Otterbox is your dream come true. The Otterbox is not really sleek or stylish, but it will protect your Pocket PC like no other carrying case. Otterbox cases are designed to be crushproof and water resistant to 100-foot depths. They also float, which hopefully means you won't have to rely on the water-resistant feature. Not surprisingly, they have a lifetime guarantee. The Otterbox is available in a variety of different sizes and colors, and includes a handy cord for keeping it attached to your person. For more information about the Otterbox, visit the Otterbox Web site at `http://www.otterbox.com`.

Pointing Tools

One accessory that you will inevitably find yourself needing is a new stylus. Whether you misplace it, it wears out, or you want to upgrade to a fancier one, the stylus is an accessory that practically every Pocket PC user will replace. A lot of different styli are on the market, including straight replacements from Pocket PC manufacturers to fancy upgrades that include ballpoint pens. There is even a small Pocket PC stylus that clips on to your finger, effectively making you the stylus. Following are some of the more popular styli that you might want to consider when the time comes to replace or upgrade your stylus:

- Platinum Pen Mini Three Action PDA Stylus
- Platinum Pen Zepher Mini Three Action PDA Stylus
- Platinum Pen Dual Action PDA Stylus
- Platinum Pen Executive Three Action PDA Stylus
- Casio Combination PDA Stylus and Ballpoint Pen
- Fellowes FingerTip Stylus
- Fellowes PenCap Stylus

Most of these styli are available for purchase at retailers that carry Pocket PCs. Refer to the Retailers section of Appendix B, "Pocket PC Resources," for more information on Pocket PC retailers.

Pocket PC Resources

THIS BOOK WAS INTENDED TO PROVIDE you with loads of insight into Pocket PC devices, what makes them tick, and how to use them more effectively. Even so, you may find yourself wanting to know more, in which case I can help direct you to other resources that will provide additional information about Pocket PCs. This appendix is broken down into three major sections that each covers a different type of Pocket PC resource:

- Web sites
- Publications
- Retailers

Web Sites

Web sites are undoubtedly the best place to go to learn more about Pocket PCs or to diagnose a particular problem. Although I am a big advocate of tinkering with computers and electronics to learn how they work, you can get a significant jump on learning tips and tricks by visiting a few informative Web sites. This book has hopefully touched on most of the more powerful Pocket PC tips and tricks, but I'm sure more are out there if you spend the time visiting some of the sites mentioned in the following sections. You'll also find these sites indispensable for product reviews, be it new Pocket PC accessories or a comparison of Pocket PC devices.

Microsoft's Pocket PC Web Site

Not surprisingly, Microsoft lays claim to the official Pocket PC Web site, located at http://www.microsoft.com/pocketpc. This site is actually divided into two subsites: Microsoft's Mobile Devices site and the Pocket PC Platform site. The Mobile Devices site focuses more on the hardware of handheld devices, and includes information about Pocket PC devices as well as larger Windows CE Handheld PC (H/PC) devices. Plan on spending most of your time on the Pocket PC Platform section.

The Pocket PC Platform site is a great source of Pocket PC information, and includes a wide variety of small technical articles designed to help you accomplish a certain task or solve a certain problem. The articles are broken down into the following categories:

- Viewpoints

- Help & How to

- Highlights

I regularly visit this site to read new articles and learn about Microsoft's official take on certain Pocket PC issues. In addition to helpful how-to articles, you'll find useful tips on how to circumvent known bugs such as the corrupted database problem with Pocket Money or the missing skins problem with the Windows Media Player. For more information on these particular problems, see Chapter 15, "Using Pocket Money," and Chapter 17, "Fun with the Windows Media Player."

→ **See Also** "Synchronizing Money for Pocket PC," **p. 242**.

→ **See Also** "Personalizing Windows Media Player," **p. 287**.

Dale Coffing's Pocket PC Page

Dale Coffing's Pocket PC Page is a great source of Pocket PC information that you are unlikely to find anywhere else. Mr. Coffing is the consummate Pocket PC tinkerer, and has loads of great insider tips and tricks on his site. To give you an idea regarding the type of information on this site, Mr. Coffing includes instructions on how to build your own Pocket PC battery extender, as well as how to make a mobile phone cable and a car adapter to power your Pocket PC on the go. You may not have the desire to go to such lengths to enhance your Pocket PC experience, but it's still interesting to learn the possibilities.

Beyond the hardware projects, Dale Coffing's Pocket PC Page also includes a lot of great Pocket PC news links, rumors of upcoming devices and accessories, and numerous suggestions for improving the Pocket PC experience. The site is located at http://www.iolnm.net/dcoffing/Casio. The "General FAQs, Tips & Tricks" section is a great place to start.

Chris De Herrera's Windows CE Web Site

Chris De Herrera's Windows CE Web site is another great site maintained by an individual with a big interest in handheld computing. It originated as an educational site for Windows CE users back with Windows CE version 1.0, and has evolved into a broad knowledge base for all Windows CE devices. There is a fairly large section of the site devoted to Pocket PC (Windows CE 3.0), including a feature comparison of Pocket PC devices, useful tips and tricks, and an archive of Pocket PC news articles. The site is also a great place to learn about the origins of Pocket PC by exploring previous versions of Windows CE.

If Chris' site isn't enough for you, he hosts a Windows CE chat on America Online's PDA Forum on the first and third Wednesday of each month at 6:30 p.m. PDT. He is also an Assistant Forum Manager for Microsoft Network's Windows CE Forum, where he hosts a monthly chat on the first Thursday of each month at 7:00 p.m. PDT. Chris De Herrera's Windows CE Web site is located at http://www.cewindows.net.

BrightHand

BrightHand is a Web site that grew out of a consulting business called BrightHand Consulting, Inc. It quickly grew from a handful of articles and a discussion board to become a broad information repository for handheld device users. BrightHand is devoted to handheld devices in general, and therefore includes coverage of both Pocket PCs and Palm devices. Although Pocket PC diehards might perceive this as a negative, the two types of devices will likely coexist, at least for the foreseeable future.

The discussion boards are probably the most valuable part of the BrightHand site, as they see a fair amount of posts. The BrightHand site is located at http://www.brighthand.com.

The Gadgeteer

The Gadgeteer is a Web site devoted to handheld devices in general, including Pocket PCs, Palm devices, and other handhelds. As opposed to other sites that include unique content of their own, the Gadgeteer mainly serves as a link repository to guide you to other Pocket PC resources scattered across the Web. Even so, its compilation of device comparisons, reviews, and FAQs is nice to have at your fingertips. The Gadgeteer Web site is located at http://www.the-gadgeteer.com.

PocketNow

PocketNow is a solid Web site devoted specifically to Pocket PC. In it you will find articles, news, reviews, device comparisons, discussion forums, classified ads, and a concise but informative FAQ. The news section of the site is probably my favorite because it reports on the entire handheld computing world. You can visit PocketNow by pointing your browser to http://www.pocketnow.com.

Pocket PC Help

Another Web site consisting mainly of links to other places on the Web is Pocket PC Help, which is located at http://www.pocketpchelp.com. Pocket PC Help is broken down into several categories including articles, news, hardware, software, and so on. One particularly interesting section of the site is Craig's Corner, where the host of the site, Craig Peacock, provides his own commentary and review of Pocket PC devices. Pocket PC Help is also one of the few Pocket PC Web sites to include a programming section.

Wired Guy

Wired Guy is a well-organized Web site devoted to both Pocket PCs and Palm devices. Wired Guy is essentially a review site, but thoroughly reviews Pocket PC hardware, software, and accessories. For more information, visit the Wired Guy Web site at `http://www.wiredguy.com`.

Publications

No one can argue that Web sites can't be beaten for up-to-the-minute information on just about anything, including Pocket PCs. However, traditional printed publications also have their place. Even Pocket PCs with their ClearType technology won't completely replace printed material in the very near future, which is why I still find myself reading magazines and newspapers on a regular basis. Add to this the fact that most magazines and newspapers have an online presence, and you simply can't ignore the value of a print publication. Following are a couple of magazines that I recommend as valuable sources of Pocket PC insight:

- *Pocket PC Life Magazine*

- *Pocket PC Magazine*

Because Web sites typically try to keep things very bite-sized, you'll find that these magazines often spend more time delving into Pocket PC topics. Print articles are also often more accurate and better written, perhaps due to the fact that it is much tougher to correct mistakes in print whereas a Web page can always be updated.

Pocket PC Life Magazine

Formerly *Windows CE Power Magazine, Pocket PC Life Magazine* aims to explore ways you can improve your life by using Pocket PCs. This is a grand ambition for a magazine, but it should be interesting to see how they pull it off. Based upon the quality of *Windows CE Power Magazine, Pocket PC Life Magazine* should be a great resource for Pocket PC users of all levels. Be on the lookout for the magazine at your local bookstore, or drop by the magazine's Web site at `http://www.pocketpclife.com`.

Pocket PC Magazine

Although the magazine was around before Microsoft officially blessed the Pocket PC name, *Pocket PC Magazine* is a great resource for users of all Windows-powered handheld devices. With Microsoft's recent shift away from Windows CE and toward Pocket PC, the magazine is following the same approach and becoming more centered on Pocket PC topics. The magazine is packed with tips, reviews, a download of the week, and a buyer's guide that is sure to grow as more Pocket PC devices and accessories are released. The magazine is available at most local bookstores, and online at http://www.pocketpcmag.com.

Retailers

Remember
For a complete list of Pocket PC retailers, please refer to Microsoft's online list of retailers at http://www. microsoft.com/ pocketpc/ retailers.asp.

Now that you know where to go to learn more about Pocket PC hardware, software, and accessories, it doesn't hurt to know where you can buy it. Pocket PCs are available through most traditional office and electronics stores such as Office Depot, Staples, Best Buy, and CompUSA. In addition to those large "brick and mortar" retailers, there are many online retailers that carry Pocket PC products. Some of the larger online retailers include Amazon.com, Beyond.com, and Buy.com.

Although a large online retailer can often offer rock-bottom prices, you might prefer dealing with an online retailer that specializes in handheld devices. Following are some online retailers that cater to the handheld market:

- **Handango**—http://www.handango.com

- **PocketGear**—http://www.pocketgear.com

- **CEShopper**—http://www.ceshopper.com

- **smaller.com**—http://www.smaller.com

- **MobilePlanet**—http://www.mobileplanet.com

Resetting Your Pocket PC

U NLIKE DESKTOP AND MOST NOTEBOOK computers, Pocket PCs never truly shut down when you turn them off. When you power down a Pocket PC, the screen turns off and the device certainly looks like it's doing nothing, but everything in memory is actually preserved. That's why when you turn on a Pocket PC, you are instantly returned to the last thing you were doing, such as editing an email document or playing a fierce game of Pac-Man. This functionality is sometimes referred to as "instant-on," and is an incredibly powerful feature.

The occasional downside of Pocket PC "instant-on" functionality is revealed when applications don't perform properly. You no doubt are familiar with applications crashing on a desktop computer, resulting in your having to reboot to clean everything up. Unfortunately, Pocket PC applications are also capable of crashing and causing problems with memory, in which case it's important to be able to restart the device with a clean slate.

At this point, it's worth clarifying that there are two different logical areas of memory in a Pocket PC: active RAM and storage RAM. I made up these designations to distinguish between RAM that acts as a "memory hard drive" to store installed applications and application data (storage RAM), and RAM that is used by the Pocket PC operating system and applications to perform various processing tasks (active RAM). Storage RAM

Inside Scoop
Special memory is being developed for desktop and notebook computers to give them "instant-on" functionality similar to Pocket PCs. That way, you won't have to sit through a two-minute boot sequence every time you turn your computer on. It also helps in terms of keeping your work active and not having to reopen applications.

Remember
Pocket PCs also have ROM, which is used to hold the Pocket PC operating system and standard applications.

is a concept that doesn't currently exist on desktop and notebook computers; all their RAM is active RAM.

Getting back to the issue of restarting a Pocket PC with a crashed application, the problem usually arises from the fact that active RAM has been corrupted by the application. It's worth pointing out that in the vast majority of situations, this problem is associated with an application that doesn't behave properly, as opposed to the Pocket PC device itself. The only sure-fire way to deal with the problem is to reset the device, which is equivalent to rebooting a desktop PC. This type of reset is known as a basic reset, or soft reset, because it clears only the active RAM. There is another type of reset called a full reset, or hard reset, that completely resets a Pocket PC to its factory settings. This second type of reset clears any data you have stored on a device, as well as any applications you have installed.

A full reset essentially clears all the RAM in a device (both active and storage). The only reason to perform a full reset is to completely reset up your Pocket PC from scratch. A full reset is somewhat akin to formatting the hard drive on a desktop PC, with the primary difference being that the Pocket PC operating system and standard applications are still present in ROM on the Pocket PC, whereas you have to manually reinstall all software on a desktop PC. As harsh as a full reset sounds, it's still a handy feature if you want to start over with the device in the same state it was in when you bought it.

Performing a Soft Reset

A soft reset is easy to perform and is identical across all Pocket PC devices. Every Pocket PC is required to have a reset button that is typically located on the back of the device. The reset button is intentionally inset so that it can't be pressed without using a pointed object such as a stylus. To perform a soft reset, locate the reset button on your device, grab your stylus, and follow these steps:

1. Turn the power on.

2. Press the reset button with the stylus and hold it for a couple of seconds.

After holding down the reset button for a second or two, the screen goes blank and then displays a starting screen. You may also hear an audible chime to indicate that the device was reset. After a few more seconds, the Today screen appears, in which case the device has been successfully reset.

Keep in mind that a soft reset deletes any data on your device that is in the process of being input or edited; in other words, anything that isn't yet saved is lost. Device settings and anything you've already saved are retained after a soft reset. You'll typically want to perform a soft reset when an application has failed, leaving the device in a questionable state. An example of such a state is the device not responding when you tap the screen or press a button, or when the animated wait icon stays up indefinitely.

Part of the soft reset procedure is the device performing a memory check to make sure that there is no problem with the memory. If a memory problem is detected during a soft reset, the device displays an error message instead of the Today screen. You are then prompted to press the Action button to continue with the reset, in which case the device attempts to repair the memory problem. If memory cannot be repaired, another error message appears indicating that the memory error is fatal, in which case a hard reset is necessary. Pressing the Action button allows you to perform a hard reset, which erases all the RAM in the system, including saved data and installed applications.

Performing Hard Reset

Just as it is sometimes beneficial to clean off the hard drive of a desktop computer and start anew, it is also sometimes necessary to perform a hard reset on your Pocket PC. You will have to perform a hard reset if memory gets corrupted and cannot be repaired. You may also want to perform a hard reset if you forget your password.

Remember
Avoid using the backup feature in ActiveSync if you suspect a memory error because the corrupted memory will be part of the backup, and will reveal itself when you attempt to restore the data. Perform regular backups when there aren't problems to avoid this situation.

Unlike a soft reset, which is uniform across all Pocket PCs, the steps required to perform a hard reset are not the same across all devices. The next few sections explain how to perform a hard reset on each of the major types of Pocket PC devices that are available as of this writing. If information about your device isn't provided here, please refer to the hardware manual, which should contain directions on how to perform a hard reset.

Casio Cassiopeia E-115 and HP Jornada 540

Following are the steps required to perform a hard reset on the Cassiopeia E-115 Pocket PC and the HP Jornada 540 line of Pocket PCs:

1. Turn the power off.

2. Remove the device from the cradle or unplug it from the USB cable.

3. Remove any CompactFlash cards that are installed.

4. Press and hold down the power button.

5. While holding down the power button, press the reset button with the stylus and hold it for a couple of seconds.

6. Press the Action button to confirm that you want to proceed with a hard reset.

7. Press the Action button again to confirm that you really want to erase all the device's RAM.

Following these steps results in the device's RAM being completely cleared, which restores the unit to its factory settings. You can cancel out of a hardware reset in steps 5 or 6 by pressing the Start button.

Compaq iPAQ H3600

Following are the steps required to perform a hard reset on the Compaq iPAQ H3600 line of Pocket PCs:

1. Turn the power off.

2. Remove the device from the cradle.

3. Remove any CompactFlash cards that are installed.

4. Open the On/Off door on the base of the device using the stylus.

5. Slide the On/Off switch to the Off position using the stylus, and wait for about a minute.

6. Slide the On/Off switch back to the On position.

7. Close the On/Off door on the base of the device using the stylus.

Compaq Aero 1550

Following are the steps required to perform a hard reset on the Compaq Aero 1550 Pocket PC:

1. Turn the power off.

2. Remove the device from the cradle.

3. Remove any CompactFlash cards that are installed.

4. Remove the main battery and the backup battery.

5. Wait at least one minute, and then replace the batteries.

Undocumented
Unlike other Pocket PC devices, the contacts stored via the Contacts application are not cleared when you perform a hard reset on the iPAQ. Contacts are automatically backed up to Flash ROM, which is why they aren't automatically cleared via a hard reset. You can disable the storage of contacts to Flash ROM in the Backup settings for the iPAQ.

Upgrading to Pocket PC

EVEN THOUGH THE POCKET PC operating system is promoted as brand-new, it's really version 3.0 of an existing operating system known as Windows CE. If you are one of the die-hard Windows CE users who own a pre-Pocket PC device, you might be wondering whether a Pocket PC upgrade is in your future. The good news is that it is technically possible to upgrade some of the Windows CE 2.x devices to the Pocket PC operating system. Sadly, the bad news is that you are at the mercy of the device manufacturer.

The reason upgrading a handheld device running Windows CE 2.x to Pocket PC isn't a no-brainer software installation is because the operating system on Windows CE devices is stored on a ROM chip. As you probably know, ROM stands for Read-Only Memory, which is a technical way of saying you can't change it. This means it is necessary to replace the ROM chip in your device to upgrade it to Pocket PC. Some devices are designed so that the ROM chip can be upgraded easily, while others aren't. I'll get into the specific devices in a moment.

You might be wondering why you just can't call up Microsoft and have them send you a ROM chip because they obviously are the folks that make the Pocket PC software. The problem with this approach is that each device manufacturer customizes the operating system for its devices, which locks you into that manufacturer's customized ROM chip. You have to deal with the device manufacturer for upgrades.

HP

Now you know you are at the device manufacturer's mercy, so let's get on with the bad news. If you own an HP handheld device with Windows CE 2.x or earlier, you are out of luck in terms of upgrading to Pocket PC. This is mainly because the hardware in HP Jornada Pocket PCs is completely new. In other words, HP doesn't want to deal with trying to upgrade older hardware to support Pocket PC, which would probably lead to technical support nightmares. Of course, you couldn't care less about HP's technical support reasoning if you hold one of those devices that can't be upgraded. To be fair, HP briefly offered a discount on Jornada Pocket PCs for owners of other HP devices, which is better than nothing but, unfortunately, not of much use to anyone now.

Casio

Casio fared slightly better than HP in providing an upgrade path for Pocket PC. Owners of Casio E-100 and E-105 handheld devices had a limited window of opportunity to send their devices back to Casio for a ROM replacement. Casio also offered a trade-in program in which you could trade in an E-100 or E-105 for a significantly discounted E-115 Pocket PC. I'm writing in past tense because both of these offers were available only during the initial launch of the E-115 Pocket PC, so beyond that timeframe you are more or less on your own.

Speaking of being on your own, if you are able to run across the Casio Pocket PC ROM, it's possible to rip apart an E-100 or E-105 device and perform your own ROM chip replacement surgery. I don't recommend this approach for the technically faint of heart, but it's an option for some. For details about how to carry out this manual upgrade, check out the following Web page: http://www.brighthand.com/ROMupgrade.html.

Compaq

After all the bad news from HP and Casio in regard to Pocket PC upgrades, it's time for something positive. Compaq is the only handheld device manufacturer to offer a clean upgrade path to Pocket PC with no apparent time limit. If you own a

Compaq Aero 1500 or 2100 series device, you can simply purchase a new ROM chip from Compaq and install it yourself with little difficulty. As of this writing, the Aero 1500 upgrade cost $69, and the Aero 2100 upgrade cost $99; the price difference reflects the increased memory in the Aero 2100.

Compaq claims that performing the upgrade is as easy as "adding a memory chip." It's a matter of unscrewing the back of the case and swapping out the chips. For more information on purchasing a Pocket PC ROM upgrade from Compaq, please visit the Compaq Handhelds Web site at http://www. compaq.com/products/handhelds.

Symbols

56Kbps modem cards (56 kilobits per second modem cards), 364

A

accessing eBooks titles, 298
accessories, 361
  carrying cases, 370-371
    Incase Design PDA cases, 371
    Otterbox, 371
    RhinoSkin cases, 370
  CF (CompactFlash) cards, 361
    CF slots, 361
  communication, 363
    56Kbps modem cards, 364
    Psion infrared Travel Modem, 364
    Sierra Wireless AirCard, 366
    Socket digital phone card, 365
    Socket network cards, 366
  memory, 362
  multimedia, 367-370
    Boostaroo audio amplifier, 367
    Casio digital camera card, 368
    Casio Freedio palm-sized printer, 369
    Casio Freedio palm-sized scanner, 369
    KeySync keyboard, 370
    Koss audio amplifier, 368
  pointing tools, 372
  storage, 362
Account Manager screen, Money for Pocket PC, 247
Account Register screen, Money for Pocket PC, 248-249

accounts
  Audible.com, registering, 316-317
  Money for Pocket PC, 244
    cash, 244
    checking, 244
    credit cards, 245
    line of credit, 245
Action button (Pocket Outlook)
  Notes application, 105
  Tasks application, 101
ActiveSky Media Player, 351, 355
ActiveSky Web site, 355
ActiveSync
  AvantGo, enabling (Pocket Internet Explorer), 168
  email, 74-75, 141, 148-150
  Ethernet, 136
  infrared communications, 176-177
  Money for Pocket PC
    accounts support, 244
    installing, 241-242
  Web content, 162-168
    installing, 163
ActiveSync CD-ROM, 66
  ActiveSync software, installing, 49-52
  eBooks, availability, 298
  maps
    copying from, 261-262
    U.S. cities, 261
  Money for Pocket PC, installing, 241-242
  Pocket Streets, installing, 259-261
  synchronizing desktop PCs with Pocket Word, 215-216
  Transcriber, installing, 186
ActiveSync Installation Wizard, 49
ActiveSync software
  backing up data, 56-57
  connections, 118
  synchronizing PCs, 47-52
    applications, 51-55
adapters, infrared ports, 176
Add Favorite screen (Pocket Internet Explorer), 162

389

C

Q-R

X-Y

Z